Naperville Public Library
Naperville, IL

W9-BNS-113

THE DYNAMIC OPTION SELECTION SYSTEM

ANALYZING MARKETS AND MANAGING RISK

Wiley Trading Advantage

THE DYNAMIC OPTION SELECTION SYSTEM

ANALYZING MARKETS AND MANAGING RISK

Howard L. Simons

JOHN WILEY & SONS, INC.

New York • Chichester • Weinheim • Brisbane • Singapore • Toronto

Published by John Wiley & Sons, Inc.

Published simultaneously in Canada.

This publication is designed to provide accurate and authoritative information in regard to the subject matter covered. It is sold with the understanding that the publisher is not engaged in rendering professional services. If professional advice or other expert assistance is required, the services of a competent professional person should be sought.

Library of Congress Cataloging-in-Publication Data:
Simons, Howard, 1954–
    The dynamic option selection system: analyzing markets & managing
risk / Howard Simons.
        p.   cm.—(Wiley trading advantage)
    Includes index.
    ISBN 0-471-32051-X (cloth : alk. paper)
    1. Options (Finance)   2. Options (Finance—Prices)   3. Risk
management.   I. Title.   II. Series.
HG6024.A35557'   1999
332.63'228—DC21   99-21805

Printed in the United States of America

10   9   8   7   6   5   4   3   2   1

*To my loving wife, Jean, who has put up with
more than anyone should have to,
and to my sons, Ariel and Samuel*

Contents

Preface

Would you be interested in writing a book?

Well, actually, no, even though the idea has been broached to me before. I'll think about it. ... All right; it would be an interesting thing to do, I guess. I'll try to give you an outline in two months. ... Six months later, here's your outline. Does this mean that I have to start writing?

This is the sort of thought process that I went through with Pamela van Giessen, my editor, at the start of this project. Why was I so uncertain about taking my life experience of the past 15 years and putting it down on paper? After all, writing about markets had become almost second nature by that point; I had first started writing for *Futures* magazine in May 1994 and had gotten to the point of generating articles on a monthly basis. Speaking about markets had also become second nature; I had started teaching in the Financial Markets and Trading Program of the Illinois Institute of Technology in August 1994. Putting together memos and presentations was almost like breathing.

A book, therefore, should have been a natural, but the commitment to writing something of this length, with this permanence, was a bit daunting. The topic was originally just to be a discourse on options, but this did not seem particularly satisfying. The topic had been covered in great detail in a wide range of books, some quite technical, others of the "how to make a million dollars" variety.

I wanted to address more, to integrate the topic of options with market analysis and risk management. I wanted to distill the observations I had made as a trading systems designer, market analyst, and trader into 10 simple principles, each of which could be written on the inside cover of a matchbook with room to spare:

1. Collective human behavior is immutable.
2. This behavior manifests itself in all aspects of markets, not just price.
3. These manifestations can be read to reveal relative anxieties.
4. Anxiety imbalances define a market's path of least resistance.
5. Risk is ever present, in favorable as well as in adverse environments.
6. Risk includes a trader's own risk aversions and affinities.
7. Risk must be managed, and this always involves a cost.
8. Options are the most direct tool for recognizing this cost.
9. Costs can be reduced via position selection and management methodologies.
10. Take care of the downside, and the upside will take care of itself.

These 10 principles are addressed in this book. Chapter 1 introduces the concepts of risk aversion and affinity and of economic utility. Chapter 2 expands these concepts into the aggregation of risks and utilities in a market. The search by price for underlying economic value and a method of parsing this out are discussed. Chapter 3 looks at the classic method of hedging with futures and dismisses it as the transformation of the external risk of the market into the internal risk of a trader's decisions. In Chapter 4, the distortions of the forward curve in physical markets and their information content are discussed. Chapter 5 integrates price analysis with the forward curve in physical markets and with volatility to produce the Market Tension Index. This analysis is extended to the short-term interest rate and currency markets in Chapter 6, which develops the sister EuroTension Index.

Chapter 7 is a detour into a policy discussion of the global currency markets. This chapter was completed in July 1998, just prior to the arrival of a global bear market triggered by the currency disruptions that began in Thailand during July 1997. The discussion is included in this book because the perpetual inability of the global community to arrive at a stable currency system is the driving force behind so many of the risks and problems we face in markets. No solutions are offered, however.

The second part of the book begins with an overview of option market mechanics in Chapter 8. The chapter is designed to be intelligible to novices and a refresher for seasoned options traders. Emphasis is placed on the concepts needed for Chapter 9, which deals with the strike selection procedures within the Dynamic Option Selection System. Chapter 10 assembles these selected strikes into trading strategies and discusses their merits and a method for selecting the optimal strategy. Once these strategies are selected, they need to be managed, and that is the topic for Chapter 11.

The reader is asked three forbearances. Several topics are discussed without revealing completely the specific formulas and algorithms for calculating them. These include the Market Tension Index and EuroTension Index formulas and both the strike selection and strategy ranking algorithms for the Dynamic Option Selection System. The second is a stylistic matter, and that is the use of *we* and *our* where *I* and *my* might be just as appropriate. This is done not as an affectation or out of a lust for royal status but rather as a reflection of a conversation between writer and reader. You, the reader, are invited to share in the logical development of the topics involved. The third is the consistent use of the masculine form of personal pronouns when the feminine would work just as well; trading problems, as far as I have been able to discern, are fairly independent of gender.

Experience has taught that some readers may find the book too quantitative and others may find it not quantitative enough. An attempt has been made to satisfy both interests; the equations displayed are there for the purpose of illumination only, not to serve as boilerplate: There are far too many technical books whose reliance on mathematical excess would not be necessary if only the author knew how to write.

On the other hand, this book is filled with charts, tables, and graphs. Perhaps that is a legacy of my having spent too many years in a corporate environment, but pictures tell a story. These are referred to often during the course of the ongoing and subsequent discussion, and I can only look forward to a hypertext version for the benefit of readers in later years.

Howard L. Simons
Glenview, Illinois
June 1999

Acknowledgments

An undertaking such as this is the product of a lifetime of experience, and, as such, involves the contributions, direct and indirect, of dozens of people, some of whom may not have recognized their value regarding one man's education and development.

My special thanks to, in chronological order, Joan Macala, a high school English teacher who cared enough to force me to learn how to write; Bela Balassa, Edward Luttwak, and Isaiah Frank, professors who awakened me to the beauty of economics and markets; Merton Miller, a matchless professor of finance; James Abboud, who taught me econometrics; James Johnston, a tireless free-market polemicist; Jeffrey Kunka, a friend in need; Leo Carcione and Peter Borish, who gave me opportunities in markets; Dean Bozek, a great trading partner and a rollicking good time; Ginger Szala, who opened, and has kept open, the pages of *Futures* magazine to me; John Bilson, who gave me the opportunity to teach; and Guillermo Matta, who promoted me to the world.

Life is not always a bowl of cherries, especially in this business. For all of those who, along the way, gave me the opportunity to meet new people, acquire new experiences, broaden my horizons, and pursue whatever additional personal interests might have been out there, I extend warm thanks. Few dull people have had such an interesting life.

THE DYNAMIC OPTION SELECTION SYSTEM

ANALYZING MARKETS AND MANAGING RISK

Introduction

On the Repetition of Folly and the Acceptance of Madness

A short drive north out of Atlanta along U.S. Highway 41 through Marietta brings you to the pine-covered foothills of the Appalachians as they cut across Georgia. The terrain is now covered with well-manicured upper-middle-class homes, many of which pay homage in their own way to antebellum architecture. One can sense just how much this area has changed over the years as Atlanta's quintessentially American prosperity has attracted hundreds of thousands of new residents. The culture of this place gets broadcast to the world over the Cable News Network, a service almost as universal as its fellow Atlanta institution, Coca-Cola. Living looks comfortable here.

The tranquillity is deceptive, as is so often the case. An interested visitor can follow the familiar and muted rusty brown signs of the National Park Service northwest out of town. The directions to the Kennesaw Mountain National Military Historical Park are clear and easy to follow, and the road cut up into the hills is designed with the maximum ease of travel in mind. The Park's visitors' center offers a selection of books and other educational materials, along with a driving tour guide for the park itself.

Visitors' center? Why do we tease ourselves in certain situations? Think of your first visit to any restaurant with a signature dish, the food that made it famous and distinguishes it from the wanna-bes destined to fail after 10 months. You peruse the menu thoughtfully and pretend to weigh all of your options, perhaps joined in your half-acted charade by an indulgent waiter, before you capitulate to the obvious and order what is already waiting for you back in the kitchen.

There is a reason to go to Kennesaw Mountain, a reason more terrifying to those who know where they are going than to the interlopers and school buses full of children out on a field trip, a reason that can make anyone who wants to see recoil in the starkest terror of all: This is who we were, who we are, and who we shall forever be.

The sign on the road is simple enough: THE DEAD ANGLE. You get out of the car, walk past carefully preserved trenches dug into the heavy soil, and come to a small crest below the top of the hill itself, a crest chosen for its commanding view of the steep hillside and open vale below . . . .

It is the morning of June 27, 1864, and the temperature is in the midnineties. Arrayed before you in that vale are the same Union forces you have been fighting for two and a half years already. You look down and think to yourself that there's no way anyone could be so stupid, so insane, so suicidal as to come up that steep hillside . . . .

Out of curiosity, you step down the hill, stopping every few feet to turn around and look at that crest above you. You repeat the process until you reach the bottom. You cannot stand at the foot of Kennesaw Mountain without wondering how these men, veteran troops who knew the odds, could stand there waiting, hearts pounding, fingertips numb, throats dry, and then charge to their certain deaths and uncertain rewards. Had they learned nothing from their experience? Maybe they had, but they were still willing to take enormous risks for uncertain benefits. And, of course, the unanswerable question: Why would I have gone up Kennesaw Mountain?

One must conclude from their undertaking that some combination of peer pressure, loyalty to their cause, and belief in their own invincibility outweighed the fear of death. Behavior such as this is just part of the human condition. We undertake needless risks, pursue goals we cannot articulate, and deliberately ignore our own experience again and again. If we acted otherwise, in the predictable and rational manner described in economics textbooks, then the social sciences would lose some of their messiness and become neat and clean like the physical sciences.

Or would they? The history of scientific thought has two threads: the gradual removal of ourselves from our self-conceived role as the center of the universe, and the collapse of every attempt to neatly codify and explain the physical world with stable rules of prediction. The urge to reject randomness and impose order is so extreme that even theories that celebrate unpredictability, such as quantum mechanics and chaos, are seen as new predictive tools.

The behavior of people in markets combines the irrational behaviors produced under situations of uncertainty and stress with the dynamic and chaotic behavior of inanimate systems. Many traders eventually stand at the foot of their own Kennesaw Mountain and believe that just once the road to triumph will be opened, as it was for the old gambler in *The Cincinnati Kid*, by making the wrong move at the right time. Worse, many others look up at the crest and know they are doing the wrong thing at the wrong time but do it anyway. In both cases, their knowledge, their fears, and their intentions, although of critical importance to themselves, are of absolute irrelevance to the defenders of the crest. It does not matter whether they have studied previous assaults, whether they have a plan, whether they have a hill-taking system, or even if they have survived previous charges. All that matters is that they are in the game.

The task of writing about markets cannot be done in a vacuum. Trading, for this author at least, is an intensely personal experience. It is primal and definite: You either win or you lose. It offers no cumulative success: Your reward for winning is that you get to try it again tomorrow. It demands ever greater knowledge, but it neither rewards preparation nor penalizes luck. It has infinite variables but only one constant: the behavior of the people involved. This is the most important part of market analysis, and one that will be revisited constantly in the pages that follow.

PART I

THINKING ABOUT MARKETS

1

In the Game

WE TRADE, THEREFORE WE ARE

Archaeologists digging and picking through the usual assortment of rubble in northern Assyria in the late 1980s kept encountering charred grains of barley in the bottom of large vessels not normally associated with baking. This led to the development of an unusual hypothesis regarding the origins of agriculture, and hence the development of modern civilizations: We started cultivating grain to ensure ourselves a supply of beer. How things change.

Of course, one cannot have the concept of ensured supply without first having mastered the concept of exchange. Although we could stretch a bit and try to convince ourselves that these first farmers were willing to donate their grain to the local brewmaster for the greater good of their community, it is far more likely that they received goods and services of value in return. Whatever method of exchange was used—probably barter—a market had to be involved.

Complex systems apparently jump from nonexistence to a near final state. In cosmology, this has been dubbed the "big bang." The parallel origin of life does not have a similar catchy name, but the end result was the same: One point in time separated the void from the universe, and another point in time separated prelife from life. Period. There was no intermediate phase or transitional state. This bright line, this sharp distinction between two very different states of affairs, and the irreducible uncertainty involved in the process, always have and always will provide us with our greatest philosophical questions: One cannot either prove or disprove either the divine or some stochastic process; one can only accept and believe.

7

The evolution of markets, like the evolution of living organisms, must have exploded from near nothingness to a rather complete state in a very short period of time. Just as an organism must exhibit all aspects of an organism to survive and propagate, markets must exhibit all aspects of a market to function and expand. Terms of trade, recordkeeping and accounting, storage, insurance, dispute resolution, and information transfer all had to originate quickly. Taxation did not have to originate quickly, but one suspects that it did, nevertheless.

If the concept of exchange is a prerequisite for the concept of ensured supply, and if markets require all of their multiple facets to function—just as there can be no partial life or partial universe, there can be no partial market—then human civilization arose out of a big bang of its own, the creation of markets. Everything we do in our socioeconomic lives today is but a footnote to this singular event. As a result, there are constants in market analysis, just as there are constants in the laws of physics and biology.

Although reasonable people can and will differ on the issue, we will submit that all markets are driven by common human behavior, and therefore markets can be analyzed and compared to one another on a consistent basis. In other words, it does not matter whether you are trading Eurodollars or soybeans; the behavior of traders will be the same in both markets. An immediate corollary to this is market behavior is independent of culture. Eurodollars traded by Americans will exhibit the same trading patterns as Eurolira traded by Italians, Euroyen traded by Japanese, and bank bills traded by Australians. Another corollary is trading patterns are independent of the level of technology used in a market: It does not matter whether we are using clay tablets, rice paper, an abacus, or the Internet—the resulting footprints of a market are the same. We can read a cotton price chart from the Civil War, stock price charts from the 1920s, and grain price charts from the early 1970s on the same basis.

The one constant between markets for different assets, between eras, and between levels of technology is the behavior of human beings. In homage to George Santayana's famous dictum that those who do not learn history are condemned to repeat it, the one thing we can learn from history is that people do not learn from history—their own or anyone else's. Maybe there is a remarkable person somewhere on this earth who has not made the same mistake twice or who has never succumbed to intuition when rational analysis was appropriate or who is immune to the emotions of fear and greed, but if so, this person does not dominate market behavior. Since the goal of this work is to both absorb the collective anxiety of the market and to minimize the need for decisions based on price forecasting, we should detour for a moment into the behavior of traders and investors.

ECONOMIC UTILITY

Most of us assume, as a matter of course, that people trade to make money, since that is the reward of a successful trading program. However, many risky activities have a negative expected return. The classic example of this is gambling. A simple stroll down the Strip in Las Vegas is a testament to our willingness to lose money; those gaudy casinos were not financed by allowing the customer to win. An economist of the behavioral school would counter quickly that gamblers must derive some additional utility other than expected winnings, such as camaraderie, free food and drink, other forms of entertainment, or simply the thrill of being in the game.

This argument carries a strong appeal for an entertainment center like Las Vegas, but does it carry equal appeal for a video poker game at a truck stop in rural South Carolina? What external utility does this activity provide? The same question can be asked in regard to state lotteries, most of which offer very negative expected returns. The behavioral answer in both cases is a short-term dream, the fleeting hope that in return for a low-cost lottery ticket or a few coins in a video poker machine, the player's life will be changed forever for the better. Never mind that the probability of dream realization is quite low, that the cumulative cost of playing the game can be a rather stiff tax on naiveté, or that the trap of gambling addiction can be worse than the life the player is trying to escape: The expected utility from playing the game must exceed the cost of playing. In more general terms, a player should purchase entry into the game if expected utility, the sum of all probability-weighted returns, exceeds the cost of entry.

$$\sum_{i=1}^{N} p_i \cdot r_i > Cost \qquad (1.1)$$

Of course, this relationship breaks down quickly as the cost of entry rises. A lottery player may assign internally a certain utility to his warm feeling on purchasing a ticket for $1, because the pain of losing $1 is, one hopes, less than any pleasure received from just being in the game. Our player may stay in at a cost of $5 or $10, but as the ticket prices rise, his willingness to accept an actuarially fair bet will decrease. You don't see very many $100 slot machines, do you? This phenomenon, known as the Bernoulli paradox, will come into play later in our discussion of appropriate strike selection for long option positions.

One of the central assumptions of utility analysis is that more is better than less, so that the relationship between utility and wealth is positively sloped. If U is our utility level at any level of wealth (W), then $U'(W) > 0$, or

$$\frac{\delta U(W)}{\delta W} > 0 \qquad (1.2)$$

The philosophical implication of this assumption is that we are all doomed to frustration and unhappiness because no matter what level of utility we achieve; no matter how large our bank accounts, we could always have more. Fortunately, most of us make choices in our life to address utility functions that cannot be measured in dollars and cents. For example, we may choose to spend more time with our children or volunteer for a nonprofit organization. Economic analysis can be extended to comparing the utility of these activities to that of income-producing activities; Gary Becker was awarded a Nobel Prize in economics for his efforts in this regard. Although our total utility function for all of our activities—our personal portfolio, as it were—is positively sloped, the mix of activities associated with generating income frequently declines as higher wealth levels are reached. In other words, the marginal utility of income declines with wealth for most of us. This is obvious at the extremes; a person struggling to survive will need to devote an extraordinary portion of his efforts to providing for necessities, whereas a wealthy person is free to pursue many non–income generating activities and may even be able to retire from the labor force at an early age.

Declining marginal utility of income, which defines risk-averse behavior, is a simple concept with immense ramifications. Let us take two investors, one with a net worth of $10,000 and one with a net worth of $10,000,000, and present them both with an opportunity to make an additional $1,000. This potential income represents a gain of 10% in wealth for the first investor but a gain of only 0.01% for the second investor. On this basis, we can assume that the first investor would value the additional $1,000 more than would the second. The opposite is true as well. A loss of $1,000 would be devastating for our first investor, but we should hope that the second investor would not be upset badly. Succinctly, what could the second investor do with $10,001,000 that he could not do with $10,000,000, or what could he not do with $9,999,000 that he could have done with $10,000,000?

Figure 1.1 **UTILITY FUNCTIONS**

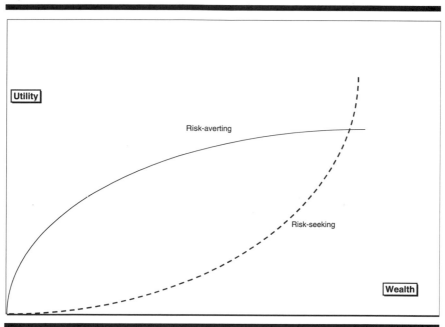

We can categorize the risk preference of investors by the second derivative of their utility functions (Figure 1.1).

$$U''(W) < 0 \quad \text{Risk-averse} \qquad (1.3)$$

$$U''(W) > 0 \quad \text{Risk-seeking} \qquad (1.4)$$

$$U''(W) = 0 \quad \text{Risk-neutral} \qquad (1.5)$$

REMEMBRANCE OF TRADES PAST

Accounting recognizes the difference between stock concepts and flow concepts, the former being a snapshot, a balance sheet, and the latter an accumulation, an income statement. Wealth, or the amount of equity in a trading account, should be a stock concept, a simple declaration of the funds available at any given moment. However, we treat our wealth level on a flow basis as well. Mentally, we give it a history.

For example, a trader who bought soybeans at $6.50 per bushel and then watched them go down to $6.25 per bushel is far more likely to jump at the opportunity to sell them out at a subsequent recovery to $6.60 per bushel than is a trader who had bought soybeans at $6.55 the day before. Why is this the case? The only thing that should matter to either trader is his expectation for future soybean prices based on supply and demand fundamentals. The recent price history of soybeans and the trader's own equity history should be irrelevant. However, the first trader, who sat through a loss of $0.25 per bushel on his position—$1,250 per futures contract on the Chicago Board of Trade—probably is very relieved that both his monetary loss and his personal anxiety, if any, are now things of the past. The second trader has no such experience and therefore no sense of relief that a loss has been avoided.

This reversion from risk aversion to risk seeking as a function of recovered equity produces one of the more common price patterns, the double top or double bottom. This is illustrated in Figure 1.2 for the June 1988 treasury bond contract. A first top formed in early February near the 94:00 price level; this top was the continuation of a rally that began in December 1987. Trading was characterized by a series of strong closes, which can be interpreted as buyers' being eager to own

Figure 1.2 A DOUBLE TOP: JUNE 1988 TREASURY BONDS

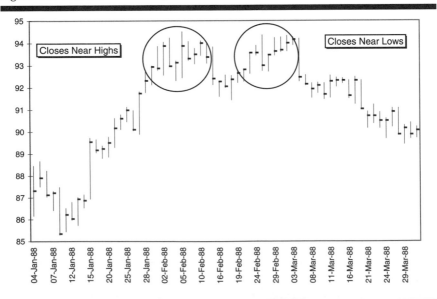

the contract prior to the next day's opening. The market pulled back quickly toward the 91:00 level, giving a loss of close to $3,000 per contract for anyone who had bought near the highs. A subsequent recovery within days to the 94:00 level produced a different set of results and a different character of trading. Not only did the market fail to make a new high, but the closes were consistently near the lows of the day, which can be interpreted as sellers' being eager to take advantage of perceived weakness.

The principles of investor psychology were encapsulated neatly by Daniel Kahneman and Amos Tversky. The first trader in our soybean example illustrates two of the Kahneman–Tversky principles. The first is that traders are risk averse in the domain of profits; we are too eager to grab a gain for the simple satisfaction of having won the trade. The second is that traders are risk seeking in the domain of losses; we are too willing to sit through a loss in the hopes that our original decision will be vindicated. Neither principle should exist if the first trader were the classical risk-adjusted profit maximizer he was supposed to be.

BOTH A COWARD AND A DAREDEVIL BE

The notion that any individual trader's risk preference can change from seeking to aversion and back again should not be surprising. We encounter this preference in many aspects of our lives, both individually and collectively. For example, most of us are unbelievably risk averse when it comes to medical expenses and are thus overinsured. Why should a person carry insurance for normal medical expenses that might amount to no more than a grocery or car repair bill, and why have we, as a society, created a mind-numbingly complex system of billing and review to administer these routine payments? The standard answer is that we fear the expense of a catastrophic illness, but another of the Kahneman–Tversky principles is that we overestimate the probability of such an event's happening and then underestimate its actual impact when it does. The result of this principle is that we are underinsured for the catastrophic event. Although our societal overinsurance for mundane medical expenses indicates risk aversion, our habits regarding life insurance or saving for retirement indicate risk seeking. Even though mercifully few among us relish a conversation on our own mortality, even fewer of us will win this game. The same holds true for its complement, growing old. A huge cottage industry has emerged to remind the baby boom generation that they are not saving enough to cover the risk that they will outlive their money, and the life insurance industry struggles to remind people that they are leaving their loved ones at too great a risk of the bread-winner's untimely demise. The very same people who would never consider employment with an organization whose medical plan was deemed inadequate probably avoid successfully the necessities of financial planning.

Lamenting this state of affairs is pointless. This is what we as human beings are, have been, and will be. Our job as investors, traders, and market analysts is to take advantage of the situation as it is presented to us and not to remake the world into some impossible ideal. This means recognizing our own vulnerability to the Kahneman–Tversky principles and sculpting a trading system, as we will later do, to turn them to our advantage:

- Since traders are risk averse in the domain of profits, even if the original logic behind the trade is still valid, a mechanical and quantitative method of taking profits is likely to be superior over time to an arbitrary profit-taking methodology.

- Since traders are risk seeking in the domain of losses, even if the original logic behind the trade has been shown to be invalid, a mechanical and quantitative method of reducing losses is likely to be superior over time to an arbitrary stop-loss methodology.

- Since all of us tend to overestimate the probability of the catastrophic and then underestimate its impact, a mechanical and quantitative methodology of structuring trades and managing positions to both capture the anxiety embedded in the first condition and the profit contained in the extreme event is likely to produce superior returns.

Any market is composed of traders, both buyers and sellers, who have different utility functions. At a given point in time, two traders with long positions and identical fundamental analyses may possess entirely different urges to hold their position, add to their position, or exit their position. Accommodating these different trades produces short-term noise in the market, but this noise can be analyzed in turn for clues as to where the underlying economic value is. Even more important, the combination of underlying signal and noise can provide clues as to the short-term anxieties of buyers and sellers, and this is often the most useful information a market produces.

2

For What It's Worth

PRICE AND VALUE

Let's start with a direct and, I hope, noncontroversial statement: Price can be known exactly, but value can only be inferred. The first part of the statement can be verified by a walk through your local grocery store or by a glance at your quote screen. What you see in each instance are prices; the items marked in the grocery store are offers to sell at a fixed price, whereas the prices on the quote screen are recordings of the interactions between buyers and sellers.

Determination of the value of the good or service transacted at that price is a much more difficult problem, as shown in Figure 2.1. A six-pack of soda sitting on the grocer's shelf is identical to a six-pack of soda at the edge of a desert. One might surmise that a parched straggler wandering in from the desert would be willing to pay much more for the soda than would a shopper making a routine set of purchases. There are several reasons behind this. The first and most obvious is that the straggler may be purchasing his continued existence, whereas the shopper may be purchasing only an inconsequential drink. The economic utility of the soda is far higher for the straggler than for the shopper. The second is the availability of substitutes. This presumes, of course, that the grocery store is well stocked with all sorts of beverages and that even if it is not, there are neighboring stores with beverages available. The third reason is that the straggler's demand curve is highly inelastic; the shopper, presumably, has an elastic demand curve and would be willing to postpone any purchases should the price be deemed unsatisfactory.

Figure 2.1 **COMPARATIVE PRICE ELASTICITIES OF DEMAND**

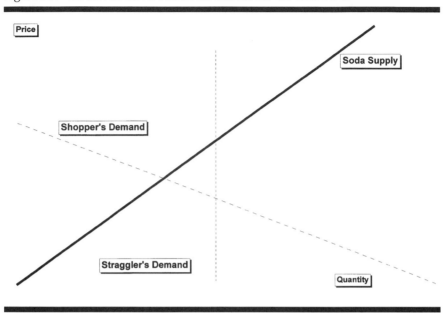

The six-pack of soda does not have a fixed intrinsic value. Its value needs to be determined within the context of both the external environment and the internal needs of both the buyer and the seller. Since the value is far higher to the straggler than it is to the shopper, the straggler is likely to outbid the shopper. The resulting price, if made visible to the world, is unlikely to be ratified in subsequent transactions by anyone other than a straggler. However, the aberrant price spike yields extremely valuable information: This is how high the price of soda can get when the buyer is desperate.

PRICE OVERSHOOTING VALUE

In terms of technical charting of price, this information presents itself as a spike top or a spike bottom, and these formations are some of the most definitive evidence of when price has become disconnected from value. A spike bottom, as shown in Figure 2.2, occurs when the low of a day is lower than both the previous day's low and the next day's low. Certain markets, such as the Standard & Poor's (S&P) 500 or crude oil, exhibit this pattern frequently.

Equities are particularly difficult to value because they represent, fundamentally, the discounted stream of expected future dividends

Figure 2.2 **A SPIKE BOTTOM: DECEMBER 1997 STANDARD & POOR'S 500**

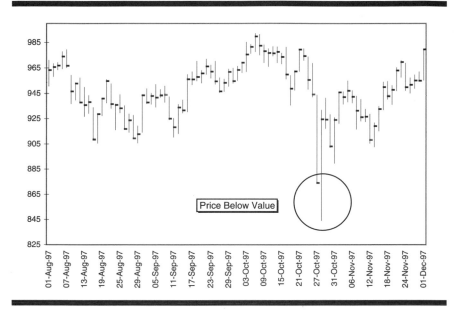

from a firm, a very uncertain quantity. This quantity is then valued in the context of all other available investments and current consumption alternatives, which muddies the intrinsic value of an equity even further. Finally, equities as a class exhibit certain characteristics of a superior good, one that becomes more desirable as its price increases. As a result, the equity market is given to sudden fits of self-doubt regarding its pricing of underlying value. Only when lower prices are rejected decisively by a determined buyer can the rest of the market become more confident in its aggregate judgment.

Crude oil spikes for a different set of reasons. Crude oil demand is almost totally price inelastic in the short term because final fuel demand is almost totally price inelastic in the short term. The limited number of refiners who buy crude oil are very competitive with each other in terms of processing costs and realize gross refining margins that are close to one another for each class of refinery. As a result, a refiner's margin and competitive position depend very heavily on his ability to buy crude oil at a relatively cheap price. Once one refiner stops a price slide, the others are almost forced to jump in and buy at the same time. The economics of the situation make the process reasonably symmetrical, with spike tops occurring almost as frequently as spike bottoms, as shown in Figure 2.3.

Figure 2.3 **SPIKE TOPS: FEBRUARY 1997 CRUDE OIL**

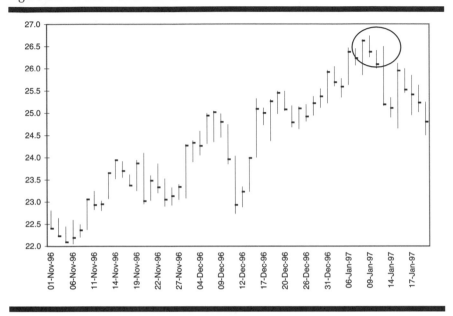

MARKET EFFICIENCY

Medieval theologians are alleged to have debated endlessly on the number of angels who could dance on the head of a pin. Modern economists have engaged in a similar exercise on the question of market efficiency. The efficient market hypothesis states in its strong form that the price of an asset reflects all available information, public and private. A close cousin of the efficient market hypothesis is the random walk model of price behavior, which states that the current price of an asset is the best predictor of the next price, where α is a drift term and ε is a randomly and normally distributed error term:

$$\ln P_{t+1} = \alpha + \ln P_t + \varepsilon \qquad (2.1)$$

Is market efficiency a viable model in markets where the utility of each price changes for important classes of participants in the market, each of whom may have a level of risk aversion or risk seeking depending on their wealth, and each of whom may have a different price elasticity of demand? The tautological answer is that prices are set at the margin by both buyers and sellers whose behavior changes instantaneously at that segment of the price spectrum. How can this model accommodate such market situations as fast markets, wherein all orders are executed at whatever the prevailing bid or asking price is and wherein carefully calculated price orders are ignored? The efficient market hypothesis should allow for those situations wherein the market participants at the margin may be efficient in their analysis, but the resulting price does not reflect their assessments on either an immediate or a continuous basis.

An allowance for such discrepancies will become increasingly important as electronic trading systems take precedence over the traditional open-outcry method of price discovery. No electronic order entry system yet available is as fast and as flexible as a floor trader. If the resulting prices are more a result of what a trader was able to execute, as opposed to what he wished to execute, then is it safe to conclude that markets have become less efficient, or would we just have to say that they are just noisier on a short-term basis?

Two postulates are offered:

- Markets are efficient in the sense that they always tend toward equilibrium. Over the shortest time frames, tick-by-tick trading, prices can be disproportionately noisy. Over longer time frames, noise diminishes in relation to the underlying signal.
- Price is a convergent search process for underlying economic value. Even if a price is a poor instantaneous representation of value, the market's acceptance or rejection of this price yields valuable information on value.

Acceptance of these two postulates allows us to both respect the efficiency of free markets and to glean useful information from price movements. The tendency toward efficiency and the tendency toward equilibrium provide us with a suitable working model. This is the lowest energy state of a market; just as a cup of hot coffee wants to reach the temperature of the room or an object held over the ground wants to fall, markets want to reach a state of perfect efficiency and a market-clearing equilibrium in which no riskless profits can be achieved.

It is important to add, given the earlier admonition about seeking predictive order in data analysis, that the information gleaned is descriptive of what has been and is not predictive of what will be. The illustrations of spike tops and bottoms above provide us with descriptive information of where price and value became disconnected from one another, but only in the fundamental supply–demand balance prevailing at the time. They say nothing about either the recent path of value or its prospective path over time.

LET THE TREND BE YOUR FRIEND

If we accept the efficient market hypothesis and the gravitational effects of market equilibrium, then we must be prepared to accept the notion that past prices contain little or no predictive power over future prices: The current price reflects all known information about this particular market, plus or minus a normally and randomly distributed error term. The autocorrelation (ρ) of a price series X at a lag of one period should be zero:

$$\rho_1 = \frac{E\left[\left(x_t - \mu_x\right)\left(x_{t+1} - \mu_x\right)\right]}{\sigma_x^2} = 0 \qquad (2.2)$$

Even the most devout advocates of the efficient market hypothesis, however, have to recognize, from visual observation if nothing else, that price paths over time do exhibit significant first-order autocorrelation. (The value of visual observation should never be minimized; the "I know it when I see it" standard for obscenity of U.S. Supreme Court Justice William Joseph Brennan, Jr., is still the best working definition extant.) Our definition of a trend is necessarily this loose: There can be no precise mathematical point when a price series exhibiting significant first-order autocorrelation suddenly transforms from a nontrend to a trend; this transformation, like beauty, must exist in some part in the eye of the beholder and nowhere else.

Figure 2.4, which charts nearby Japanese yen futures over the period between 1993 and 1998, exhibits rather linear price movement, both up and down, for protracted periods, and its autocorrelation at lag 1 is a highly linear .9805. Should we conclude from the trending path of the yen that the market is being inefficient in not capturing what appears to be a time-dependent function? Of course not. Even if we ignore the understandable hesitancy of traders to lay a ruler down on a piece of graph paper and call it a trading system, the trending path of the yen is not at all inconsistent with market efficiency if we allow for value changing over time.

SIGNAL: THE PATH OF VALUE OVER TIME

Price is a convergent search process for an underlying economic value determined by fundamental factors. Since changes in price depend on changes in value in all but the shortest time frames, price cannot lead value; it must react to value, as shown in Figure 2.5. This process produces not only price trends but all other identifiable market patterns as well. A price trend begins when value changes and price must subsequently change to reflect the new reality. A price trend ends when price overshoots underlying value, as in the case of the spike top or spike bottom. A consolidation of a recent trend occurs as price converges toward the new equilibrium in value.

When value changes, large price changes are required to reflect the new reality. Therefore, in the early phase of a new trend, *inter*day price change dominates *intra*day price range. This is seen on a price chart as a tightly channeled directional move, perhaps with some gapping (today's low higher than yesterday's high, or today's high lower than yesterday's low). The explosive price changes for the Japanese yen seen in Figure 2.4 during 1995 are accompanied by very little backing-and-filling, profit-taking, or countertrend movement. This is a market that knows where it wants to go and is determined to arrive there with as little ceremony as possible.

Figure 2.4 **A TRENDING MARKET: JAPANESE YEN FUTURES, 1993 TO 1998**

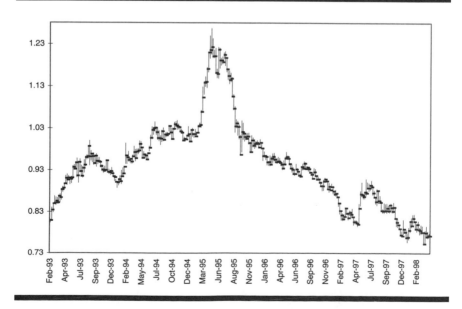

On the other hand, when price catches up to value and begins oscillating around the underlying value in a test to see whether there are sellers at higher prices and buyers at lower prices, *intra*day price range dominates *inter*day price change. The narrow consolidation seen for the Japanese yen in Figure 2.4, during the second half of 1994, is characterized by several trips through a confined price range, producing almost no net price change.

Value changes as a function of changes in the supply–demand balance within a market. In the case of the Japanese yen over the period between 1993 and 1998, demand for the yen surged between 1993 and 1995 when the foreign exchange market perceived weak dollar and trade protection policies from the new Clinton administration, and then demand for the yen collapsed as the Bank of Japan engaged in an increasingly loose monetary policy. In both periods, the market might have been slow to recognize the duration and magnitude of these broad, secular policies, but being *imperfect* in judging the underlying fundamentals and being *inefficient* in pricing the underlying fundamentals are two different things.

ADAPTING TO THE MARKET

If a change in underlying value is required to produce a trend in price, and if price oscillates imperfectly about underlying value, then the observed movement in price can be broken down into a signal, the change in underlying value, and noise, the price movement not associated with a change in value. This signal, which must be inferred from actual market data, is descriptive of what has been, not predictive of what will be. However, its structure yields information on the efficiency of price's search for value, and this information can be incorporated into subsequent trading constructs.

A settlement, or closing, price is but one price observation in a trading day. The significance of this price as being representative of the trading day as a whole is diminished by the range of the trading day. Can one conclude reasonably that the settlement price for a Eurodollar contract on a day with a 10–basis point range is more representative of the market's activity than when the day's range is only 2.5 basis points? The proliferation of nonpit trading activities on electronic exchanges has lowered the anxiety level of traders who used to need to close positions on a given day; when treasury bond futures traded only during the day, they closed within three ticks of their high or low over 36% of the time, as compared to a little over 26% of the time during 1998. This ongoing trend within the futures industry

Figure 2.5 **RELATION OF PRICE TO VALUE**

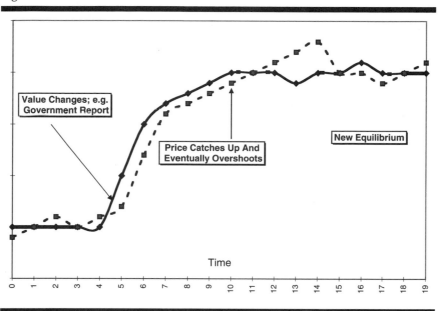

should continue to lower the significance of the settlement price even further.

We already have submitted that a trending market is character-ized by the dominance of interday price change over intraday price range and that a sideways or trading range market is characterized by the domination of intraday price range over interday price change. A measure to unify these two price concepts is necessary. What should this descriptive time series look like? If we could draw a line through a price series, we would want the descriptive line, L, to have minimal absolute differences between itself and the price series:

$$\min \sum_{i=1}^{N} |P_i - L_i| \qquad (2.3)$$

At the extreme, this would be achieved by employing the fastest mov-ing average possible, a one-day moving average that would have no memory of any prior event. This one-day moving average would be the underlying price series itself, and it would indeed minimize Equa-tion 2.3 by virtue of being equal to zero.

However, we would also want the descriptive time series to have some degree of smoothness to capture the underlying trend of the price series while eliminating some of the noise. The sum of the absolute differences between points on the descriptive line L should be minimized as well:

$$\min \sum_{i=1}^{N} |L_{i+1} - L_i| \qquad (2.4)$$

At the extreme, this would be achieved by employing the slowest moving average possible, an N-day moving average where N would be equal to the number of observations in the series. The resulting average would have a constant value equal to the arithmetic average of the series. This N-day moving average would minimize Equation 2.4 by virtue of being equal to zero.

Our descriptive line L needs to minimize these two qualities simultaneously. In other words, the ideal moving average, or trend, will be the locus of points derived from an underlying price series whose sum of absolute differences between itself and the original series is minimized, and whose own sum of absolute first differences is minimized as well.

In a world where price observations were entirely signal and no noise, where one price represented the market's best estimate of underlying economic value, we could combine these two measures and derive the basis for our adaptive moving average with no further work:

$$\min \sum_{i=1}^{N} |P_i - L_i| \cdot |L_{i+1} - L_i| \qquad (2.5)$$

Since prices are imperfect estimates of underlying economic value, we must include the effects of this noise in our effort to parse information on the change in value out of the our data on change in price. Once this initial discussion of volatility effects is complete, we will return to complete the discussion of the path of value over time.

VOLATILITY EFFECTS

The discussion to this point has assumed that a given price is, at any given point in time, the market's best estimate of underlying value; if this was not the case, then why did the transaction occur between consenting buyer and seller? However, we have seen the effects of risk aversion and risk seeking on the part of traders, and we can never ignore the various mechanical interferences in a market, such as short-term illiquidity, fast markets, and the like. Thus, each transaction occurs at the mode of a probability distribution around the reported price, a distribution determined by the short-term utility functions of both buyer and seller and by the market's temporary environment. The more inelastic the price curves and the greater the degree of risk aversion or risk seeking, the wider this probability distribution will be. This measure of price dispersion over time is the historical volatility of a market, which is only somewhat related to the implied volatility of an option market discussed in Chapter 8.

Standard historical volatility measures focus on the daily percentage price changes in a market. Most early studies converged on these percentage changes' being normally distributed, the so-called lognormal distribution. The assumption in the original Black–Scholes option pricing model was that price changes were lognormally distributed. Later studies began weighing in with percentage price distributions conforming more to a leptokurtic distribution, one that closely resembles the normal distribution, but with fatter tails and a higher, narrower peak than the standard distribution shown in Figure 2.6.

The leptokurtic distribution is intuitively pleasing to market analysts. It states that we have a greater than expected probability of nothing happening—the higher, narrower peak—and a greater than expected distribution of significant price movement—the result of a major shift in value. Leptokurtosis also conforms to both the natural risk aversion of those with a profit and the risk seeking of those with

Figure 2.6 **THE STANDARD NORMAL DISTRIBUTION CURVE**

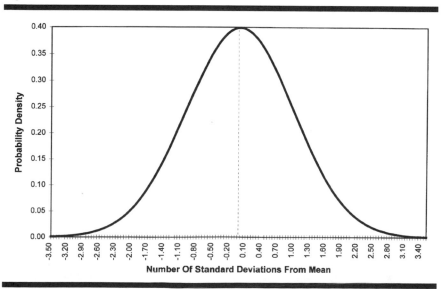

a loss. This is seen best by examining the cumulative normal distribution, the area under the familiar bell curve of Figure 2.6.

A simulation can be conducted with any audience, such as a group of students. Tell them they are wheat farmers whose break-even price for their crop in the field is $3.50 per bushel. Now start moving the hypothetical price available in the market higher in $0.10 increments, each time asking the questions "Would you sell any of your wheat crop forward at this price?" and "How much, in percentage terms, of your crop would you sell?" The results for this experiment have been invariable. By the time the price gets to $3.90, well over 80% of the crop has been sold. As the price moves higher and higher, the ersatz farmers lose their risk aversion and become quite greedy over their last percent of wheat available for sale. Much of this greed is self-flagellation for the mistake of having sold the bulk of their crop at a price now seen as way too low. Of course, they would love to sell more here, but they are simply out of goods to sell.

Unsurprisingly, the opposite behavior occurs in buyers. Tell a group of students they are flour millers whose break-even price occurs at $3.60 per bushel, and repeat the price-climbing exercise above. Once the price climbs over $3.60, buyers disappear; who, after all, wants to lock in a certain loss on his wheat purchases? Now introduce the concept of risk of ruin, a price level that is high enough to ensure business failure and its associated costs, both personal and financial. As this point is approached, panic buying emerges. However, much of the potential wheat crop has been sold already to parties outside of the flour milling business, say to professional speculators.

The intersection of panic buying and the combination of unwillingness and inability to sell results in huge price increases over a very short period of time. The same is true on the other side; huge price decreases can occur when sellers are facing a risk-of-ruin decision and buyers have already covered their purchase requirements. These are the very same price spikes illustrated in Figures 2.2 and 2.3.

These price spikes can be seen in a different fashion in Figure 2.7. At 1.65 standard deviations over the mean, 95% of the cumulative probability has occurred, and at −1.65 standard deviations under the mean, only 5% of the cumulative probability has occurred. Since both 0% and 100% cumulative probabilities are limits and not definite values, the number of standard deviations from the mean a price can move is bounded $-\infty < \sigma < \infty$. Until a price is equal to zero, at which point there will be no sellers—and the logarithm of zero is $-\infty$, or until a price is equal to ∞, at which point there will be no buyers—and the

Figure 2.7 **THE CUMULATIVE NORMAL DISTRIBUTION**

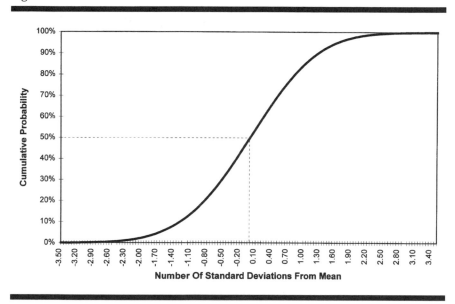

logarithm of ∞ is ∞, the price can continue to move either lower or higher, respectively.

The economic damage that can occur in these last few percentage points of a price distribution is astonishing, as many have discovered under unpleasant circumstances. None of this should come as a surprise, since for any given level of price volatility, we can calculate the odds of a price level being exceeded. First, for any year fraction, τ (days/365), remaining on a risk and for any volatility level, σ, we can calculate the confidence interval for a price given Z, the number of standard deviations of the normal distribution required to produce the confidence interval:

$$Range = \text{Price}_{t0} \cdot \pm e^{\,\sigma\sqrt{\tau}Z} \qquad (2.6)$$

We can now rearrange Equation 2.6 to isolate the upper and lower bounds of the price range in terms of odds:

$$\ln(\frac{UpperBound}{\text{Price}_{t0}}) = \sigma\sqrt{\tau}Z$$
$$\ln(\frac{LowerBound}{\text{Price}_{t0}}) = -\sigma\sqrt{\tau}Z \qquad (2.7)$$

Since the current price, the historical volatility, and the year fraction remaining are all known, then we can impose a Z value and calculate both our bounds and our odds of staying within those bounds. A two-tailed confidence interval of 1.96 standard deviations from the mean will give us a central confidence band of 90% with two 5% tails. If we have a base price of $10 on an asset, a volatility of 15%, and 30 days left, our bounds will be

$$Range = 10 \cdot \pm e^{.10 \cdot \sqrt{30/365} \cdot 1.96}$$

or $9.45 on the lower bound and $10.58 on the upper bound. Our odds of staying below the upper bound of $10.58 are .95/(1 − .95), or 19:1, and we have identical odds of staying over the lower bound of $9.45. The two bounds do not have identical absolute differences between themselves and the original $10 price; this is a reflection of the log-normality of price behavior.

A visual image of Equation 2.6 is important in understanding risk. We can illustrate this in several different combinations of the three determining variables, year fraction, volatility, and confidence interval at 1.96 standard deviations. First, let us examine the combination of volatility and year fraction on our upper bound from an initial $10 price at a two-tailed confidence interval at 1.96 standard deviations, as shown in Figure 2.8. The effect of volatility is linear, as could be deduced quickly from Equation 2.6, but the effect of time is curvilinear, with the degree of curvature increasing in higher volatility environments and accelerating as time remaining approaches zero.

Next, as shown in Figure 2.9, we can depict the upper bound over a combination of volatility and confidence intervals at our initial 30-day time horizon. Once again, the effect of volatility is linear, while the effect of expanding the confidence interval accelerates as the interval widens and increases in a higher volatility environment.

Finally, in Figure 2.10, we can depict the upper bound over a combination of confidence interval and time at a constant 10% volatility. Neither effect is linear; the upper bound expands as a function of both a wider confidence interval and as a function of more time remaining over the interval.

In all cases, any combination of higher volatility, a broader confidence interval, or more time over which the risk will remain open will increase the implied price range. Over the short-term time frame where only a small number of price observations are available, volatility is the only variable that will have a significant operating impact.

Figure 2.8 **UPPER CONFIDENCE BOUND AS A FUNCTION OF TIME AND
VOLATILITY**

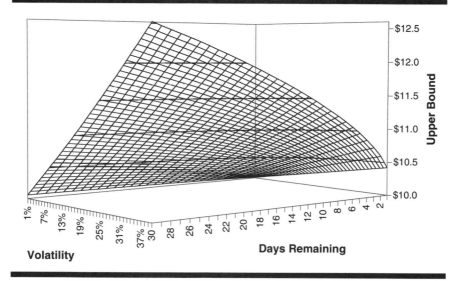

Figure 2.9 **UPPER BOUND AS A FUNCTION OF VOLATILITY AND
CONFIDENCE INTERVAL**

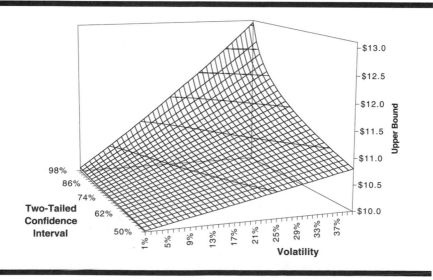

Figure 2.10 **UPPER BOUND AS FUNCTION OF TIME AND CONFIDENCE INTERVAL**

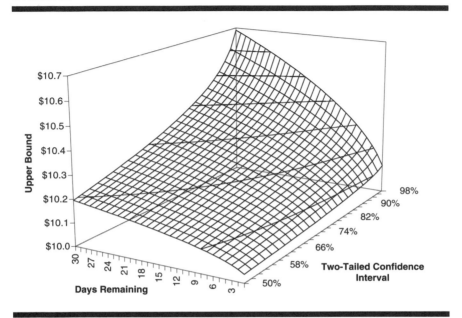

MEASURING VOLATILITY: RANGE AND CHANGE

Our earlier discussion of price movement posited that a trending market, one whose autocorrelation at lag 1 approached a unitary value, was characterized by the domination of interday change over intraday range. This represents a more rapid movement by price toward value, which also reflects greater market certainty: One does not run after anything in large, bounding steps without some degree of confidence as to the location of the target. If volatility represents uncertainty, as it does given the effects of higher volatility on confidence intervals and probable price ranges seen above, we must conclude that a large degree of interday price change is characteristic of a low-volatility market.

The opposite is true as well. A nontrending market is one in which either price is oscillating narrowly about a confined value—a tightly consolidating market, for example—or one in which value itself is oscillating within a broad band and is frustrating the attempts of price to locate it. In either case, intraday range dominates interday range. The degree of certainty as to the path of value over time is low, and this higher uncertainty expands the confidence interval and probable price ranges. The higher degree of uncertainty represented by the large daily price ranges is characteristic of a high-volatility market.

Standard historical volatility measures focus on the annualized returns, the logarithm of the ratio of consecutive closing prices, of a price series over an N-day period. These measures, however modified, classify any series with large interday price changes as volatile, but this is wholly contrary to the economic meaning of uncertainty.

$$\sum_{i=1}^{N}\left[\frac{(\ln(\frac{C}{C_{t-1}}))^2 \cdot 260}{N}\right]^{\frac{1}{2}} \tag{2.8}$$

This problem can be circumvented by combining the two concepts of intraday price range and interday price change into a single measure, Parkinson's high-low-close volatility, and then modifying the measure to account for true daily ranges by taking either the maximum of today's high price and yesterday's closing price or the minimum of today's low price and yesterday's close:

$$\sum_{i=1}^{N}\left[\frac{\left[.5\cdot\left(\ln\left(\frac{\max(H,C_{t-1})}{\min(L,C_{t-1})}\right)\right)^2 - .39\cdot\left(\ln\left(\frac{C}{C_{t-1}}\right)\right)^2\right]\cdot 260}{N}\right]^{\frac{1}{2}} \tag{2.9}$$

This high-low-close volatility expands as uncertainty expands and intraday price range dominates interday price change, and it contracts as interday price change dominates intraday price range; therefore it is far more representative of the true economic relationship between uncertainty and volatility. This relationship is illustrated in detail in Chapter 5 as we discuss the development of the Market Tension Index.

VOLATILITY AND SIGNAL: THE ADAPTIVE MOVING AVERAGE

We left the construction of the adaptive moving average at Equation 2.5, restated below, with the promise to return with the inclusion of volatility and its effects:

$$\min\sum_{i=1}^{N}|P_i - L_i|\cdot|L_{i+1} - L_i| \tag{2.5}$$

Each half of the relationship, $|P_i - L_i|$, which is the difference between the current price series and its optimal moving average line L, and $|L_{i+1} - L_i|$, which is the first difference of the line L itself, is both increased in value and decreased in its ability to represent the true underlying value by higher volatility. We need, therefore, to divide both halves of the relationship to avoid overweighting the segments in time of the underlying price series that are volatile, the segments in which price is struggling to converge to underlying value:

$$\min \sum_{i=1}^{N} \frac{|P_i - L_i|}{Vol} \cdot \frac{|L_{i+1} - L_i|}{Vol} \tag{2.10}$$

Finally, we need to put this into an operating context by solving for the number of days in which the average value of this function is minimized. A 1-day moving average is meaningless, and a very long moving average loses meaning for most price series as well. Two bounds will be imposed arbitrarily, one at 4 trading days and one at 29 trading days: A period of 3 days or less includes too little information to be useful, and a period of 6 trading weeks or more contains too much information to be useful. After taking the average over the N-day period from 4 to 29 days, we select the value N that minimizes Equation 2.11. This N-day moving average adapts to the market's underlying structure and the efficiency of price in locating the underlying economic value, and will be referred to as the adaptive moving average. The value of N that minimizes Equation 2.11 will be referred to as the N-day speed and will be used in the subsequent system of market classification.

$$\frac{1}{N} \cdot \sum_{i=1}^{N} \frac{N}{Vol^2} \cdot |(P - MA)| \cdot |\Delta MA| \tag{2.11}$$

CLASSIFYING MARKET STRUCTURE

The French word *triage*, which describes the act of dividing something into three categories, entered common usage during World War I. Battlefield casualties were classified into the categories of (1) beyond hope and therefore unworthy of receiving scarce medical assistance, (2) superficially wounded and likely to recover without scarce medical assistance, and (3) those who would need scarce medical assistance to survive. Our task is analogous but is mercifully free of the unbearable moral burdens faced by triage officers.

Markets, too, can be divided into three categories: (1) markets in an identifiable trend in which price is moving rapidly behind value, (2) markets in a sideways condition in which price has matched value and is now waiting for either further confirmation or reversal of the change in underlying value, and (3) markets in which value itself is oscillating so that price's path is of a transitional nature.

A trending market exhibits an inertia of sorts; so long as price is pursuing a still-changing underlying value, the trend should remain intact—and indeed may remain intact for a very long period of time, as the bull market in equities during the 1990s demonstrated. A trend will endure until one of two things happens: a decisive rejection of a price in excess of value—our spike tops and bottoms—or a gradual fizzling out into a sideways market, a devolution into a consolidative structure indicative of price's convergence to underlying value.

What should the relationship between an adaptive moving average and the underlying price series be in a trending market? Since a trend is characterized by price trying to catch up with a changing underlying value, we should not expect the adaptive moving average to cross the underlying price series; it should always trail the underlying series. In a trending market, interday price range dominates intraday price range, so we should expect the price series itself to exhibit tightly channeled behavior. A slow-moving average, one with a high N-day speed over 20 days, will trail the channeled price series and can be used to classify the market as trending. This is illustrated in Figure 2.11, a chart of the closing price of the June 1998 Digital Access Exchange (DAX) stock index futures and its 25-day moving average. At the last data point, May 22, 1998, the 25-day moving average minimized Equation 2.11. The DAX price series, trending upward at the time, outstrips the upward pace of the adaptive moving average.

A sideways market, unsurprisingly, exhibits many of the opposite characteristics. Unless the market involved is inherently nonvolatile—as was our earlier example of sand—we should not expect underlying value to remain confined within a narrow zone for very long, since the very nature of active markets creates a set of dynamic and chaotic feedback loops between price and the supply–demand balance that create a new and different underlying economic value. Sideways markets, therefore, are temporary. They begin with the successful convergence of price to underlying value and end when a new path of value over time emerges. Which way will value emerge from the consolidation—in the direction of the previous trend or opposite of the previous

Figure 2.11 **A TRENDING MARKET: JUNE 1998 DIGITAL ACCESS EXCHANGE (DAX) AND 25-DAY MOVING AVERAGE (MA)**

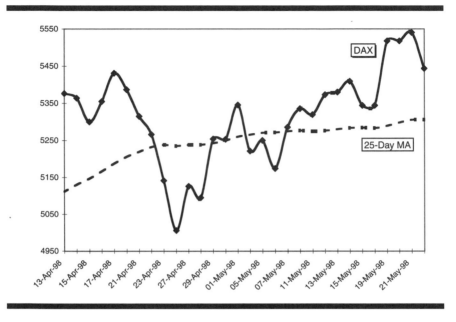

trend? If the market is at all efficient in the fundamental sense—and we should always assume that it is—the price at the end of a consolidation must be a very close representation of underlying economic value and therefore will have no predictive information as to the next change in value. In other words, we need to wait for the market to tell us its next move.

What should the relationship be between an adaptive moving average and the underlying price series in a sideways market? If a sideways market is defined by a successful convergence on value by price, we should expect the adaptive moving average line to cross through the price frequently. Moreover, in a sideways market, intraday price range dominates interday price change, so the movement of the price series itself should not be channeled tightly. A fast-moving average, one with a low N-day speed below 10 days, will slice through such a price series frequently and thus can be used to classify markets as sideways. This is illustrated in Figure 2.12, a chart of the closing price of the June 1998 Canadian dollar future and its 4-day moving average. The 4-day moving average minimized Equation 2.11 on May 22, 1998. The Canadian dollar had, at this writing, hit a short-term bottom, indicating that price has converged to a new, lower value, and its

Figure 2.12   **A SIDEWAYS MARKET: CANADIAN DOLLAR AND 4-DAY MOVING AVERAGE**

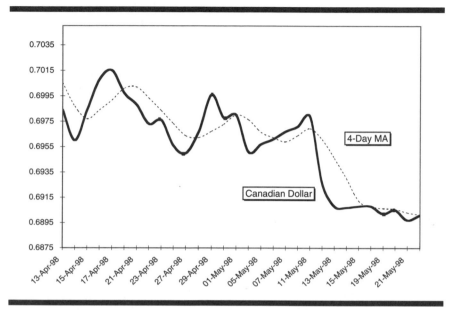

4-day moving average had already started to cross the underlying price series.

Transitional markets combine characteristics of both sideways and trending markets. As is the case in a sideways market, price in a transitional market is a close representation of value, but as is not the case in a sideways market, value itself in a transitional market is moving over time. Unlike a trending market, however, the move in value of a transitional market is not persistent and unidirectional; rather, it is bidirectional, with short-lived feints in either direction. Transitional markets are also temporary, for eventually a persistent move in value over time will manifest itself.

What should the relationship between an adaptive moving average and the underlying price series be in a transitional market? In a transitional market, interday price change does not dominate interday price range or vice versa. Price moves are not tightly channeled, as they are in a trending market, so we should expect the adaptive moving average to cross the price series frequently, but since value itself is changing direction frequently within a range, we should expect to see the adaptive moving average of price trailing the movement of price. A medium-speed *N*-day moving average, one between 10 and 20 days, can be used to classify markets as transitional. This is illustrated in Figure 2.13, a chart of the closing price of the June 1998 Italian government bond (Buoni del Tesoro Poliennali [BTP]) future and its 14-day moving average, the minimization point for Equation 2.11 on May 22, 1998. The BTP bonds rejected higher prices at the end of April, twice rejected lower prices in mid-May, and rejected one more attempt to move higher in late May. This broad range of uncertainty and the large and rapid moves from one end of the range to the other are consistent with an underlying value bouncing within the boundaries of the range.

THE PRICE–VALUE RELATIONSHIP: THE ADAPTIVE MOVING AVERAGE TREND OSCILLATOR

If the adaptive moving average is a distillation of the path of value over time, then the relationship between price and this average should provide a snapshot of the divergence between price and value. At the one extreme, if the price is equal to the adaptive moving average, then price instantaneously is providing a good representation of value, as it is in Figure 2.13 for the Italian BTP bonds. On the other

Figure 2.13   A TRANSITIONAL MARKET: ITALIAN BTP (BUONI DEL TESORO POLIENNALI) BONDS AND 14-DAY MOVING AVERAGE

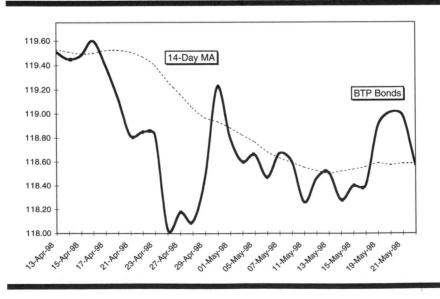

hand, as the market accelerates further and further into a trend, we should expect the difference between price and the adaptive moving average to grow large, as is the case in Figure 2.11 for the DAX stock index. In all cases, higher volatility lowers the probability that any given price represents underlying value.

To measure the difference between price and the adaptive moving average on a consistent basis, we need to adjust for the high-low-close volatility as defined in Equation 2.9 for any N-day trend speed:

$$\frac{(P - AMA)}{Vol} \tag{2.12}$$

Finally, since the difference $(P - AMA)$ will vary widely from market to market depending upon the ordinal magnitude of prices, we need to normalize the measure in Equation 2.12 for the price level itself:

$$\frac{(\frac{(P - MA)}{Vol})}{P} \tag{2.13}$$

This last measure is the adaptive moving average trend oscillator, which we will encounter again in Chapter 5 as part of the Market Tension Index.

3

Taking Care of Business

ON THE PERMANENCE OF RISK

Not having a position is a position. If you do not have an explicit trading position in the turnip market, then you have told the world in no uncertain terms that the cost of your gathering the information and of assuming all of the other overhead necessary to trade turnips is greater than the potential rewards in the turnip market. Otherwise, it would be economically irrational for you not to be trading turnips. This statement is true even if your business and your personal sustenance operate completely outside the orbit of the turnip world.

Even though a person standing outside the turnip market may choose to trade turnips and subject himself to the market's risks, he is not naturally at risk regarding the price of turnips. Only those whose economic lives are entwined somehow in the turnip market, either as producers and sellers or as consumers and buyers, are at risk with respect to the price of turnips, and these people are always at risk, regardless of wherever turnip prices happen to be at the moment. All producers/sellers are "long" the market and will suffer if turnip prices fall, and all consumers/buyers are "short" the market and will suffer if turnip prices rise.

All participants in the turnip market have a linear profit profile in turnips. Their distribution of expected returns is lognormal. This combination is the identical profit profile of a speculator in the market and will be referred to as the speculative profit profile. The word *speculation* and its derivatives have acquired a negative connotation over the years; the terms were linked to such paragons of virtue as Joseph Stalin and Mao Tse-tung and their very pockmarked walls. Admittedly, speculators throughout the ages have served the vital economic role of restoring free markets at times and places when and where governments have disrupted them, and no one likes the operator of a black market even as he lines up to purchase from the only source of supply available. The assumption was always made, therefore, that speculators were economic parasites on par with ticket brokers, rock-concert promoters, and other manifestations of the all-purpose enemies of the people. This is all so unnecessary. The word *speculate* derives from the Latin verb for "to watch," and that is the beginning and end of it. A speculator watches the market, gathers information, takes a risk, and accepts the consequences of his actions.

These speculative risks are intrinsic to one's economic role, and as such, they are always present in one form or another until they are removed. They are neither good, bad, nor ugly; all business depends on the prudent acceptance of risks to make a fistful of dollars—perhaps a few dollars more.

RISK TRANSFORMATION AND HEDGING

The time-honored method of neutralizing price risk is acquiring a position with an opposite profit profile, a process commonly known as hedging. The process's elegant simplicity derives from the linear and additive nature of profit profiles, as illustrated in Figure 3.1. A long cash market position will benefit from higher prices, usually on a one-for-one basis, and as a result, its profit profile across the dimension of price moves as a 45-degree line from the southwest to the northeast. A short futures market position will benefit from lower prices, and its profit profile across the dimension of price moves as a 45-degree line from the northwest to the southeast. The opposite profit profiles hold true for the case of a short cash market position combined with a long futures market position.

Until a hedge is emplaced, both long and short participants in the market are said to be "floating" on the price; their economic position rises and falls with changes in the prevailing market. Both sides can "fix" their price by executing an opposing futures market trade at a time of their choosing. Once price fixing has occurred, the external price risk is eliminated from an accounting standpoint except for minor basis fluctuations.

What is always excluded from this time-honored presentation is the decision point of where to emplace the hedge. The blithe assumption often is made that the hedge will be emplaced at the price that will guarantee an operating profit—or prevent a loss or provide some level of personal and professional satisfaction or some other reason

Figure 3.1 THE CLASSIC HEDGE SCENARIO

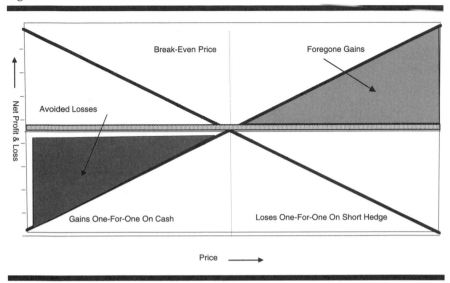

proffered after the fact. None of these oft-cited reasons is acceptable. The reality of the situation, hard though it may be to accept, is that this form of trading is nothing more than a speculation on price. As such, it does nothing to eliminate risk; it merely transforms the external risks provided by the market—which have been removed in the accounting sense by fixing the price—into an economic risk, one defined by opportunity gains and losses. The net result of the replacement of definite accounting risk with indefinite economic risk is that no risk has in fact been removed.

Before we begin to demonstrate this last point, it should be emphasized that there are indeed reasons to trade at a particular price, all of which are discussed later in this chapter. These include the facilitation of cash market transactions through the disconnection of the price from the underlying physical transaction and the demonstration of an appropriate floor or ceiling price to facilitate the extension of credit.

Now we return to the assertion that hedging at a particular price level simply reconstructs the linear profit profile of an unhedged cash market position. Despite the known tendencies of traders to be risk averse in the domain of wins and risk seeking in the domain of losses discussed in Chapter 1, let us assume that we will have a uniformly risk-neutral utility function across the entire price spectrum, which is giving ourselves a little bit more than we deserve. Let us also assume that we are incapable of adding value as a price forecaster, that our price predictions are no better than the random walk of the efficient market hypothesis. This sort of market behavior will give us the log-normal distribution of prices and the cumulative normal distribution curve seen in Figures 2.6 and 2.7 and shown together in Figure 3.2.

As demonstrated in Equations 2.6 and 2.7, these curves allow us to predict the probability of a price's reaching a certain level, at which point we can calculate the expected return of that price. If we use an example of an asset priced at $5.00, a volatility of 25%, and 50 days left in the life of the hedge, we can construct an absolute return map, one not weighted for the probability of this move's occurring, for any number of standard deviations of the price change. Superimposed on this gain and loss graph is the normal probability density curve, described in Equation 3.1, which highlights the low likelihood that these large, high-impact price moves will occur:

$$Density = \frac{1}{\sqrt{2\pi}} e^{-\frac{1}{2}x^2}$$
(3.1)

The expected gains and losses are simply the product of the two lines in Figure 3.3, the profit and loss of a certain standard deviation price change multiplied by the probability of its occurrence. The max-

Figure 3.2 **NORMAL DISTRIBUTION OF PERCENTAGE PRICE CHANGES**

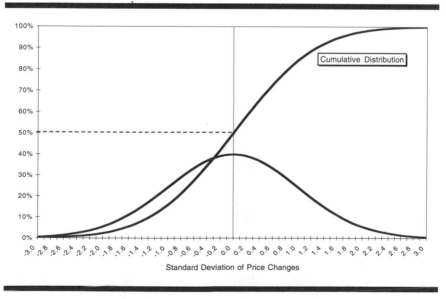

Standard Deviation of Price Changes

Figure 3.3 **ABSOLUTE GAIN AND LOSS FOR A $5.00 ASSET**

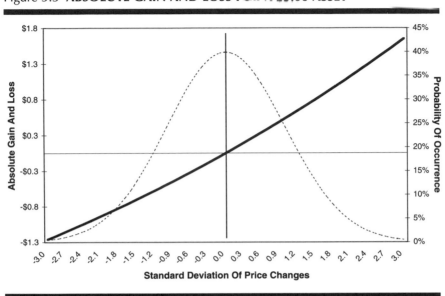

imum expected gains and losses do not occur at the maximum price movements, for these price movements are too infrequent, but rather toward the –1 and 1 standard deviation of price change levels. Superimposed on this expected gain and loss line is the cumulative normal probability distribution, described in Equation 3.2, which will be used to calculate the expected cumulative profit profile by summing the area under the curve:

$$Cumulative = \int_{-\infty}^{\infty} \frac{1}{\sqrt{2\pi}} e^{-\frac{1}{2}x^2} dt \qquad (3.2)$$

The curve of the expected cumulative profit profile in Figure 3.4 is a snapshot in time, one taken with 50 days of risk remaining. This curve can be summed over the cumulative normal probability distribution and then generalized over the entire life of the risk to illustrate how expected cumulative gains and losses expand with time, as shown in Figure 3.5.

The cumulative area of this surface is linear across time, as we can see in Figure 3.6 by taking the sum of expected returns over each day. Since the original profit profile of the unhedged position was linear as well, we can restate our original proposition that hedging, as commonly understood, does not eliminate risk but simply sweeps it under

Figure 3.4 **EXPECTED GAIN AND LOSS FOR A $5.00 ASSET**

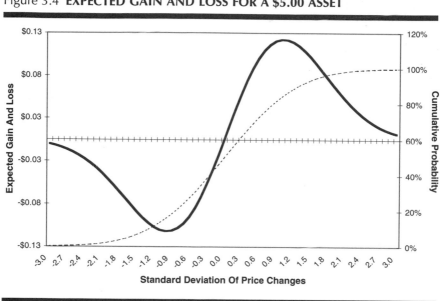

Figure 3.5 **CUMULATIVE EXPECTED RETURN AS A FUNCTION OF TIME**

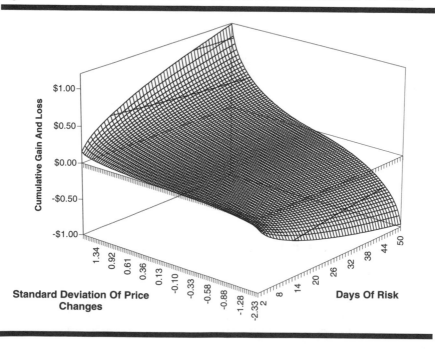

Figure 3.6 **CUMULATIVE EXPECTED RETURNS PER DAY**

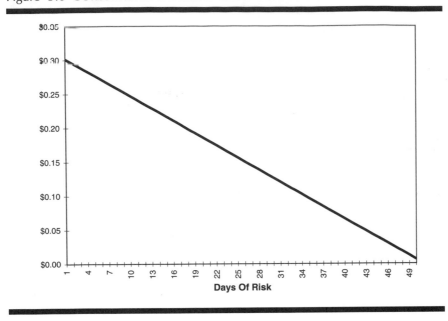

the rug. The values in Figure 3.6 are always positive as an artifact of the lognormal distribution of price changes.

Unless a trader adds value to the equation by having positive net expected returns from his trading decisions, there is no gain from hedging. Since a trader can be right in the absence of any underlying cash market position—one does not need to be a hedger to trade—the hedging activity is really a speculative activity. Moreover, the very nature of speculative trading demands risk-seeking behavior, and as discussed in Chapter 1, this leads to a refusal to accept small losses and to a willingness to accept the risk of larger losses.

True hedging is quite rare, and justifiably so. Businesses prosper by managing their risks, not by insuring 100% of their exposure in an absolute manner.

DISCONNECTING THE PRICE FROM THE PHYSICAL TRANSACTION

The world would be a far more civil place if people would simply agree to disagree more often. In a perverse way, this has been a hall-mark of civilization's advance. One must assume that commerce originally depended on a simple barter system, the legacies of which are still with us. Barter depends on multiple levels of negotiation between the parties, the first of which is what each good is worth in terms of the other, and the second of which is determining the relative anxiety levels of each party. The more anxious negotiator loses the negotiation but sets the price for all others to see, since it is his variance between price and underlying economic value that is reported.

The first critical evolution in commerce came with the advent of money as a medium of exchange, a storehouse of value, and a measuring system. Pricing all goods and services in terms of money instead of each other means that exponentially fewer prices need to be determined. For an economy with N goods and services, we need only N prices in terms of money but $(N^2 - N)/2$ prices in terms of barter arrangements. Although money certainly lowered the cost of commerce for all parties involved, it only simplified the first negotiation— what something is worth in monetary terms—and did not affect the relative anxiety negotiation at all.

The second critical evolution in commerce came with the advent of futures and forward contracts as a method of allowing both the buyer and the seller to fix prices not in direct negotiation with each other but rather in an open market. After these advances, the parties had only to agree to engage in the underlying physical transaction, a much easier decision to make, since this decision is defined by the business itself. A soybean farmer needs to sell his soybeans, and a soybean crusher needs to buy soybeans. Otherwise, both parties will eventually cease conducting business.

Table 3.1 illustrates a hypothetical soybean disconnection transaction between Farmboy Enterprises, the producer, and Crushco, the buyer. Both parties are quick to agree on the need for the physical transaction for 1 million bushels (1 MM Bu) of soybeans but are unable to agree on the price. The two parties enter into an exchange of futures for physicals (EFP) transaction wherein Farmboy trades its long soybeans for a long futures position at the prevailing price of $6.00 per bushel and Crushco trades its short position in cash soybeans for a short futures position at the same price.

Each party now has an equal and opposite price risk in the futures market, and both sides are floating on their price. Each side is free to fix the price at a time of its own choosing by offsetting the futures position. Once this is done, the financial risk of the transaction disappears for both parties but is replaced by an unequal and opposite set of economic risks: Farmboy will forgo gains over $6.30 per bushel, whereas Crushco will forgo gains below $5.75 per bushel. The cost of this arrangement is that each party must accept market risk in the accounting sense while their price remains floating. In all cases,

Table 3.1 **HYPOTHETICAL DISCONNECTION TRANSACTION**

Events/Conditions	Actions Taken	
	Farmboy	Crushco
Day 1: exchange of futures for physicals transaction with futures at $6.00		
Physical transaction	Sells 1 MM Bu	Buys 1 MM Bu
Financial transaction	Receives 200 futures at $6.00	Pays 200 futures at $6.00
Financial risk	Incurs long futures price risk	Incurs short futures price risk
Economic Risk	Incurs no incremental risk	Incurs no incremental risk
Day 2: price surges to $6.30 on forecast of extended dry weather		
Financial transaction	Sells 200 futures at $6.30	
Financial risk	None	Incurs short futures price risk
Economic risk	Forgoes gains > $6.30	Incurs no incremental risk
Day 5: price collapses back to $5.75 after heavy rains		
Financial transaction		Buys 200 futures at $5.75
Financial risk	None	None
Economic risk	Forgoes gains > $6.30	Forgoes gains < $5.75

Bu = bushels; MM = million.

whether payment is in barter, money, or futures, both parties remain at market risk in the economic sense after the price is fixed.

There is no magic involved in both parties' receiving a better price—nor would there be any chicanery involved if both parties received a more unfavorable price—after each party fixed its prices separately from the underlying transaction: They transacted price not with each other but with anonymous third parties. Engineers and physicists will be happy to note that there is a conservation of risk as well: Both parties traded their financial accounting risk for the economic risks associated with their respective opportunity gains and losses.

In exchange for the modest transaction costs involved, several benefits accrue to society as a whole. The most important of these is that since the two parties can ignore the negotiations intrinsic to barter and monetary transactions, they can both focus on finding the lowest-cost trading partner, one whose business is most complementary to their own. This allows for the minimization of transportation costs and other service-related costs associated with all physical transactions. A second benefit comes in the area of planning and certainty; once a physical transaction has been consummated, the business objectives of the firm take one more step toward completion, and this allows the firm to focus on its remaining objectives with presumably greater energy and efficiency. A final benefit to society is that although the firm has transformed only the nature of its risk, it has converted the risk into a form that is much easier to manage; it is far easier to convert the linear profit profile of the futures market position into the truncated profit profile of an option position than it is for a cash market position to do so.

Even though claiming societal benefits for price disconnection may sound grandiose, please consider that all such trades lower costs and risks. It is true that no firm ever prospered by buying insurance, but it is also true that few risky and innovative industries could stay in business for long without insurance. On a more personal note, ask yourself whether you would be willing to take on the risk of home ownership without the ability to insure this asset. Now consider the societal benefits of home ownership: stable communities, development of facilities, the personal benefits to children of growing up in their own home, and so on. Risk management matters.

FLOORS, CEILINGS, AND MARGINS: DO MARKETS FORECAST?

The greatest gain from risk transformation through the use of futures and forwards, however, comes from allowing marginal producers and consumers to stay in business by raising their credit quality. If Farmboy Enterprises was a cash-poor operation dependent on credit to stay in business until the harvest arrived, it would certainly help matters if it could show a bank that it has a minimum price, or floor, secured. The same applies on the other side of the transaction; Crushco may need to demonstrate a maximum cost, or ceiling.

If we extend the above disconnection transaction beyond the current crop cycle, we may find Farmboy and Crushco engaging in a series of transactions far out in time. Does this mean that the two parties have intersecting price forecasts, an equal assessment that the transacted price represents the expected underlying economic value that will pertain at that point in time, or do these transactions simply mean that at that particular price, each party will be able to secure a sufficient portion of its cost structure or revenue stream to protect its operating margins and to reassure its creditors?

Farmboy may, for its part, believe that $6.00 is an absurdly low price for soybeans, and Crushco may be equally unhappy about paying that amount. Both firms may have completely divergent price forecasts based on their understanding of prevailing supply and demand balances. Both firms may be risk seeking at the $6.00 price: Farmboy may be bullish on the market and thus willing to gamble on the chance that prices will move higher, whereas Crushco may be bearish on the market and equally willing to gamble on the chance that prices will move lower. Does the $6.00 trade price contain any information whatsoever on either side's outlook for the soybean market? No, but the $6.00 price does provide useful information on industry economics. If hundreds of soybean farmers are in the same position as Farmboy, and $6.00 remains the minimum price at which the marginal producer can stay in business, farm equipment suppliers know that they will not be able to raise their prices if soybeans approach $6.00. Soybean buyers will know that supply will start to leave the market once this price is approached. Industry forecasters will know that fewer acres will be planted in soybeans as this price is approached, and both the corn and cotton industries may need to prepare for the shift in planted acres. Signals will be sent to the South American soybean industry as well. Finally, the forward curve of soybean prices over time will reflect this valuable information on the relative anxieties of buyers and sellers.

4

Take My Risk, Please

A healthier diet and more frequent exercise will add years to your life, but at the wrong end. We might want to insert those extra years into a prolonged youth, but this is not possible: Time moves in only one direction, and it does so at a predictable rate. Try though we might, there is no way for us to trade a group of years in our eighties for a few months of youth.

This dilemma is not so stark in our economic lives, however. We can and do trade present consumption for future consumption through our decision on how much to save. Several factors enter into the saving decision, including one's age, anticipated future income requirements, wealth level, and confidence in the security of one's present income, but the key linking variable between consumption and saving is interest rates. All else held equal, the supply of savings should increase as a function of rising interest rates, as higher borrowing costs discourage present consumption and higher returns on savings encourage savings.

A similar logic pervades the market for commodities over time. A producer has an alternative between selling his production now or at some point in the future, and a buyer can either buy now or defer his purchases. The two prices should be linked by the cost of carrying the commodity available for sale now forward in time. At the point of indifference, the relationship should be:

$$\text{Future} \equiv \text{Spot Price} \cdot (1 + r)^t + \text{Physical Costs} \qquad (4.1)$$

Equation 4.1 is the standard cost-of-carry model for futures prices. It represents a powerful attractive force in the world of markets, a sort of financial law of gravity. Like gravity, it can be defied in many ways, but its presence never goes away. The enforcement mechanism for the standard cost-of-carry model is cash-and-carry arbitrage. We can rearrange Equation 4.1 so that if the future is greater than or equal to the current spot price plus the costs of storage, the combined capital and physical costs, then we can buy the cash commodity, place it in storage, and sell the future. Of course, just as nature abhors a vacuum, markets abhor providing traders with riskless arbitrage opportunities, so deviations from the cost-of-carry model are quite common in physical markets, in short-term interest rate markets, and in currency markets.

Market deviations from a pure carry structure convey information about the relative anxieties of buyers and sellers, about supply–demand imbalances, and about aggregate market expectations. These deviations in turn create a feedback loop into the market because they influence the costs of trading for buyer and seller alike. First, however, we should look at the cost-of-carry model as it applies to the one commodity most consistently in a full carry— gold.

A GOLDEN CONSTANT

The classic illustration of cost of carry exists in the gold market; the storage costs of gold are very low relative to its underlying value, and neither supply nor demand is particularly seasonal. We can calculate the carry rate between the spot and nearby futures contracts (F_1 and F_2, respectively) of gold futures as traded on the New York Commodity Exchange (COMEX) and later on the New York Mercantile Exchange (NYMEX) using Equation 4.2; since gold futures trade at 2-month intervals, we must take the nominal return to the sixth power to annualize it:

$$Carry\ Rate = \left[1 + \frac{F_2 - F_1}{F_1}\right]^6 - 1 \qquad (4.2)$$

Over the period between 1983 and 1997, this implied carry rate maintains a nearly linear relationship with the 90-day U.S. treasury bill rate, as shown in Figure 4.1. The positive coefficient of 1.067 accounts for the presence of physical carrying costs, such as warehouse fees and insurance, in the carrying charge. The R^2 of the relationship, .699, is surprisingly low given the generally high liquidity of gold futures and the cash market stocks of gold readily available for arbitrage strategies should the carrying relationship become distorted.

Figure 4.1 **IMPLIED CARRY RATE FOR GOLD FUTURES VERSUS 3-MONTH TREASURY BILL RATE DISTRIBUTION, 1983–1997**

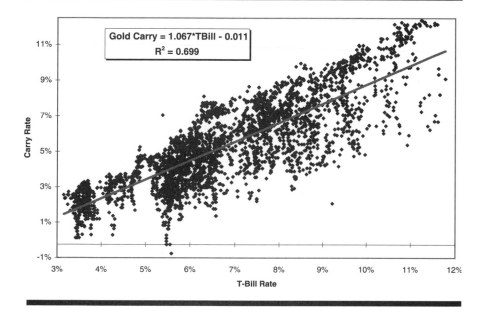

The source of the variance is in the day-to-day fluctuations of the implied carry rate for the gold futures, and not in the treasury bill rate; the daily variance of the implied carry rate is .0581%, as opposed to a daily variance of only .0357% for the treasury bills. The relationship between the two rates of return exhibits a general consistency, with the implied carry rate normally below the treasury bill rate, as shown in Figure 4.2.

DEVIATIONS FROM THE COST OF CARRY: BACKWARDATION

The gold market is very much the calm exception in a fretful world. Gold buyers—the brief burst of buying during the late 1970s excepted—are not particularly eager to secure supplies at a fixed price given the decades of visible supply in the market. Gold-mining companies have made active use of forward sale arrangements to guarantee the economic viability of their operations as discussed in Chapter 3, but the amount of gold mined each year is but a fraction of the supply already sitting in central bank vaults.

Figure 4.2 **IMPLIED CARRY RATE FOR GOLD FUTURES VERSUS 3-MONTH TREASURY BILL RATE TIME SERIES, 1983–1997**

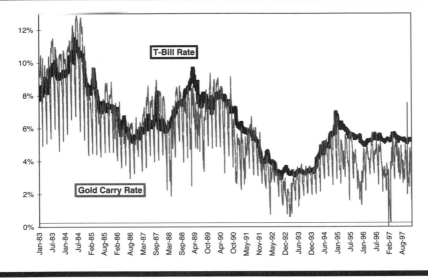

Other markets do not enjoy such luxury. The commodity is either consumed finally, as is the case in foodstuffs and fuels, or processed into another product where it will remain until recycled, as is the case in metals. In instances in which the commodity producer is in a singular business—a copper mining firm whose sole business is dependent on copper prices, for example—and the buyers are processors whose operating margins are a function of many factors other than the single input of a given commodity price, the commodity producer is likely to be the more anxious party in the transaction.

It is unlikely for producer anxiety to be uniform across time horizons, however. A producer who needs to demonstrate a floor price to secure longer-term financing will need to sell forward over a horizon equivalent to the maturity of his financing. The producer does not need to sell forward over short-term horizons, since the material probably has been sold already to a cash market buyer or it has been placed in storage and hedged to a longer time horizon. If prices rise, the seller's ability to move more product into the market for immediate delivery will be constrained by actual market demand, so the seller will look to hedge even more production forward. Since sellers become risk averse in the domain of profits, the effects of producer anxiety are most noticeable through lower prices at longer-term time horizons.

The opposite holds true for buyer anxiety. The cost of the commodity in question is but one component of the final processing margin. The buyer will limit purchases to whatever is needed to maintain operations and will keep inventories to a minimum. As prices rise, the buyer is likely to become more risk seeking in the domain of losses and convince himself that the present price level is both unjustified and bound to fall. The cost of inventory maintenance is deflected back to the seller wherever possible. Since buyers become risk seeking in the domain of profits, the effects of buyer anxiety are most noticeable through higher prices at shorter-term time horizons.

The combination of producers eager to sell forward and buyers deferring their purchases to the last possible date leads to the market condition called backwardation (or inversion, in most agricultural markets). Once prices start to rise, both buyer and seller expect them to fall, but they manifest their expectations in different forms.

John Maynard Keynes theorized that anxious producers needed to offer a discount to speculators to sell their risk—commercial buyers being unwilling to extend their purchase commitments that far into the future—and that this discount produced a natural return for speculators willing and able to buy the distant months. Keynes's hypothesis, the concept behind such products as the Goldman Sachs Commodity Index (GSCI), requires stable or rising cash market prices to realize this natural return, and such a market outcome is by no means certain. This subset of backwardation is referred to as normal backwardation. We will examine later whether these natural returns on holding commodities exist.

Table 4.1 lists the attributes often associated with a backwardated market. Each of these points is discussed below. Point 3, the relation-

Table 4.1 **ATTRIBUTES OF BACKWARDATION**

Attribute	Description/Properties
1. Shape of forward curve	Declines with time
2. Relationship to spot cash price	Futures below cash; converge upward
3. Cash market supplies	Scarce
4. Prevailing cash price trend	Generally rising
5. Price expectations	Falling
6. Hedging cost	Paid by sellers
7. Rewards	Buying early
8. Convenience yield	Positive
9. Cash-and-carry arbitrage	Impossible
10. Method by which lending is achieved	Sell near/buy far
11. Limits to curve	Profit of selling supply > processing

ship between backwardation and supply scarcity, will be the subject of a small case study for the corn market at the end of this section.

The first two attributes, the declining forward price curve over time and the convergence upward to the cash price, are confirmed readily by visual inspection. Copper is a commodity readily suited for backwardation; marginal mines need to secure a floor price to guarantee operating profitability and thus are eager to sell forward, but copper buyers, such as brass mills, have every incentive to practice just-in-time inventory. The cheapest place to store copper is in the ground. If demand for copper surges, there is no way for mines to bring additional supply to market quickly, since the supply pipeline is capacity constrained in terms of such factors as mine operating rates and railroad and port schedules. The London Metals Exchange (LME) offers contracts on copper on both a spot and a 3-month-forward basis. As shown in Figure 4.3, the cash price generally exceeded the 3-month forward, and often by a significant amount, between early 1994 and the sharp downturn in copper prices in late 1997 associated with the collapse of the east Asian economies.

Some of these periods of excessive backwardation can be linked to the market manipulations of Sumitomo over this period, but a longer-

Figure 4.3 **LONDON METALS EXCHANGE (LME) COPPER BACKWARDATION**

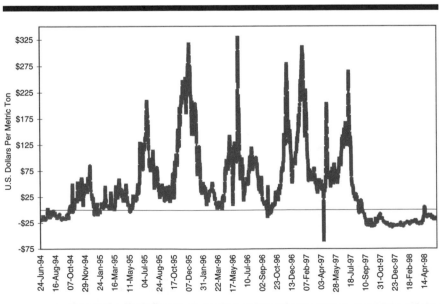

Figure 4.4 **COPPER BACKWARDATION, 1959–1998**

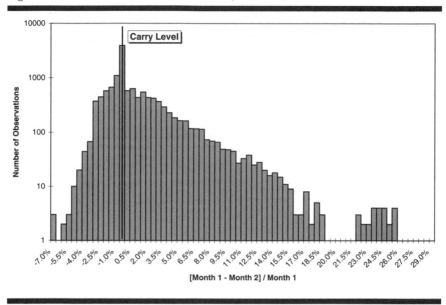

term view of copper shows a very consistent pattern of open-ended backwardation and limited carry. Data for the spot and first nearby copper futures traded at the COMEX (now part of the NYMEX) are available since 1959. A histogram of copper backwardation taken as a percentage of the underlying price, $(Month_2 - Month_1)/Month_1$, is presented in Figure 4.4 along with a market line depicting the level required for carrying copper from one contract month to the next. The majority of observations are of copper in backwardation.

A more interesting observation is the asymmetry of the histogram: Although only a scattered number of observations get down to a level of carry as large as 7% of the spot month price, a large number of observations exceed 7% backwardation, and there are a smattering of observations at the extreme backwardation levels of over 20% of the spot month price. Many readers will recognize this asymmetry as the profit profile of a call option; that correct conclusion is discussed later in this chapter.

Since backwardation occurs when both buyer and seller agree that the present price is unsustainably high and therefore should fall in the future, points 4 and 5 in Table 4.1, we should expect to see a connection between price and backwardation. This connection has held in copper since 1982, as illustrated in Figure 4.5.

Figure 4.5 **COPPER BACKWARDATION AS A FUNCTION OF PRICE**

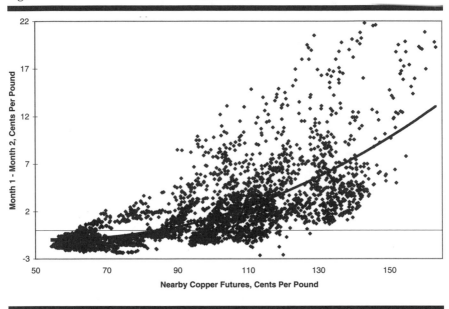

The call option–like nature of backwardation is even more apparent in Figure 4.5 than in Figure 4.4. The carry discount never gets deeper than $0.03 per pound, regardless of the ordinal price level of copper. As the price of copper rises, backwardation not only tends to rise apace but actually accelerates in a quadratic manner: A regression of backwardation against price yields a relationship of

$$\text{Backwardation} = 2.96 - .148 \cdot \text{Price} + .0012 \cdot \text{Price}^2 \qquad (4.3)$$

The residuals of the regression from Equation 4.3 display increasing variance as a function of the price, further evidence of increasing anxiety in the market on behalf of both buyers and sellers as the price rises, as stated in point 5 of Table 4.1.

The data displayed in Figures 4.4 and 4.5 illustrate the historical limits to copper backwardation in two ways. In Figure 4.4, we see only a small number of data points where backwardation exceeds 20% of the spot month price. In Figure 4.5, we never see copper backwardation in excess of $0.22 per pound. Without any fundamental knowledge of any copper processing industry, we can conclude that at these levels of backwardation a processor will find it more profitable to return the copper to the market than to process it into any product. This is one illustration of point 11 in Table 4.1.

Our sixth attribute of backwardation is that hedging costs are paid by the seller as part of the inducement to speculative buyers in the back months to assume the risk of lower prices. These hedge costs fall into two categories. The first is the difference between the current cash market price and the discounted price in the future, or the difference between what something is worth now and what an anxious seller is willing to receive. This is conceived readily by imagining someone's selling a pound of copper worth $1.00 today for $0.95—or an equivalent value in a foreign currency—3 months from now. This cost is direct and measurable and can be accommodated readily by anyone's accounting system. The second cost is the difference between the full carry level and the current cash market price, or the difference between what one should have received in a market free from anxiety and what something is worth now. This is conceived readily by imaging someone's lending $1.00 now with the expectation of receiving $1.015 3 months from now.

In the example above, a seller of $1.00 worth of copper should receive $1.015 3 months from now but receives only $0.95. The true economic cost of hedging is *$1.015 – $0.95*, or $0.065. If we annualize this, we can see that the cost of hedging is:

$$\left[1 + \frac{1.015 - .95}{.95}\right]^4 - 1, \text{ or } 30.31\% \tag{4.4}$$

This cost of hedging is rather considerable, and it begs two questions. The first, and most obvious, is why would anyone pay such an economic penalty? The only rational answer is that the hedger fears the possibility of a price decline greater than $0.065 per pound of copper over the next 3 months. We can calculate the odds of such an occurrence by using our lower bound range formula from Equation 2.7 and rearranging; we will use a 15% volatility:

$$\ln\left(\frac{LowerBound}{Price_{t0}}\right) = -\sigma\sqrt{\tau}Z \tag{4.5}$$

$$\ln\left(\frac{.95}{1.00}\right) = -.15 \cdot \sqrt{\frac{91}{365}} \cdot Z \tag{4.6}$$

The value of Z can be solved for quite easily as .6848, which corresponds to a cumulative probability of 75.33%, or odds of 3.05 : 1 that the price will stay over $0.95 during the next 3 months. If the hedging firm is exposed heavily to copper, it is exposed to a nontrivial probability of losing money on its copper position. The final hedging decision needs to be based on the firm's ability and willingness to afford such a loss.

The second question is simply the opposite of the first: Why would any buyer of cash copper pay $1.00 now when it is available for $0.95 3 months from now? The answer is given within the question: A processor of copper needs copper continuously and probably needs to keep minimal stocks of copper and other raw materials available as working inventory. Shutting down a production line incurs a substantial number of costs and should be considered only when the entire operation is both presently and prospectively unprofitable.

The annualized hedging cost seen in Equation 4.4 is the cost a buyer pays for the convenience of having inventories available, and thus is referred to as convenience yield in point 8 of Table 4.1. It can be conceived of as the rate of price increase that would be required to justify holding inventories over the hedging period. All markets in backwardation exhibit a positive convenience yield, all markets in perfect carry exhibit a convenience yield of zero, and all markets in contango—a discount of the front month greater than the full carry level—exhibit a negative convenience yield.

The positive convenience yield of a backwardated market precludes cash-and-carry arbitrage, or the profitable storage of surplus inventories, point 9 of Table 4.1. A reverse cash-and-carry arbitrage, defined by selling cash market inventories and buying distant futures, is possible, and as is discussed below, this allows the holder of a hedged cash market inventory to realize the call option potential embedded in the inventory. The positive convenience yield paid by a buyer in a backwardated market also implies that there is a reward for buying as early as possible to minimize the backwardation spike as delivery date approaches, and that lending is achieved by selling the near month and buying the far month, points 7 and 10, respectively, in Table 4.1.

Backwardation as a Call Option

We have mentioned several times that backwardation has characteristics of a call option. Before we discuss options in greater detail, though, it is vital to make the comparison now so that we may complete the discussion of the attributes of backwardation listed in Table

4.1 and provide one more illustration of the table's point 11, the limits to backwardation.

A call option is the right, but not the obligation, to purchase an underlying asset on or by a fixed time at a fixed strike price. A fixed premium is paid for this right, and for reasons discussed later, this premium represents a borrowing on the part of the buyer—just as the purchase of a near month and sale of a far month in a backwardated market represents a borrowing on the part of the buyer of the near month. This right becomes more valuable as the price of the underlying asset increases relative to the strike price, and it becomes more valuable without limit: If the price of the underlying asset keeps increasing, then the value of the call option will keep increasing.

Backwardation contains an embedded call option. We can illustrate this directly by substituting a long cash market position for a long spot month future, resulting in a long cash–short nearby month future spread, not an unusual situation in any market. If the cash market position was acquired by taking delivery on a long futures position at an arbitrage profit, the owner of the cash position has a known downside—a profit, in this instance—which is analogous to the known downside of a long call option position.

As an example, let us assume that we can buy soft red winter wheat, the kind that trades on the Chicago Board of Trade, for $3.025 per bushel for September 1998 delivery. It costs $0.048 per bushel per month to store wheat; let us assume that we have a 5.5% cost of short-term capital. Our full carry price for December wheat is:

$$\$3.025 + 3 \cdot \$0.048 + 3.025 \cdot (.055 \cdot \frac{91}{365}), \text{ or } \$3.21125 \qquad (4.7)$$

If our grain elevator operator is willing to take a speculative long position in wheat, he may wait until December wheat is at $3.25 before he sells. He is now assured a profit of $3.25 – $3.21125, or $0.03875 per bushel, an annualized gain of $(1 + \$0.03875/\$3.025)^4 - 1$, or 5.22%, a rate of return roughly in line with the risk-free rate. This is the elevator's accounting rate of return.

The economic rate of return is something quite different. During the period between the expiration of September futures and delivery on the December futures, the elevator is now in position to deliver cash wheat to anyone who finds himself, for whatever reason, in sudden need of wheat for immediate, and not December, delivery. The elevator can sell the wheat and buy back December futures, whereas a flour miller can buy the wheat and either sell December futures as a hedge or simply do nothing at all. Although the flour miller's needs simply are for immediate delivery of wheat, one might assume that his best course of action would be to do nothing at all, but he may have to sell December futures as an exchange of futures for physicals (EFP) transaction to facilitate the deal with the elevator operator, who is looking to buy back his short December futures.

At what premium on the December futures will the elevator be willing to part with its wheat? One would hope that it would be some number that would exceed his assured 5.22% rate of return, which is now his worst-case outcome. What is the greatest premium of cash wheat to December futures that a flour miller will be willing to pay? The answer depends on the physical costs of the mill and the economic damage that would result from having to either purchase flour in the cash market for redelivery to the mill's customers or default on delivery obligations. Let us arbitrarily cap this premium at $0.75 per bushel and, in deference to point 11 of Table 4.1, state that at this level, a flour miller at the margin will make far more money selling wheat back to the market than he ever will processing it into flour.

We now can calculate the potential annualized economic return on the hedged wheat in storage:

$$\max\left(\left(\left[1+\frac{(Cash-Fut)-(3.25-3.025)-0.048\cdot\frac{d}{30}-(.055\cdot\frac{d}{365})\cdot3.025}{3.025}\right]^{\frac{(365)}{d}}-1\right),5.22\%\right) \quad (4.8)$$

where the (Cash − Fut) term represents the premium of the cash wheat in storage over the December future, and d is the number of days in which the wheat will remain in storage. Experienced option traders will recognize the similarity between Equation 4.8 and the value of a call option's intrinsic value at expiration, max(Future − Strike, 0). Since the minimum annualized return under the conditions posited is 5.22%, we must reach the conclusion that the market is paying us to own a call option!

One final piece of data is needed to complete the analysis, and that is the probability of us ever realizing the full value of this embedded call option. There are two intersecting probabilities here, the first being the probability that a flour miller somewhere will require immediate delivery of cash market wheat, and the second is the probability distribution that the premium of cash wheat over the December future will follow. Neither probability can be known in advance; these are truly situations where past performance does not predict future results. Figure 4.6 illustrates what the nonannualized return will look like once the call is made on the elevator to sell cash

Figure 4.6   **EXPECTED ECONOMIC RETURN ON HEDGED INVENTORY**

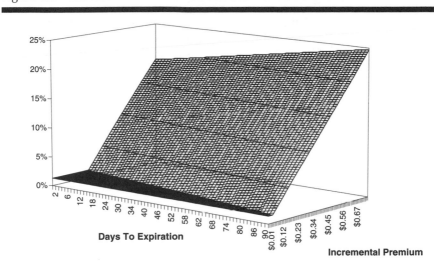

market wheat under our familiar lognormal distribution of prices with a 15% volatility.

Unlike a normal call option, however, the economic return of a hedged inventory can be limited by the willingness of a potential buyer to return supplies to the market instead of processing or consuming them. If we extended Figure 4.6 to incremental premium levels beyond $0.75, our arbitrarily imposed limit, we would see the economic return graph flatten out to an asymptotic level at each time horizon.

Backwardation and Supply Scarcity: Corn

Extracted commodities, such as crude oil and copper, are produced continuously, but agricultural commodities are produced on discrete seasonal schedules. Supply responses from farmers lag price signals in the market, as do livestock herd sizes. Once the vagaries of weather are added to this cycle, periodic shortfalls and surpluses of deliverable grain stocks result.

The level of corn stocks carried over from year to year is built largely from supplies deliverable against the December contract. For example, corn grown during the summer of 1998 will be delivered against the December 1998 contract, and supplies will be carried over into 1999. Since some corn is delivered against the September contract,

July usually is considered the last contract for the old crop, the one grown in the preceding year. Any scarcity of deliverable stocks should produce backwardation—inversion—between the May and July contracts as corn buyers scramble to ensure themselves an available supply. Even though the same logic holds true for the July–September and September–December spreads, those spreads reflect expectations for the current growing season.

Table 4.2 reflects the carryover stock-to-usage ratio and the average May–July spread over the 2-month period when May was the spot futures contract for each crop year since 1987. One year, 1996, stands out for its strong inversion. In that year, the carryover stock-to-usage ratio fell to .05, the lowest value in the period. The year with the second lowest ratio, 1997, also witnessed an average inversion. Figure 4.7 illustrates the May-to-July spreads for each year over the period when May is the spot month future.

Backwardation and Seasonality

The crop year in corn is one example of how seasonal factors affect intermonth spreads in the futures market. Since the production of corn is noncontinuous, a better example of seasonal factors in backwardation can be seen in such fuels as natural gas and heating oil. In normal conditions, the forward curves for both commodities unsurprisingly peak in the winter months, decline in an apparently backwardated fashion into the summer, and then revert to a carry struc-

Table 4.2 **INVERSION IN CORN PRICES**

Year	Carryover/Average Usage Ratio	May–July Spread
1987	.66	−4.49
1988	.55	−7.54
1989	.27	−0.09
1990	.17	−1.48
1991	.20	−7.24
1992	.14	−5.26
1993	.25	−5.07
1994	.11	−2.78
1995	.17	−6.24
1996	.05	16.97
1997	.10	0.61
1998	.14	−7.68

Figure 4.7 **MAY-TO-JULY CORN SPREAD**

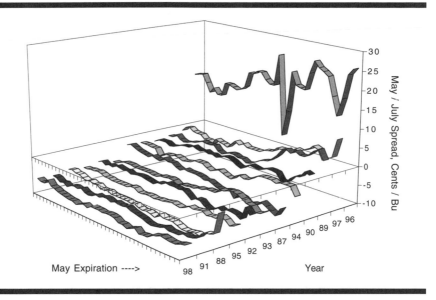

ture. This is obvious, in Figure 4.8, for natural gas but less so for heating oil; the deeply depressed price levels of spot heating oil at the time of the snapshot provided ample opportunities for cash-and-carry arbitrage in this market, and the pattern of buying cash heating oil and selling futures over the winter months between 1988 and 1998 buffered this curve's normal shape.

In actuality, the seasonal patterns for natural gas and heating oil have been diverging for some time, and this tells an interesting story in terms of industrial organization, market behavior, and the use of futures markets. The spread between the spot and nearby futures contracts for natural gas, depicted in Figure 4.9, swings sharply between backwardation levels and deep carry levels, with the normal seasonal pattern being for maximum backwardation as a percentage of the underlying spot price occurring in November and December and for the deepest carry occurring in August and September. In the short life of natural gas futures, covering several weather cycles and a wide range of supply–demand balances, this pattern has been remarkably stable.

The natural gas industry is somewhat unusual in that the major value added is in the transport, not in the production or in the minimal processing required to transform raw natural gas at the wellhead into a clean, dry, homogeneous product ready for use as either a fuel

Figure 4.8 **FORWARD CURVES FOR HEATING OIL AND NATURAL GAS**

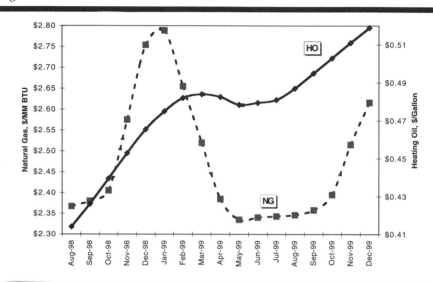

Figure 4.9 **NATURAL GAS SPOT–NEARBY SPREAD AS A PERCENTAGE OF NEARBY PRICE**

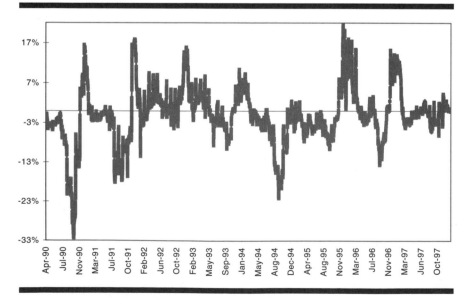

or as a chemical feedstock. Even though the product is storable and many local distribution companies (LDCs) do operate a system of storage caverns, less than 5% of natural gas is stored throughout the supply chain. More importantly, almost none of this gas is stored by end users, most of whom lack storage facilities.

Moreover, although some large industrial fuel users can switch to a cheaper fuel during a price surge, few residential or commercial customers have this capability. If backwardation is caused in part by a surge in immediate demand relative to supplies and is broken when buyers find it more economic to return their supply to the market rather than consume or process it, then natural gas is tailored for nearly unbreakable surges in backwardation: At what price will a residential customer cease buying heating fuel during a cold snap? This removes the incentive for the middlemen in the natural gas transport chain—the pipelines and LDCs—to cap their own purchase costs. The economic penalty for buying and storing extra natural gas that will then go unsold can be large, but the penalty for paying a spot market premium that can then be passed on to customers is nearly absent.

The heating oil market, which should have a largely similar seasonal cycle, exhibits different behavior. As seen in Figure 4.10,

Figure 4.10 **HEATING OIL SPOT–NEARBY SPREAD AS A PERCENTAGE OF SPOT PRICE**

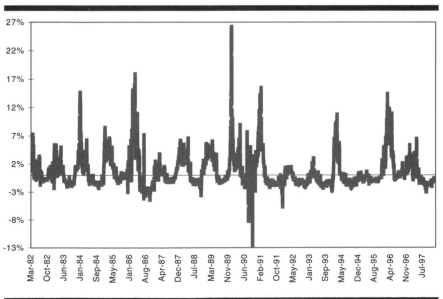

although the maximum levels of backwardation still occur in the winter months, there is no countercycle of deep carry in the summer months, the anomaly at the start of the Persian Gulf War in 1990 excepted. In fact, the maximum carry levels at other times around 3% of the spot month futures price are very close to the maximum carry percentages seen earlier in copper. This suggests market behavior that stops the carry level from deepening, the building of inventories at either cash-and-carry arbitrage levels or at minimal storage cost levels.

Unlike the natural gas industry, the heating oil industry is characterized by storage all through the supply chain. Refiners build inventories for subsequent sale because they cannot possibly meet seasonal demands otherwise; these stocks are referred to as primary inventories. Commercial middlemen also need to keep supplies on hand in what are called secondary inventories. Finally, consumers, including commercial and industrial users of other petroleum distillates, such as diesel fuel, keep supplies on hand in what are called tertiary inventories. A natural gas customer may be locked into a particular supplier by the constraints of the physical pipeline structure, but a heating oil customer can shop around for the lowest price and the most reliable service. Unlike the LDCs in natural gas, a supplier in the heating oil market will suffer economic penalties if he tries to pass on higher costs. In response, the entire heating oil market has modified its behavior. There is nothing anyone can do about external disturbances, such as the Persian Gulf War, or about the annual temperature cycle. Heating oil buyers—and this includes buyers of related petroleum distillates—can use a variety of hedging strategies to cap their costs and to build inventories in anticipation of peak demand. If this behavior modification has occurred, then we should be able to see a dampening pattern of seasonality in the market.

We can take the backwardation history of the NYMEX heating oil contract over the 18-year period between 1980 and 1997 inclusive and run a seasonal adjustment analysis on it using a standard U.S. Census Bureau X-11 seasonal adjustment process. As seen in Figure 4.11, our highest average monthly backwardation—those months with seasonal adjustment factors well over 1.00—occurs in the winter and the deepest carry levels—those months with seasonal adjustment factors well below 1.00—occur in the summer. This is as expected.

What may not be expected, however, is the decreasing spread between the seasonal factors as time moves on. This can be illustrated simply by subtracting the smallest monthly seasonal backwardation factor, that of August, from the largest, that of February. The resulting curve, shown in Figure 4.12, is consistent with the premise that a change in behavior occurred over time. The period covers diverse

Figure 4.11 **MONTHLY BACKWARDATION FACTORS IN HEATING OIL, 1980–1997**

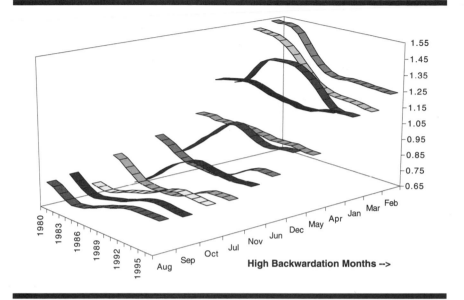

Figure 4.12 **HEATING OIL BACKWARDATION: AMPLITUDE OF SEASONAL FACTORS**

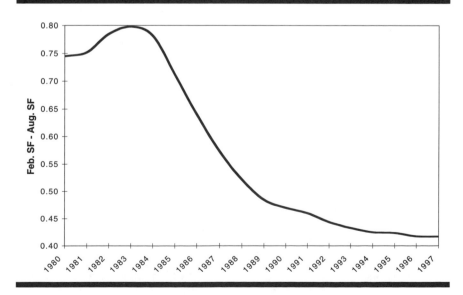

cycles of weather, price, and the economy, the distortions of the Persian Gulf War, the deregulation of natural gas, the advent of exchange-traded heating oil options in 1989, and the growth of an over-the-counter (OTC) market in customized heating oil derivatives. What was constant over this period? Only the increasing sophistication of participants in both sides of the heating oil market. The dampening of seasonal cycles illustrated in Figures 4.11 and 4.12 does not prove that increasing acceptance of sound risk management practices reduces backwardation and its associated price spikes in a market, but the dampening is consistent with the data. One wonders whether the exaggerated cycle of sharp backwardation and deep carry seen in Figure 4.9 for the natural gas market would be buffered similarly if the industry's organization were closer to that of heating oil.

Backwardation, Speculation, and Natural Returns

The theory of normal backwardation holds that speculators need to be provided with a discounted price in the distant months to assume the risk of sellers. How much should a speculator be willing to pay? At the very maximum, a speculator should pay the price he expects to prevail in the future discounted by the risk-free rate; this allows the speculator to earn a minimum of the risk-free rate, although in practice, any self-respecting speculator should demand to earn more. This price limit to speculative buying is referred to as the expected future spot price.

We can infer the expected future spot price by reverse cash-and-carry arbitrage, which consists of selling a cash market position forward and buying the future at a level that will cover the costs of capital and storage over the time horizon of the future. This is simply a rearrangement of Equation 4.1, the standard cost-of-carry model:

$$\text{Spot Price} \equiv \frac{Future}{(1-Costs)^{t}} \tag{4.9}$$

Since very few speculators are interested in reverse cash-and-carry arbitrage for the simple reason that they do not have the cash market position to sell forward, all of this falls into the category of easier said than done. The speculative buyer in a distant month is assuming two rather large risks: (1) that the current cash market price will remain stable or increase and (2) that the shape of the forward curve will remain in backwardation. Cash market prices in active markets are not stable; this is almost the definition of an active market. As we have illustrated in Figures 4.3, 4.9, and 4.10, the forward curve of commodities in backwardation frequently lapses into carry, both on a seasonal and on a nonseasonal basis. All that the theory of normal backwardation holds is that the discounted future price should converge upward to the cash price over time; if one removes the short cash market position from the reverse cash-and-carry arbitrage, all that is left is a speculative long position that will converge to whatever the spot market price will be at expiration. This can turn into a spectacularly bad trade.

A speculator in crude oil during the Persian Gulf War market could have bought distant months at a large discount to the spot month future and then waited for the upward convergence to work its inevitable magic. We can illustrate this trade by buying March 1991 crude oil at the close on December 10, 1990, at $25.74. February crude oil was at a $0.78 backwardation premium at the time, and given the strong likelihood that hostilities would emerge sometime in January 1991, it had the elements of a reasonable speculative trade, one that would gain in price as well as convergence. After crude oil prices fell after initiation of the air war on January 17, 1991, backwardation did in fact converge to only $0.26, a convergence gain of $0.52. This did little to offset the fall in March futures to $18.99, a loss of $6.75, for a combined loss of $6.23.

The extreme example in Figure 4.13 notwithstanding, speculators do buy forward in backwardated markets, so we must conclude that they expect to make a return on their investment and that the gain on holding a discounted forward month will exceed their cost of capital on a risk-adjusted basis, where S_i and F_i represent the sale price and purchased future prices, respectively:

$$\frac{1}{N} \sum_{i=1}^{N} \frac{S_i - F_i}{F_i} \geq RF \tag{4.10}$$

If Equation 4.10 holds true over time, we should be able to see reasonably consistent returns on the GSCI. However, as seen in Figure 4.14, this has not been the case since the inception of the data in March 1994. Although it is true that the period from 1994 through 1998 has been generally deflationary, and that only a brief period during 1996 saw any sort of commodity price increases coupled with backwardation, the entire notion of a natural return on commodities may be suspect.

First, we should address the issue of whether commodities are an asset class. Any financial asset has an economic return independent of

Figure 4.13 **PROFIT AND LOSS PROFILE FOR MARCH 1991 CRUDE OIL PURCHASE**

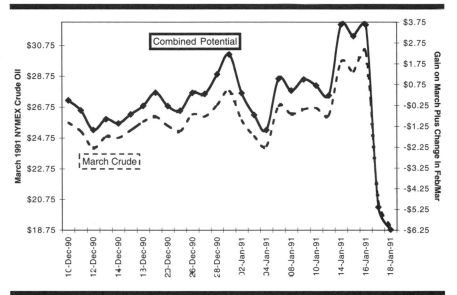

Figure 4.14 **GOLDMAN SACHS COMMODITY INDEX (GSCI) TOTAL RETURN INDEX**

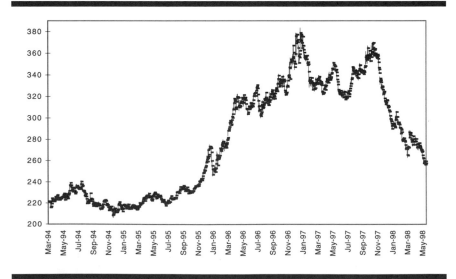

its owner. If 100 different people buy treasury bonds or Intel stock or syndicate shares in an office building, they will all receive the same return. Different investors may assign a different value to a given stock or bond depending on their investment objectives, existing portfolio, and risk tolerance, but once they acquire the asset, they will enjoy the same investment characteristics as any other buyer. All investors should be able to arrive at the same price for a bond by using known and accepted formulas involving interest rates, time to maturity, and credit risk. The same cannot be said for physical commodities. A corn miller can derive a different return from 5,000 bushels of corn than will a hog farmer, a distiller, or a grocer. The potential value added or processing margin is different for different buyers, and therefore each class of buyer should be willing to pay a different price for the corn.

Second, we should address a far more controversial—nearly religious—issue, whether commodity prices rise or fall over time. Our position is simple and direct: In a free market, factor input prices fall over time as productivity and efficiency increase. If a given factor input—whether it be land, capital, labor, or any physical commodity—increases in real price without a concomitant increase in its productivity, then either its supply will increase, demand therefore will decrease, or some combination thereof will ensue.

The temptation always is to believe otherwise, that the eighteenth-century logic of Thomas Robert Malthus will assert itself and that the world will start to exhaust its resources. It has not happened yet; it will it never happen in the future. Not only does every mouth consuming resources come with a pair of hands to produce resources, but the very definition of valued resources changes. An observer in the midnineteenth century might fret about impending shortages of fodder for horses and mules or about the ever-increasing scarcity of whale oil for lamps. Technological change made these concerns irrelevant, as subsequent technological changes have led to unprecedented levels of prosperity on a global basis. For us to think otherwise would be for us to deny the human capacity for ingenuity, and that capacity does not appear to have a limit.

The third and final point we need to address, and one that we will address in greater detail in our discussion of financial markets, is whether inflation is a permanent feature of the economic landscape. If this is the case—and this view certainly had its adherents by the late 1970s—then ownership of tangible assets was a natural hedge against depreciating financial assets. Let us assert quickly that inflation is not a given, and although it certainly has been tamed since the early

1980s, it has not yet gone to zero on a global basis. We can, however, take a look at almost any basket of commodities and find no evidence of nominal price increases, let alone any evidence of inflation-adjusted price increases. Figure 4.15 depicts the course of two commodity baskets that measure different segments of the economy, the *Journal of Commerce* (JOC) Industrial Price Index and the Bridge/Commodity Research Bureau (CRB) World Commodity Price Index, over the period from April 1988 through June 1998, indexed to 100 in April 1988.

One would be hard pressed to find any secular nominal price trend over this period; indeed, the values of both indices in June 1998 are virtually identical to the initial values in April 1988. Both indices have risen and fallen over the period, but there simply is no conclusive evidence of rising nominal commodity prices over time. This is not to say that there will never again be periods of strong physical commodity markets, for whether caused by supply disruptions from both natural and human causes or by surges in demand born from strong economic growth, commodity price levels will surely see periods of gain. However, these gains will never be sustainable so long as free markets are allowed to operate.

Figure 4.15 *JOURNAL OF COMMERCE* (JOC) INDUSTRIAL INDEX AND BRIDGE/COMMODITY RESEARCH BUREAU (CRB) WORLD COMMODITY PRICE INDEX, 1988–1998

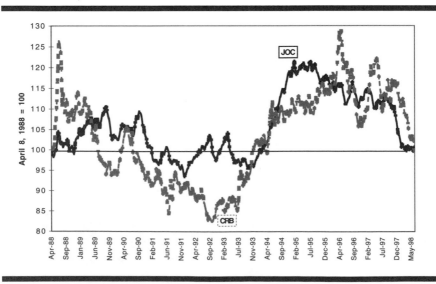

Conclusions

We began our discussion of the topic of the standard cost-of-carry model for futures markets by describing it as a financial law of gravity, a powerful attractive force, but one that is defied in many ways. Backwardation is the most important of these deviations in the physical commodity markets. Three aspects of backwardation were touched upon incompletely, with the idea that a further discussion would need to be developed: the effects of backwardation on hedging strategies, the linkage between intermonth spreads in futures and the option markets, and the linkage between backwardation and volatility.

We now turn to the other principal deviation from the standard cost-of-carry model, contango.

DEVIATIONS FROM THE COST OF CARRY: CONTANGO

The attributes of backwardation listed in Table 4.1 have, as do most economic processes, a set of near opposites for the situation defined by excess supplies in a market, contango. They are listed in Table 4.3, which can be viewed as a parallel guide to Table 4.1.

Attributes

The most important aspect of a contango market is the one that should not exist in a perfect world, and that is the inability and/or

Table 4.3 **ATTRIBUTES OF CONTANGO**

Attribute	Description/Properties
1. Shape of forward curve	Increases with time
2. Relationship to spot cash price	Futures above cash; converge downward
3. Cash market supplies	Abundant
4. Prevailing cash price trend	Generally falling
5. Price expectations	Rising
6. Hedging cost	Paid by buyers
7. Rewards	Selling early
8. Convenience yield	Negative
9. Cash-and-carry arbitrage	Possible
10. Method by which lending is achieved	Buy near/sell far
11. Limits to curve	Storage costs

unwillingness of buyers to engage in cash-and-carry arbitrage. However, there are physical limits to storage space and to the amount of capital buyers wish to commit to the building of inventories. In addition, the price of storage should increase as the demand for storage increases; one must assume that buyers will fill their lowest-cost storage space first.

Although a histogram of backwardation should and does resemble the profile of a call option, as illustrated in Figures 4.3 through 4.6, the histogram of contango levels should resemble a stairstep, a declining pattern that pauses as each incrementally more expensive level of storage is filled. We can illustrate this in the case of crude oil by generating a histogram—Figure 4.16—of negative spot month to nearby month spreads in crude oil futures. Each vertical bar in the figure represents the number of observations at that spread, whereas the solid line represents a five-value average of that spread value and the two adjacent spread values higher and lower. The shadowed boxes indicate the zones where the number of observations plateau at a lower discount than seen previously. These zones occur approximately between –$0.22 and –$0.37, between –$0.43 and –$0.58, and between –$0.76 and –$0.88. The three zones correspond to the approximate spread levels required to finance storage in tanks and pipelines, in barges, and in tanker vessels, respectively.

Figure 4.16 **DISTRIBUTION OF NEGATIVE INTERMONTH SPREADS IN CRUDE OIL**

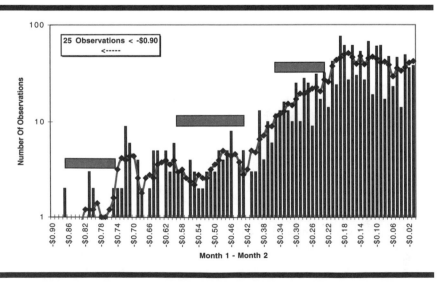

The cash-and-carry storage cost limit to contango, point 11 in Table 4.3, is a much easier boundary condition for a market to hit than is the limit to backwardation, the point at which a processor returns supplies to the market. Backwardation can move higher swiftly because reverse cash-and-carry is a much more difficult and less desirable trade to execute than is cash-and-carry arbitrage, but contango markets tend to develop slowly as buyers build hedged inventories and as suppliers eventually reduce the volume of goods moving to market.

The mixes of relative anxieties for backwardation and for contango are quite different, as defined in points 3 through 5 in Table 4.3. Speculative buyers do not need to be induced into assuming risk from commercial sellers in distant months; instead, a contango market is characterized by the need for commercial buyers to either step up their current demand or build inventories. Sellers are not worried about the price level in distant months; they believe that the current supply glut is temporary, so that although cash market prices are falling now, they will be stable or rising in the future. Buyers share this rising price expectation, but as is not the case for backwardation, they will be paying a penalty for buying in the distant months.

We can rearrange the facts in Equation 4.4 so that the copper market is in contango: cash copper will be selling for $0.95 per pound and a 3-month future will be selling for $1.015 per pound. We can add, for good measure, that copper prices have fallen from $1.25 over the past 2 months. If a brass mill or wire producer has purchased all the copper it needs for immediate use and does not wish to tie up additional capital and resources in building copper inventories even at the arbitrage profit level, it would still cost the same 30.31% annualized rate that we saw in Equation 4.4. Paying this rate of return implies that there is a negative return on holding cash inventories, which is the equivalent of saying that the convenience yield in a contango market is negative—point 8 in Table 4.3. Lending is achieved by the opposite action: buying a cash position or near-month future and then selling a distant future—point 10 in Table 4.3.

Buying the future at this negative convenience yield is simply a speculative long trade. It does not have any of the embedded optionality found in the hedged cash position. Even worse, since the future is priced at a level greater than its cost-of-carry fair value, the buyer in a forward month will be paying the combined cost of capital and physical storage costs and therefore needs the future's price to rise at a rate sufficient to cover those costs. Since these carrying costs diminish as a function of time, we expect that the overvalued future will converge downward to the cash market price as a function of time and that each succeeding future will be priced higher than the shorter-dated futures—our points 1 and 2 in Table 4.3. This is a handicap that few speculators would wish to assume. Thus, is it buyers who pay the hedge cost in a contango market and sellers, selling early in the cycle, who gain an economic advantage—our points 6 and 7 in Table 4.3.

Conclusions

The focus of this entire book is and must be the relevance of the forward curve for trading strategies and hedging applications. The forward curve is the market's thermometer for relative anxiety between buyer and seller. We can use this information as part of our own single indicator for measuring this relative anxiety, the Market Tension Index.

5

The Beating Heart

DIMENSIONS OF MARKETS: TREND, STORAGE, AND INSURANCE

The central tragedy of the Information Age is that too many people now know how to use computers, saddling us with 15 pages of indecipherable paperwork for every visit to the doctor and a blizzard of meaningless statistics spewing forth from every televised sporting event.

Enough. A torrent of numbers is mere data, but a single number can contain useful information when interpreted properly. We have now developed all the component statistics required for integration into this single number, which we will call the Market Tension Index (MTI). The MTI captures all three dimensions in which a market trades.

The first dimension is price. In Chapter 2, we established a methodology for analyzing the search by a market for its underlying economic value and, in so doing, developed the adaptive moving average and its associated trend oscillator and high-low-close volatility measure. The trend oscillator incorporates the effects of market structure—our classification of a market as being trending, sideways, or in transition—and high-low-close volatility as well as the estimate of where price is in relation to its underlying economic value. As any component of an index should, the trend oscillator has a point at which it equals zero, the point at which the current price equals the adaptive moving average.

The second dimension is the market for storage and its effects on price expectations. In Chapter 4, we established a methodology for analyzing the information contained in the forward curve of physical commodities and its associated convenience yield. Convenience yield as well has a point at which it equals zero, the point at which the market is in full carry.

The third dimension is the market for insurance. Although we have not yet entered into our discussion of option markets, the implied volatility in an option represents the market's price for insurance. If implied volatility exceeds the underlying volatility, in this case represented by the high-low-close volatility, then the market is exhibiting excess demand for insurance. This index component is equal to zero when implied volatility equals high-low-close volatility. Excess volatility will be measured as:

$$\ln\left(\frac{I.Vol}{HLCVol}\right) \tag{5.1}$$

The three dimensions can be combined into a single index. The developmental case study we will use will be on crude oil, which is eminently well suited for such an analysis: It has monthly contracts, a well-developed market for storage, nonseasonal production, periods with both backwardation and contango, and an actively traded option market. The only drawback to the crude oil market over the period from 1989 through 1998 is the Persian Gulf War; the New York Mercantile Exchange (NYMEX), for reasons best known to its managers, persisted in maintaining wholly inadequate daily price limits. As a result, both intermonth spreads and implied volatilities were distorted during this period; the front-month contract always traded without a limit, and both a shadow spread market and a shadow option market, based on where the nonspot months should have been trading, evolved.

Once we have developed the construction of the MTI for crude oil, we will study a second case, for soybeans, which both lacks actively traded monthly contracts and is highly seasonal in its production cycle.

ORTHOGONALITY

We can describe the physical location of any point in space by providing coordinates of length, width, and height. These coordinates are perfectly orthogonal to each other; one does not need any information on length and width to describe height, and so on. Pure orthogonality among market indicators is practically impossible to achieve, because

Figure 5.1 **CONVENIENCE YIELD AND EXCESS VOLATILITY**

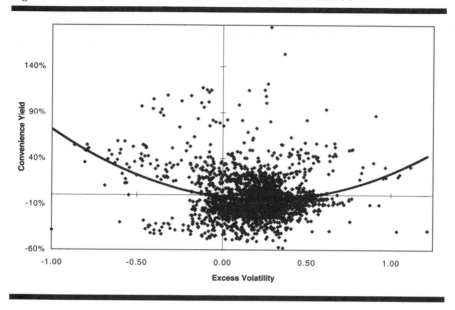

all our data are generated from the common source of price. All we can do is minimize the overlap between indicators.

First, we can take a look at the relationship between convenience yield and the excess volatility measure, as shown in Figure 5.1. The relationship between convenience yield and excess volatility is weakly quadratic; at moments of both great and weak demand for price insurance in the option market, convenience yield tends to be higher, but this relationship is not a strong one:

$$CY = -.0251 - .2399 \cdot XSVol + .0533 \cdot XSVol^2, R^2 = .0645 \qquad (5.2)$$

Next, we can examine the relationship between convenience yield and the trend oscillator, as shown in Figure 5.2. We should expect the relationship between these two indicators to be somewhat linear, as both strongly positive trend oscillators and strongly positive convenience yields are associated with rising, backwardated markets, and both strongly negative trend oscillators and strongly negative convenience yields are associated with falling, contango markets. The linearity exists, but once again, the relation is not as strong as one might expect it to be:

Figure 5.2 CONVENIENCE YIELD AND TREND OSCILLATOR

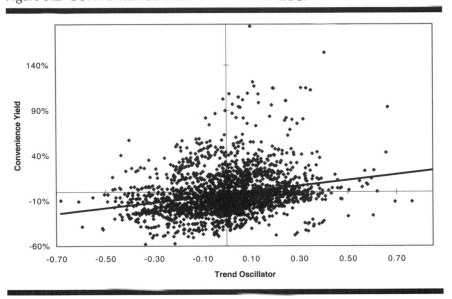

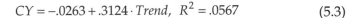

$$CY = -.0263 + .3124 \cdot Trend, \ R^2 = .0567 \tag{5.3}$$

Finally, we can examine the relationship between excess volatility and the trend oscillator, as seen in Figure 5.3. Excess volatility tends to develop as price moves toward extremes. If a trend movement is strong, it cannot be sustained forever, and therefore there should be a great deal of anxiety in regard to the present price. The converse is not exactly true: There is an asymmetry of trend when implied volatility is less than high-low-close volatility. Low-anxiety markets in crude oil tend to be associated with weak downtrends. From a fundamental point of view, this should not be surprising; the cost of hedging for producers is likely to be greater than the avoided losses from lower prices, and fuel consumers are not worried about weakly declining prices. Once again, the relationship, although visible, is rather weak:

$$XSVol = .1396 + .0889 \cdot Trend + .8591 \cdot Trend^2, \ R^2 = .0483 \tag{5.4}$$

None of the two-way relationships between the three index components is particularly strong, as we can see in Table 5.1, a correlation matrix of the components. The same observation holds true in the variance–covariance matrix of the components, as seen in Table 5.2.

Figure 5.3 **EXCESS VOLATILITY AND TREND OSCILLATOR**

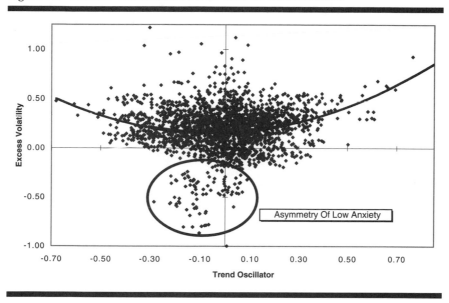

Subcomponents of the MTI have some interesting relationships as well. First, we can take a look at the relationship between convenience yield, which represents the willingness of refiners to build and maintain inventories, to the underlying price of spot month crude oil futures. In Figure 5.4, we can see that low and rising levels of convenience yield, such as seen in midsummer 1990 or in winter 1993–1994, appear to lead the movement of price higher. High and falling levels of convenience yield appear to have a much longer leading effect on subsequent changes in price, on the order of 6 months. In other words, a rebound from a contango market is ratified quickly by a change in price, whereas a break in backwardation has a much slower price effect.

Table 5.1 **CORRELATION MATRIX OF MARKET TENSION INDEX COMPONENTS**

	Convyld	XSVol	Trend
Convyld	1.0000		
XSVol	−0.1128	1.0000	
Trend	0.2380	0.0756	1.0000

Convyld = convenience yield; XSVol = excess volatility.

Table 5.2   **VARIANCE–COVARIANCE MATRIX OF MARKET TENSION INDEX COMPONENTS**

	Convyld	XSVol	Trend
Convyld	0.0578		
XSVol	–0.0062	0.0522	
Trend	0.0105	0.0032	0.0336

Convyld = convenience yield; XSVol = excess volatility.

A second relationship of interest is that between the absolute level of implied volatility and convenience yield. Just as convenience yields are bounded on the downside by the storage-cost limits to contango, implied volatility is bounded on the downside by a value of zero, the volatility that represents perfect price certainty. As convenience yields rise toward backwardation, volatility rises as a quadratic function of convenience yield, confirming the acceleration of market uncertainty in backwardation as both buyers and sellers agree that the current price is too high and bound to fall:

$$\text{ImpVol} = .2886 + .1535 \cdot \text{CY} + .1908 \cdot \text{CY}^2, R^2 = .1649 \qquad (5.5)$$

Figure 5.4 **CONVENIENCE YIELD AND PRICE**

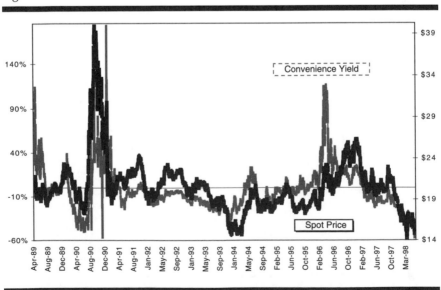

High values of implied volatility are observed at deep contango levels as well, and these are linked to instances of very sharp and sudden falls in the spot price that are soon corrected; crude oil is given to spike bottoms in a manner similar to the Standard & Poor's (S&P) 500, as seen in Figure 5.5.

DISTRIBUTION OF THE MARKET TENSION INDEX

Once the three index components are combined into the MTI, we still need to understand its distribution and whether it is an unbiased descriptor of market behavior. For the crude oil sample used, the MTI follows a normal distribution with strongly positive kurtosis; most observations are clustered around zero and there are very few extreme events. Both the mean and the skewness of the series are positive, which reflects the general risk background of the crude oil market: Although there are a large number of events, most of them unpleasant, capable of removing supply quickly from the market, there are very few events capable of adding supply quickly. As a result, both refiners and speculators are much more anxious about rising prices than about falling prices.

Figure 5.5 **CRUDE OIL: IMPLIED VOLATILITY VERSUS CONVENIENCE YIELD**

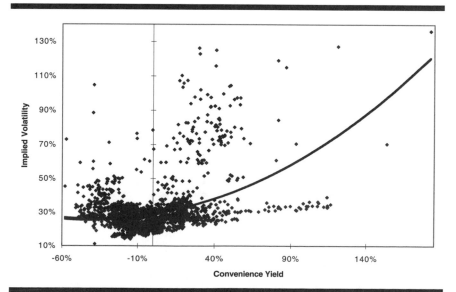

Statistically, however, the mean of the MTI is zero at a very high degree of confidence. The summary statistics for the crude-oil MTI are presented in Table 5.3, and the formula for calculating the critical number of standard deviations for hypothesis testing, Z, of the Student's distribution, is presented in Equation 5.6:

$$Z = \frac{\overline{X} - \mu_o}{\sigma / \sqrt{N}} \tag{5.6}$$

If we wish to test the hypothesis that the mean of the MTI for crude oil is indeed zero, our value of Z with the 2,296 observations available is –2.964. The probability that the mean of the MTI for crude oil is not zero, on a two-tailed t-test with 2,295 degrees of freedom, is 0.3065%.

The MTI's strongly positive kurtosis is illustrated neatly in Figure 5.6, a cumulative probability graph of the index. The one extreme outlier on the positive side, an MTI value of .2694, occurred on August 22, 1990, in the early stages of the Persian Gulf War rally; the veracity of this number is somewhat suspect because the second month future was limited to a $1.00 per barrel gain, whereas the spot month future gained more than $2.50. Implied volatility also surged to a value of more than 70%, nearly double the high-low-close volatility of 38.14% on that day. The extreme negative values occurred on March 11 and 12, 1998, as prices collapsed to their post–Persian Gulf War lows, contango fell to –$0.40 per barrel, and implied volatility surged to more than twice high-low-close volatility levels.

CRUDE OIL MARKET TENSION INDEX AS A TRADING INDICATOR

Establishing the MTI as a statistically well behaved indicator based on three reasonably orthogonal components would be just a pointless

Table 5.3 **SUMMARY STATISTICS FOR CRUDE OIL MARKET TENSION INDEX**

Aspect	Value
Mean	0.0004
Standard deviation	0.0150
Skewness	1.2915
Kurtosis	76.1581

Figure 5.6 **CUMULATIVE NORMAL PROBABILITY DISTRIBUTION OF CRUDE-OIL MARKET TENSION INDEX (MTI)**

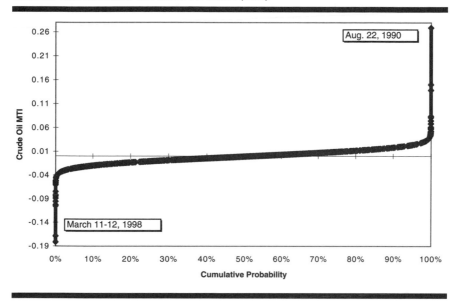

academic exercise if the MTI had no applicability for a trading system. Fortunately, this is not the case. The MTI, taken in combination with the market structures established in Chapter 2—sideways, trending, and transitional—turns out to be a robust instrument for establishing 1-day-ahead price changes in crude oil. Our trading rule matrix, listed in Table 5.4, is simple. All trading signals generated from this matrix are for one-day ahead positions only.

The most interesting aspect of the trading rule matrix is the dominant role of convenience yield within trending market structures. Any increase in the MTI within an upward-trending market is useless

Table 5.4 **TRADING RULE MATRIX FOR MARKET TENSION INDEX**

	Buy	Sell
Trending market	Convenience yield > 0 and ΔMTI > 0	Convenience yield < 0 and ΔMTI < 0
Transitional market	ΔMTI < 0 and MTI_{t-1} > 0	ΔMTI > 0 and MTI_{t-1} < 0
Sideways market	ΔMTI > 0	ΔMTI < 0

MTI = Market Tension Index.

as a buying signal unless the convenience yield component of the MTI is positive as well. This stricture prevents us from getting moved into a long position on a minor trend crossover and prevents us from buying in markets in which refiners are not willing to maintain more than a working inventory position. The same holds true for declining markets; we will not be forced into selling on minor trend crossovers unless refiners are telling us that they have more than adequate levels of supply.

Transitional markets are the most difficult; they are the states in between the confident pursuit of value by a trending price and the oscillation of price around value. The trading rule for these markets confirms the uncertainty contained in such a market state. A buy signal occurs as the MTI is weakening from positive levels, and a sell signal occurs as the MTI is strengthening from negative levels. Such trades are countertrend in nature.

The sideways market is one to be played for a breakout from the existing confined range, and therefore it has the simplest trading rule of all, following the change in the MTI. Since new trends must emerge from a change in underlying value, a trading system that follows these initial moves should be profitable.

The cumulative trading history of this integrated MTI system is depicted in Figure 5.7. The trading history begins in April 1989 and

Figure 5.7 **CUMULATIVE EQUITY GROWTH OF MARKET TENSION INDEX (MTI) AND SPOT MONTH CRUDE OIL**

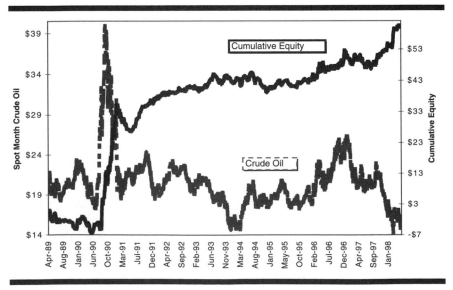

therefore covers more than 9 years of crude oil markets, including the Persian Gulf War, two periods of deep contango, and a strong rally in 1996 that also brought the market into a high level of backwardation. The large equity gains seen during the Persian Gulf War, during both the price surge and subsequent drop, should be expected given the trending nature of this market and the unmistakable signals of convenience yield. What is more encouraging, however, is the ability of the system to continue grinding out a positive equity path, nearly $30 per barrel, in the years since the war through markets that were both rising and falling, trending and otherwise.

CONFIRMATION OF THE MARKET TENSION INDEX: THE SOYBEAN MARKET

Duplication of the MTI analysis in another market should raise the comfort level we have in the indicator. Soybeans, like crude oil, are a volatile, highly storable commodity with an actively traded option market. Unlike crude oil, soybean futures are not monthly in their spacing; the active contract months are January, March, May, July, September, and November, and the August contract can become active for a few weeks in the summer. The intermonth spreads in crude oil tend to conform to the non–carry market convention of a bullish position's being long the front month and short the back month, whereas soybeans more generally conform to the carry market convention of a bullish position being long the back month and short the front month. Soybean production is seasonal in nature and is subject to a South American crop cycle as well as the traditional North American crop cycle.

One of the chiefs tenets of technical market analysis is that markets can be compared to one another consistently. With this in mind, we shall try to establish the MTI as a tool of soybean market analysis by establishing a parallel demonstration to the crude oil market.

First, we can compare convenience yield and excess volatility. Unlike the case for crude oil, implied volatility for soybean options generally is less than the high-low-close volatility. One possible interpretation here is that soybean prices are so frenetic in their search for value that market participants are less willing to purchase insurance than they should be; the belief may be that the market will return to their desired price level, and soon.

The relationship of convenience yield to excess volatility seen in Figure 5.8 is once again weakly quadratic, with a slight skew toward higher convenience yields at lower excess volatility, but the relation is not even as strong as it was for crude oil:

Figure 5.8 CONVENIENCE YIELD AND EXCESS VOLATILITY

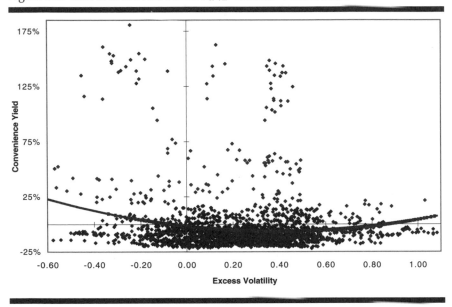

$$CY = -.0187 - .2365 \cdot XSVol + .2962 \cdot XSVol^2, R^2 = .0298 \qquad (5.7)$$

The relationship between convenience yield and the trend oscillator shown in Figure 5.9 for soybeans is weakly negative, as one could expect from a carry market. Once again, the relation between the two MTI components is more orthogonal than it is for crude oil:

$$CY = -.0367 - .0995 \cdot Trend, R^2 = .0066 \qquad (5.8)$$

The relation between excess volatility and the trend oscillator, as seen in Figure 5.10, is more defined, however, for soybeans than it is for crude oil. Excess volatility tends to disappear as prices weaken, suggesting that soybean growers are hesitant to buy price insurance in bear markets. The opposite is true for strong price markets, which suggests that soybean buyers, such as crushers and exporters, become very anxious about capping their costs. In an interesting parallel to the crude oil market, low anxiety tends to be associated only with downward trends in price. Once again, from a fundamental point of view, this should not be surprising; the cost of hedging for growers is likely to be greater than the avoided losses from lower prices, and buyers are not worried about weakly declining prices. The statistical relationship, although far stronger than that for crude oil, is still weak overall.

Figure 5.9 **CONVENIENCE YIELD AND TREND OSCILLATOR**

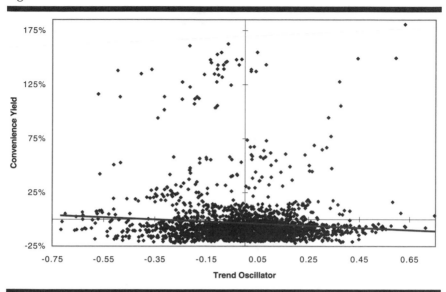

Figure 5.10 **EXCESS VOLATILITY AND TREND OSCILLATOR**

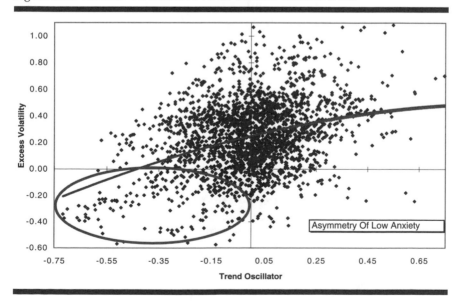

Table 5.5 **CORRELATION MATRIX OF MARKET TENSION INDEX COMPONENTS**

	Convyld	XSVol	Trend
Convyld	1.0000		
XSVol	−0.1066	1.0000	
Trend	−0.0809	0.3509	1.0000

Convyld = convenience yield; XSVol = excess volatility.

$$XSVol = .2499 + .4765 \cdot Trend - .2259 \cdot Trend^2,$$
$$R^2 = .1261 \tag{5.9}$$

As was the case for crude oil, none of the two-way relationships between MTI components is particularly strong, as we can see in the correlation matrix in Table 5.5, although the relation between the trend oscillator and excess volatility is stronger than we would like it to be. The variance–covariance matrix of the index components, shown in Table 5.6, simply confirms these relationships.

The relations between MTI subcomponents tell an interesting story in soybeans, just as they did for crude oil. The relation between convenience yield and the price of spot month soybean futures is depicted in Figure 5.11. The convenience yield is nearly always negative and appears comfortably stable near an annualized rate of −20%. Only on rare occasions does it spike high, and those occasions are the brief supply disruptions that occur before the arrival of a new crop, as seen during 1988 and 1997. Higher prices per se do not move convenience yield forward during those periods when soybeans are trading as a carry market.

The relation between implied volatility and convenience yield seen in Figure 5.12 once again confirms the patterns in the soybean

Table 5.6 **VARIANCE–COVARIANCE MATRIX OF MARKET TENSION INDEX COMPONENTS**

	Convyld	XSVol	Trend
Convyld	0.0582		
XSVol	0.0070	0.0739	
Trend	0.0038	0.0187	0.0385

Convyld = convenience yield; XSVol = excess volatility.

Figure 5.11 **CONVENIENCE YIELD AND PRICE**

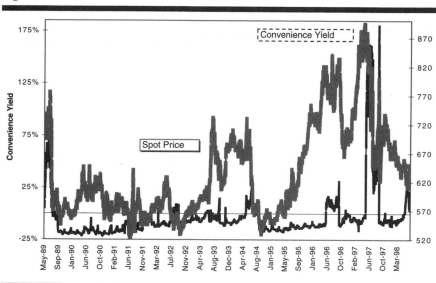

Figure 5.12 **SOYBEAN IMPLIED VOLATILITY VERSUS CONVENIENCE YIELD**

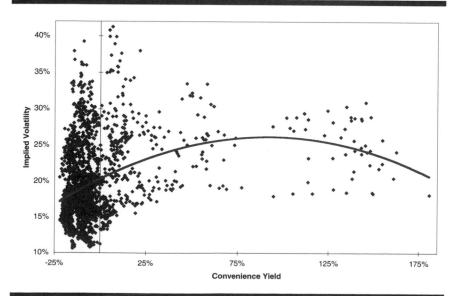

market of (1) a comfortable level of convenience yield, (2) a general rise in volatility as convenience yield rises, but (3) the unwillingness of buyers in the market to acquire extra insurance in market disloca-tions. The relation is concave to the origin, which is the opposite of the one seen in the crude oil market.

$$\text{ImpVol} = .2034 + .127 \cdot \text{CY} - .069 \cdot \text{CY}^2, R^2 = .1023 \qquad (5.10)$$

The MTI components for soybeans are not quite as orthogonal for soybeans as they are for crude oil. We can account for these dif-ferences by the difference between a carry market and a noncarry market and by the strong asymmetry of anxiety in the soybean mar-ket. With these cautions in mind, we proceed to the next phase of the comparison.

Distribution of the Market Tension Index for Soybeans

Once again, we need to examine the summary statistics for the MTI, presented in Table 5.7. The mean of the MTI series is weakly positive, confirming the generally tepid soybean markets seen over the period from 1989 through 1998. The skew of the series is strongly positive, which confirms the great asymmetry in anxiety in this market between buyers and sellers. The MTI series is still highly kurtotic—its values are still peaked around zero—even though this kurtosis is far less than that for crude oil. The Z statistic in a Student's distribution to test the hypothesis that the mean of the MTI series is zero is 6.37 with 2,303 degrees of freedom; the probability that the mean of the series is not zero is 1.36%.

The lower kurtosis for soybeans as compared with crude oil is somewhat misleading in the sense that there are serial outliers in the soybean MTI. On the positive side were a string of highly positive numbers from the period from July 1 through 7, 1997. This 4-trading-

Table 5.7 **SUMMARY STATISTICS FOR SOYBEAN MARKET TENSION INDEX**

Aspect	Value
Mean	0.0018
Standard deviation	0.0136
Skewness	2.0302
Kurtosis	49.9837

day period contained an unusual mix of very negative implied volatility combined with a strongly positive convenience yield. The price trend was positive over this time segment. However, a little more than 2 months later, in September 1997, a string of exceptionally low MTI numbers occurred in the same combination of factors—but this time within a negative price trend. The location of these two sets of outliers is highlighted in Figure 5.13.

Soybean Market Tension Index as a Trading Indicator

The value of any indicator is in its ability to generate trading profits. We can construct a trading history of the spot soybean contract using the identical rule matrix and the identical logic for soybeans as we did for crude oil. The resulting equity path, shown in Figure 5.14, is encouraging. The soybean market lacked the huge anomaly of the Persian Gulf War to generate profits, and the market generally has suffered through choppy and unrewarding trading periods since 1989. Still, the equity path grinds higher to produce over $6.60 per bushel in gains. It would certainly be interesting to see how the MTI indicator would have performed during some of the supercharged soybean markets of the 1970s and early 1980s.

Figure 5.13 **CUMULATIVE NORMAL PROBABILITY DISTRIBUTION OF SOYBEAN MARKET TENSION INDEX (MTI)**

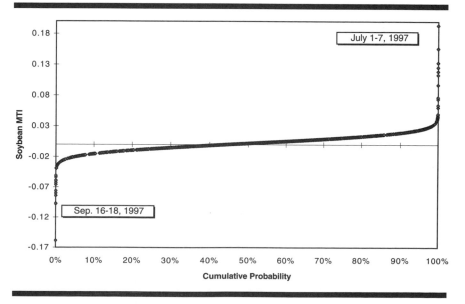

Figure 5.14 **CUMULATIVE EQUITY GROWTH OF MARKET TENSION INDEX (MTI) AND SPOT MONTH SOYBEANS**

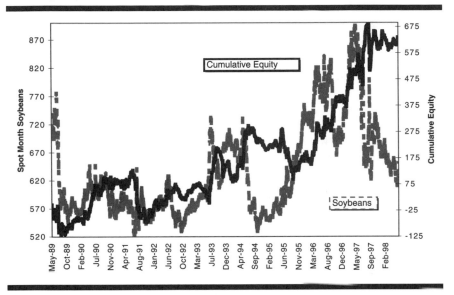

THE MARKET TENSION INDEX AND MARKET EFFICIENCY

How can one reconcile the trading simulations displayed above and the undocumented satisfaction this author has had with the MTI over the period from 1995 through 1998 with the tenet that there should be no consistent gain over time from any form of market analysis? The answer may lie in the difference in markets between *what* and *why.* Any descriptive indicator can tell us what happened, and all experienced traders strain to read market entrails in search for the why.

Our focus, established at the outset, is that markets and prices are the product of human traders, the study of whom is a far more complex and inscrutable task than is the sterile study of numbers in a single dimension. The initial premise of the MTI was that the integration of the other two dimensions of a market, insurance and storage, into the common dimension of price should paint a picture of anxiety and that trading this aspect of a market would be a more fruitful course of action than would simply trading price alone.

We will return to the concept of a different tension index, one for short-term interest rates and, by extension, currencies, in Chapter 6.

6

The Shape of Things to Come

FORWARD RATES

Our discussion so far of price expectations has remained in the world of physical commodities, with their quirky characteristics of seasonal production and consumption, storage costs, and supply–demand mismatches. It is now time to shift our attention to the far larger and better-behaved world of financial instruments and examine how they handle relative anxiety. Our focus initially is on short-term interest markets, which extend seamlessly into currency markets.

Just as convenience yield is the defining measure of expectations in the physical markets, forward rates are the defining measure of expectations in interest rate markets. A forward rate is the rate of interest between two points in the future, starting at the earliest future date. This rate is equivalent to the market's unbiased expectation of what prevailing interest rates will be at that future date. If 2-year interest rates are 5.75% and 1-year rates are 5.25%, then the forward rate between year 1 and year 2, starting at the end of year 1, will be:

$$\frac{[1+.0575]^2}{1+.0525} - 1, \text{ or } 6.2524\% \tag{6.1}$$

This is demonstrated readily in Table 6.1. The end value of the two strategies, buying a 2-year note at 5.75% (and, for the sake of purity, reinvesting the intervening coupons at the very same 5.75%) and buy-

Table 6.1 **COMPARISON OF YIELDS FOR 1- AND 2-YEAR NOTES**

	Two-year Note		Two 1-year Notes	
	Rate	Value	Rate	Value
End year 1	5.75%	$1,057.50	5.25%	$1,052.50
End year 2	5.75%	$1,118.31	6.25%	$1,118.31

ing a 1-year note, then reinvesting the proceeds at the market's expectation of 6.2524%, will yield the same ending value.

The example in Table 6.1 was for a positively sloped, or normal, yield curve, one in which the more distant rate exceeded the near rate. A positively sloped yield curve is characteristic of a market that expects interest rates to rise over time and in which lenders demand to be compensated for the increased risk of lending over longer maturities. The forward rate from year 1 to year 2 exceeds the rate at the 2-year horizon, and this also is characteristic of a positively sloped yield curve.

We just as easily could have constructed a negatively sloped, or inverted, yield curve, one in which the near rate exceeded the more distant rate. A negatively sloped yield curve is characteristic of a market that expects interest rates to fall over time and in which borrowers are hesitant to extend their credit demands to longer horizons. In a market with a negatively sloped yield curve, the forward rate from year 1 to year 2 will be less than the rate at the 2-year horizon. The relationship among forward rates, the horizon rate (the longer maturity over the forward rate period), and the market's expectation for interest rate movements is summarized in Table 6.2.

Yield curve shapes often describe policy and general economic environments as well. An inverted yield curve is associated with a constrictive monetary policy by the central bank. If, for example, the Federal Reserve sells treasury securities on the open market and thus withdraws reserves from the banking system, it expects the federal funds rate to rise relative to longer maturities. The opposite is true as

Table 6.2 **RELATIONSHIP OF FORWARD RATE, HORIZON RATE, AND MARKET EXPECTATIONS FOR INTEREST RATE MOVEMENT**

	Yield Curve Slope	Rate Expectation
Forward rate > horizon rate	Positive	Rising
Forward rate < horizon rate	Negative	Falling
Forward rate = horizon rate	Linear	Neutral

well: A relaxation of monetary policy effected by Federal Reserve purchases of treasury securities on the open market should drive the federal funds rate down.

The expectations of the short-term interest rate market for changes
in monetary policy and the course of credit demand can be illustrated
by the relationship of the forward rate to the base level of interest
rates. Figure 6.1 depicts the 9-month Eurodollar rate—the rate for 3-
month Eurodollar certificates of deposit starting at that contract's
expiration date—to the forward rate between 6- and 9-month
Eurodollar futures divided by the 9-month rate. A ratio in excess of
1.00 corresponds to the positively sloped yield curve–rising rate
expectation displayed in Table 6.2.

The limited ability of the market to correctly anticipate changes in
interest rates recalls Paul Samuelson's wisecrack about the stock market's correctly predicting nine of the last six recessions. For example,
the Federal Reserve pursued an expansive monetary policy during
the latter half of President George Bush's administration, and
Eurodollar rates correspondingly fell between 1991 and 1993. As these
rates were falling, the forward rate structure of the market was anticipating higher rates well before the Federal Reserve began driving the
federal funds rate higher in February 1994. Conversely, the two most

Figure 6.1 **NINE-MONTH EURODOLLAR RATES AND 6- AND 9-MONTH
FORWARD RATES**

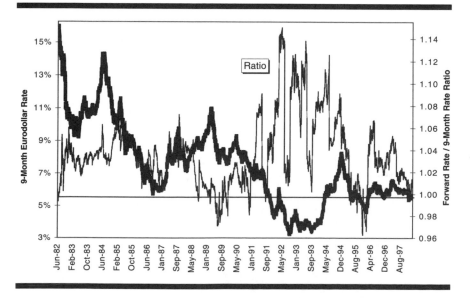

notable forays into expectations of falling rates, mid-1989 and late-1995, were followed quickly by small increases in Eurodollar rates.

The persistence of rising interest rate expectations gives us a clue as to where relative anxiety lies in this market. Fixed-income investors were decimated between 1950 and 1981 by rising inflation. The calamitous increases in inflation and interest rates seen in the late 1970s and early 1980s persist in the collective memory of this market and in the institutional memory of the Federal Reserve, and both parties have vowed *never again*. The assumption, therefore, is that any whiff of inflation will be met by both a tightening of credit by the Federal Reserve and an increased inflation premium imposed by the bond market itself; economist Edward Yardeni has dubbed the latter response the action of "bond market vigilantes." The opposite set of policy assumptions, that any weakening in the economy will be met by an infusion of credit and a lower inflation premium in the bond market, simply does not exist.

THE RATIONAL EXPECTATION GAME

The apparent inability of the short-term interest rate market to forecast changes in interest rates correctly, and its general bias toward anticipating higher future interest rates, is irrelevant. As we saw in Chapter 3 in our discussion of Farmboy Enterprises and Crushco, markets are not forecasting devices; they are measuring devices. What we see in the forward rate structure is not only the market's best unbiased estimate of where interest rates will be in the future but also a measurement of relative anxiety between borrowers and lenders as well as the effects of rational expectations. Consider this postulate:

All credible forecasts are inherently self-defeating.

Even though this assertion may sound outlandish at first, it is actually a tribute to both rational economic behavior and the general efficiency of markets. If, for example, a consensus builds among economists and market analysts that interest rates will begin rising in 6 months, this will imply a positive yield curve and forward rates higher than the horizon rate. A rational borrower, confronted with these expectations, will accelerate his borrowing, if he can, to an earlier time horizon. A rational lender will do the exact opposite and will reduce the volume of funds available for lending at shorter horizons. As a result, the credible forecast of higher interest rates in the future will have the effect of increasing short-term rates immediately by shifting loan demand toward—and fund supply away from—the shorter-term horizon. The immediate rise in interest rates will dampen economic activity somewhat and will both reduce future credit demand and increase the supply of future funds. Interest rates at the horizon, when it arrives and in the absence of intervening developments, should be lower than originally forecast.

The self-defeating nature of credible forecasts is by no means limited to the interest rate market. Many primary production industries, such as steel, chemicals, paper, and the like, are plagued by cycles of excess capacity. The reason is simple, of course: Rational company management will approve the addition of new production capacity only when it can be justified by current conditions. This is obvious in both extremes. One cannot imagine proposing the construction of, say, new polyethylene capacity at a time of excess production and low prices, since the additional capacity will only exacerbate the current environment. Similarly, one cannot imagine standing in the way of adding capacity at the very time when supplies are tight, prices are high, and, most importantly, your competitors are expanding to supply your customers if you cannot.

One of the central tenets of game theory, the Nash equilibrium, developed by the eponymous cowinner of the 1995 Nobel Prize in economics, holds that in a multiple-party noncooperative game, a player's best move is the best reply to his opponents' moves. The mere announcement of plans to add production capacity can alter an opponent's own plans. This strategy has been so common in the computer software field that it has been given a name, *vaporware*, which designates the announcement of a new competitive product that may never come to market on time.

This sort of game goes on between interest rate markets and central banks on a regular basis. The Federal Reserve, for example, has an extraordinarily limited toolkit with which to operate. It can increase or decrease the supply of reserves in the banking system through its open market operations, it can raise or lower the discount rate it charges member banks, and it can change loan reserve and stock margin requirements. The last set of tools is used so infrequently as to not get the market's attention, and changing the discount rate is a major policy signal that usually ratifies, rather than creates, a change in market interest rates.

This leaves open market operations as the principal tool of the Federal Reserve. With this single instrument, the Fed tries to affect the federal funds rate, the inflationary expectations built into the yield curve at longer maturities, the value of the dollar against other major currencies, and, while it is at it, levels of output and employment.

Milton Friedman received a well-justified Nobel Prize in economics for demonstrating that this single tool operates only with long and variable lags, and the entire rational expectations school of economics holds that expected changes in monetary policy can have no effect on output and employment—only on inflationary expectations. In other words, the Federal Reserve cannot affect real interest rates, and its effects on nominal interest rates at horizons longer than covered by the federal funds market are uncertain.

This leaves the central banks with the power of moral suasion, which is a more polite description than "bluff and bluster." Traders in the interest rate and currency markets, who can profit by pricing expected policy changes into securities, are often happy to oblige the central banks in this exercise. As a result, new economic data, government reports, speeches, and testimonies are all filtered through the prism of whether this will prompt the central bank to alter its interest rate policy. The tendency is to instantly capitalize in the extreme all such potentialities, regardless of whether they make sense in the longer term. Central bankers are happy to indulge these illusions, since the potentialities ratify their own self-importance and get the market to alter the level and forward structure of interest rates without any actions on their part.

THE EUROTENSION INDEX

We developed, in our discussion of the physical markets, a framework for the ideal forward curve, one that conformed perfectly to the pure cost of carry between contract months. Financial markets present a more circular problem, since the carrying cost of the commodity being held in inventory is a direct function of the commodity itself; it is as if the cost of holding cotton inventories was a function of cotton prices themselves. If we borrow money in the short term to finance the purchase of longer-term debt securities, then the carrying cost will fluctuate with the market's price for the short-term debt.

So long as the total return on the financed longer-term debt security exceeds the holding cost, then the transaction will be profitable. The best way to ascertain whether this will be the case is to examine the market's current expectation for what future short-term financing costs will be, and that is the forward rate structure. An inverted yield curve, one characterized by forward rates less than the horizon rate, is the ideal environment in which to purchase longer-term securities, since carrying costs should decline over time.

The relation between the expected carrying cost and the present carrying cost, which we can define as the forward rate divided by the horizon rate, and which we displayed in Figure 6.1, serves the same purpose as does the convenience yield for the physical commodities: It embodies in a single number the expectations of the market for the course of interest rates. Moreover, just as the convenience yield has a known balance point at the moment of full carry, the forward rate–to–horizon rate ratio has a balance point when the ratio equals 1.

Before we substitute this forward rate–horizon rate ratio for the convenience yield in a tension index, which we call the EuroTension Index (ETI) in reference to the *Euro-* prefix for many short-term interest rate instruments, we should make the same examination for orthogonality that we did for both crude oil and soybeans. The relation between the forward rate–horizon rate ratio and excess volatility, as defined in Equation 5.1, is shown in Figure 6.2.

The same weakly quadratic relationship exists between these two indicators as existed between excess volatility and convenience yield in the physical markets. This is somewhat surprising in the sense that the high-low-close volatility level in the Eurodollar futures market is always well below the implied volatility level in the Eurodollar options market and that the anxiety level in the Eurodollar market is skewed toward the expectation of rising interest rates. One might be

Figure 6.2 **FORWARD RATE RATIO VERSUS EXCESS VOLATILITY**

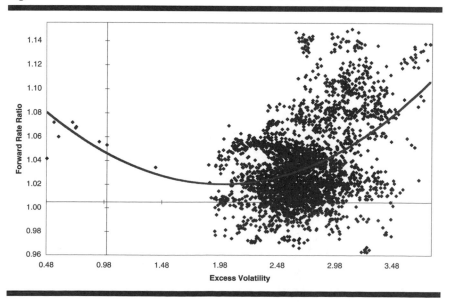

forgiven for expecting a strongly linear relationship between these
two variables, but the r-squared of the linear relationship is only .1223,
as compared to the quadratic relationship shown below in Equation
6.2. Both abnormally high and abnormally low excess volatility in the
Eurodollar market appear to be associated with a consensus that rates
will rise soon.

$$FRR = 1.1194 - .1044 \cdot XSVol + .0262 \cdot XSVol^2, R^2 = .1587 \qquad (6.2)$$

Next, in Figure 6.3, we can examine the relationship between the
forward rate–horizon rate ratio and the trend oscillator. As we
should expect, the relationship is weakly linear and negatively
sloped. The slope is not as negative as one might expect, as seen
below in Equation 6.3, owing to the market's bias toward a positively sloped yield curve, but the general relationship between negative price movement and the expectation of further negative price
movement is intact.

$$FRR = 1.0315 - .021 \cdot Trend, R^2 = .0157 \qquad (6.3)$$

Figure 6.3 **EURODOLLAR FORWARD RATE RATIO AND TREND
OSCILLATOR**

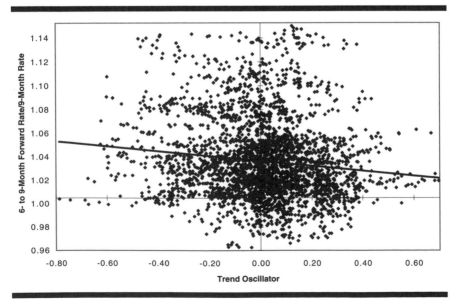

Finally, we can examine the relation between excess volatility and the trend oscillator, as shown in Figure 6.4. This relation is virtually nonexistent; there is no reason to expect one to exist. The short-term interest rate market is so expectation driven that the trend oscillator, a lagging indicator, is of no relevance to the degree of insurance demanded by the market. This is confirmed in Equation 6.4:

$$XSVol = 2.7071 - .1377 \cdot Trend, \, R^2 = .0068 \tag{6.4}$$

The correlation of matrix of the individual ETI components is presented in Table 6.3. The correlation between the forward rate–horizon rate ratio is stronger than we would like, but the historical record displayed in Figure 6.2 indicates that this relation, while correlated, is unlikely to be causal. The variance–covariance matrix of the index components tells the same story as well, as shown in Table 6.4.

DISTRIBUTION OF THE EUROTENSION INDEX

Once we combine the three index components into the ETI, we need to understand its distribution and ascertain whether it is an unbiased

Figure 6.4 **EXCESS VOLATILITY VERSUS TREND OSCILLATOR**

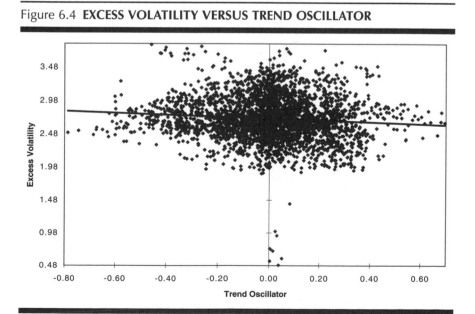

Table 6.3 **CORRELATION MATRIX OF EUROTENSION INDEX COMPONENTS**

Aspect	Value		
Forward rate ratio	1		
Excess volatility	0.3498	1	
Trend	−0.1255	−0.0826	1

descriptor of market behavior. The ETI follows a normal distribution with—as was the case in the MTI for the physicals—strongly positive kurtosis reflecting the preponderance of nonevents in the market. Both the mean and the skew of the ETI distribution are negative, which reflects the general risk bias in the interest rate markets over the period examined. Table 6.5 summarizes statistics for the ETI.

If we wish to test the hypothesis that the mean of the ETI for crude oil is indeed zero, our value of Z with the 3,357 observations available is −3.4342. The probability that the mean of the ETI for the Eurodollar is not zero, on a two-tailed t-test with 3,356 degrees of freedom, is 0.0602%.

The negative skewness and peaked kurtosis are visible in Figure 6.5, the cumulative probability distribution of the Eurodollar ETI. The large negative values all occurred with a single span of time in late May and early June of 1993, a period that corresponded to a combination of a negative price trend, a high forward rate–horizon rate ratio indicating further rate increases, and strong excess volatility. The large positive values occurred within two separate periods noted within the graph and were characterized by nearly opposite conditions. Interestingly, neither set of extreme ETI values was characterized by the sort of quantum shifts in yield level characteristic of short-term interest rate markets; rather, they were characterized by shifts in the other two dimensions, rate expectations and volatility, that comprise the ETI.

Table 6.4 **VARIANCE–COVARIANCE MATRIX OF EUROTENSION INDEX COMPONENTS**

Aspect	Value		
Forward rate ratio	0.0011		
Excess volatility	0.0039	0.1120	
Trend	−0.0008	−0.0055	0.0402

Table 6.5 **SUMMARY STATISTICS FOR EURODOLLAR EUROTENSION INDEX**

Aspect	Value
Mean	−0.0006
Standard deviation	0.0095
Skewness	−1.6860
Kurtosis	10.8272

THE EUROTENSION INDEX AS A TRADING INDICATOR

We now arrive at the same juncture as we did in the development of the MTI in the physicals—a test to see whether we can apply the simple set of trading rules set forth in Table 5.4 to the Eurodollar futures contract (Table 6.6). The forward rate–horizon rate ratio can be substituted into the spot occupied by convenience yield in that table.

The trading history shown in Figure 6.6 is encouraging. With the exception of an abrupt drop in equity at the start of the simulation at a time when Eurodollar options were new, the cumulative growth

Figure 6.5 **CUMULATIVE NORMAL PROBABILITY DISTRIBUTION OF EURODOLLAR EUROTENSION INDEX (ETI)**

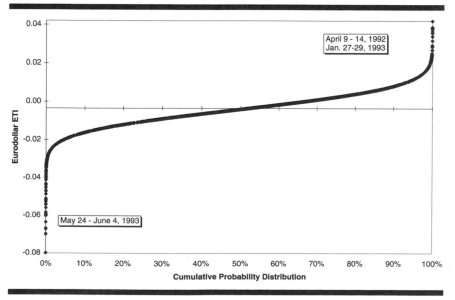

Table 6.6 **TRADING RULE MATRIX FOR EUROTENSION INDEX**

	Buy	Sell
Trending market	Forward rate/horizon rate > 1 and $\Delta ETI > 0$	Forward rate/horizon rate < 1 and $\Delta ETI < 0$
Transitional market	$\Delta ETI < 0$ and $ETI_{t-1} > 0$	$\Delta ETI > 0$ and $ETI_{t-1} < 0$
Sideways market	$\Delta ETI > 0$	$\Delta ETI < 0$

Figure 6.6 **CUMULATIVE EQUITY GROWTH OF EUROTENSION INDEX AND FIRST NEARBY EURODOLLAR**

path has been smooth. As the overlaid price history of the first nearby Eurodollar future indicates, the environment, although nowhere near as erratic as the interest rate environment of the late 1970s and early 1980s, had significant changes in the overall direction of interest rates.

We can now extend our analysis of the expectation structure of a single short-term interest rate into the relationship between two separate short-term interest rates plus an exchange rate.

7

The Original Sin

We opened the discussion in Chapter 1 by noting the earliest connections between markets and civilization, a connection possibly based on brewing. As commerce grew larger and more sophisticated, barter systems were replaced by money systems, which confer major advantages in that the price of all goods and services can be expressed in terms of a single concept, money.

Money must be easy to transport, hard to duplicate or counterfeit, and easy to recognize. Precious metals, gold especially, fit these requirements, and gold has been recognized ever since as a commodity of value. Although various early civilizations did not recognize it at the time, gold also eliminated what has become the Achilles' heel of all subsequent economic growth, the problem of exchange rates: All one had to do to exchange goods and services between economies was exchange gold, a form of money universally recognized, and one that could be converted into a different national denomination simply by melting and recasting.

As economies grew and as international trade became more extensive and more complex, gold continued to provide an anchor not only for individual currencies but for national accounts as well. The theory was simple: A country running a trade deficit would eventually run out of gold to pay for its imports of goods and services and thus would be precluded from running up further deficits. Since gold is coveted universally and in a near primal fashion, many concluded that anything capable of exhausting reserves of gold, such as trade deficits, was inherently undesirable.

SEARCHING FOR AN ANSWER

The converse was that trade surpluses, which led to increased reserves of gold, were an appropriate goal of national policy. This view, dubbed mercantilism, may not be the root of all evil, but it is a pretty good substitute therefor. Since its development in seventeenth-century France, it has encouraged all manner of misguided economic policies, up to and including the recent export-oriented economic policies of Japan and Korea, among others. Mercantilism's twin is protectionism, which is a device with which politicians can allocate rewards to favored producers by imposing a consumption tax or tariff on the importation of competing imports. These producers are protected from the normal competitive impulses to increase their efficiency, and consumers are protected from paying lower prices.

In reality, a trade deficit or surplus is neither good nor bad. One must view trade imbalances through the prism of whether imports are an economic cost or benefit. Since wealth is our ability to consume, not what we have produced, imports represent an economic benefit: Others are willing to exchange their goods and services for our money, goods and services that they cannot now consume themselves. The money they receive, which creates a capital account surplus equal to the current account deficit for the importing nation, must eventually be invested in securities denominated in the currency of the importing nation. A country running a current account deficit enjoys both the fruit of goods produced cheaper elsewhere and the benefits of portfolio investment. Since there are no free lunches in economics, the cost of current account deficits shows up in a lower level of domestic output and greater levels of debt service.

One can summarize the near permanent trade imbalance between the United States and Japan by saying that Americans got the cars and cameras and stereos while the Japanese got treasury bonds. The net result of the increased American consumption of goods and services has left the most important point of comparison—which country enjoys a higher standard of living—scarcely open to debate.

FINDING A BALANCE: THE EVOLUTION OF THE PRESENT SYSTEM

The conundrum of trade imbalances has been a permanent feature of the international economic landscape for as long as there has been trade. The early gold standards solved the problem of exchange rates by pricing goods and services in a single, uniform commodity, but the periodic balance-of-payments crises that arose whenever importers ran out of gold with which to finance trade hurt both the importing country, which could no longer afford its imports, and the exporting country, which lost a market. Moreover, the supply of gold never could increase as rapidly as trade could grow. This was a similar problem to that created by gold-based money supplies in domestic economies: The artificial constraint on the supply of money led to deflationary pressures, which in turn bankrupted debtors.

By the middle of the nineteenth century, the dominance of the British Empire in world trade and finance presented a new alternative to gold: the use of the British pound as an international currency. Various national currencies were then priced in terms of British pounds as well as gold. The British in turn strove to maintain a stable relationship between the pound and gold so as to avoid disruptive cycles of inflation and deflation. Although the gold–pound standard worked better than a simple gold standard alone, the world was still faced with the ultimate constraint of physical gold supplies themselves. We might find it amusing today to think of a connection between gold rushes in California, Alaska, Siberia, and South Africa and the stability and growth potential of the global economy, but such a connection existed. Even with these gold finds, the period between 1890 and the outbreak of World War I was characterized by deflationary pressures.

The aftermath of World War I saw the ascendancy of the U.S. dollar to a central role in the international monetary system, but this was a role accepted only reluctantly by an isolationist United States still uncertain whether it wanted to have anything to do with the world leadership. The question became more critical after the disastrous decision in 1924 by Winston Churchill, then chancellor of the Exchequer, to refix the pound to its 1914 value. This resulted in a heavily overvalued pound that penalized British exporters and subsidized British importers. The Federal Reserve sought to aid the Bank of England in its attempts to maintain an artificially high pound by keeping U.S. interest rates low via a loose monetary policy. The excess supply of dollars found its way into financial assets—the Roaring Twenties— but was otherwise notably unsuccessful in stemming the growing British trade deficit.

The Federal Reserve became alarmed over the growing speculation in American financial markets and began raising the discount rate in August 1929. This rate increase coincided with both a normal, inventory-led recession in the industrial sector and the imminent passage of the steep Smoot–Hawley tariff. The combination of a rapidly shrinking money supply, the implicit tax increase of the tariff, and an economic recession led to the Great Depression. In 1933, the U.S. government, faced with increasing demands for redemption of its paper currency for gold, ended the gold standard in the United States and actually made it illegal for Americans to own gold bullion and other monetary forms of the metal. A link to silver remained.

The new international economic order for the post–World War II era was crafted at the Bretton Woods Conference in 1944. The designers of the system, principally John Maynard Keynes of the United Kingdom and Harry Dexter White of the United States, were determined to avoid the disasters of competitive devaluation and protectionism they had witnessed during the Great Depression. The centerpiece of the global monetary system was to be the U.S. dollar, which was to maintain a value of $35 per ounce of gold—even though the formal link between the dollar and gold had been broken in 1933, never to return. The implicit understanding was that the United States would act to provide the world trading system with sufficient liquidity to finance the postwar economic recovery while striving to maintain price stability. All other currencies, many of which had lost their convertibility in the Great Depression and World War II, would be pegged to the U.S. dollar in a fixed exchange rate system. A system of international financial institutions, such as the International Bank for Reconstruction and Development, better known as the World Bank, and the International Monetary Fund (IMF), were created to foster cooperation. The IMF's charter mission was to provide short-term credits for countries in serious current account deficit; the noble idea was to allow growing economies to continue importing necessary goods and services.

The Bretton Woods system worked quite well through the 1950s and the first half of the 1960s, which were periods of rapid growth, low inflation, and expanding trade. However, economic prosperity always has a way of making people confuse a bull market for brains, and this tendency was especially pronounced in politicians who had grown enamored with the power and potential of central government. Thus did President Lyndon Johnson embark upon the colossal expansion of the domestic welfare state at the same time he embarked upon the expansion of the Vietnam War and at the same time the space program and the interstate highway system were both claiming large shares of national resources. Johnson hid the cost of these ventures from the American people by forgoing tax increases, instead using his considerable powers of persuasion to get the Federal Reserve to maintain an expansive monetary policy.

The result was predictable: a combination of higher inflation, shown in Figure 7.1, and interest rates, a deepening trade deficit, and growing pressure on the dollar as the ability of the United States to maintain the nominal $35 per ounce of gold peg came into question.

Figure 7.1 **THE CONSUMER PRICE INDEX 1913–1998: 1982–1984 = 100**

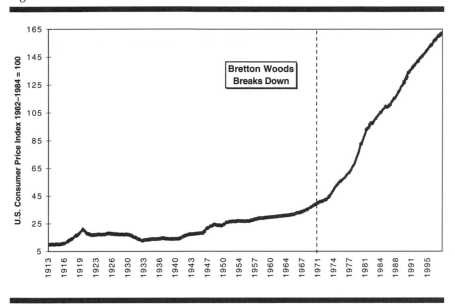

When the French presented claims on gold in 1968, the United States suspended convertibility of the dollar to gold on the international front, just as it had done domestically 35 years earlier. The economic mismanagement of the Johnson administration actually worsened during the first Nixon administration. On August 15, 1971, President Richard Nixon and his wholly unqualified treasury secretary, John Connally, imposed a 10% import surcharge, completed the break with gold, imposed wage and price controls, and devalued the dollar 10%.

For the next year and a half, the world's leading economic powers struggled with the question of how to reassemble the international monetary system. After more than a century of a peg to the British pound and gold, a peg to the pound and the dollar and gold, and finally a peg to the dollar, a process begun in December 1971 was finalized in March 1973 to try something absolutely revolutionary in world economic history: a system of floating exchange rates.

A GOOD IDEA AT THE TIME

The concept of whether a currency is properly valued has occupied the attentions of international economists since the work of Alfred Marshall in the late nineteenth century. The workings of a free market should transmit signals about the efficiency of resource allocation within an economy. Trade flows, as noted in the eighteenth century by David Ricardo, should transmit information about the competitive advantages between trading partners; in fact, the best argument in favor of free trade is that it allows each trading partner to concentrate on its most efficient production sectors and import the goods and services produced more cheaply elsewhere.

In a fixed–exchange rate system, a single price, the rate of exchange, enters into all import and export decisions. If this exchange rate is not a perfect reflection of the relative demand for goods and services between the two economies—and it can be instantaneously perfect only by accident in a complex modern economy—then a set of macroeconomic impacts, listed in Table 7.1, results.

These distortions are anything but trivial. The mispricing of a single good in a nontraded sector has ramifications within related economic sectors, but the mispricing of an exchange rate sends signals to reallocate resources through the entire domestic economy and into all competing foreign economies as well.

The mechanism to correct this mispricing in a fixed–exchange rate system originally had been the flow of gold, then the flow of reserve currencies. After the demise of the Bretton Woods system, there was no real correction mechanism: Gold was demonetized, the dollar was pegged to the increasingly useless promise of the United States to

Table 7.1 **THE EFFECTS OF IMPROPER CURRENCY VALUATION**

Policy/Policy Goal	Overvaluation	Undervaluation
Current account balance	Favors importers; leads toward deficit	Favors exporters; leads toward surplus
Capital account balance	Leads toward surplus	Leads toward deficit
Investment flows	Favors making direct investment	Favors receiving direct investment
Labor flows	Favors highly skilled	Favors unskilled
Savings propensity	Favors immediate consumption	Favors deferred consumption
Price stability	Deflationary pressure	Inflationary pressure
Interest rates	Downward pressure on rates	Upward pressure on rates
Monetary policies	Pressure to expand money supply	Pressure to contract money supply
Political rewards	Favors importers and creditors	Favors exporters and debtors

maintain its value, and there was no other reserve currency worthy of the name. Without a correction mechanism for exchange rates, all economies would be in the dark regarding the efficiency of resource allocation, both domestically and internationally, a situation recognized by most as an invitation to economic disaster.

One solution, advocated most strongly by Milton Friedman, was to let currencies trade in a free market so they could find their optimal value relative to one another. The system would be self-adjusting: An increased trade deficit would lead to an increased supply of the importer's currency on the open market, which would then lead to a decreased value for that currency, which would then lead to decreased imports and greater exports, which would by definition erase the current account deficit. It was simple, elegant, intellectually appealing, and in many ways seemed too good to be true.

It was.

First, the floating exchange rate concept assumed that all goods and services traded were price sensitive in the short term. However, petroleum, the most plentiful physical goods in international trade, was and still is denominated in dollars. The arrival of the first oil shock of the 1970s shortly after the advent of floating currencies put the system to a severe test as the demand for dollars to pay for petroleum increased even as the growing inflation in the United States should have led to a weaker dollar. A second class of goods in international trade, grain, also jumped in both price and in demand for U.S. exports at the same time. The same held true for supplies of military hardware; much of which was sold to the newly flush petroleum exporters of the Middle East. Finally, the United States dominated the world export market for computers and high-technology goods. The resulting surge in demand for dollars to finance these items of world trade once again was accommodated by the Federal Reserve, which was trying to ease the fierce recession and bear market of 1973–1974. This renewed burst of monetary creation led to double-digit inflation in the United States and a major crisis of confidence in the dollar, which in turn led to the appointment of Paul Volcker to the chairmanship of the Federal Reserve in October 1979.

Second, the notion that governments would allow their currencies to float freely was politically naive in the extreme. The same impulses that earlier led to mercantilism and protectionism then led to the notion that governments would need to step in periodically to correct the free market's assessment of a currency's appropriate value. The appropriate value could be stronger, if a country was faced with the prospect of increasing interest rates, or it could be weaker, if the country was faced with a growing trade deficit. In either case, as we shall soon see, the governments were playing a loser's game with their tax-payers' money.

Third, proponents of floating currencies held a belief in something dubbed a J-curve. Picture a country's economic fortunes lying on the leftmost curve of the J. As time moves forward to the right, the immediate effect is a lower state of welfare than the initial state, but with the further passage of time, one will travel to the right-hand, ascending, curve of the J. The J-curve was used to justify the short-term disruptions that would occur when a currency deprecia-tion was used as an instrument of national policy; these disruptions usually involved higher inflation and interest rates, and—contrary to the best hopes of policy makers—a higher current account deficit as surging import costs overwhelmed whatever export gains were purchased via a depreciated currency. The United States pursued a J-curve policy regarding the dollar between 1985 and 1987, and then again between 1993 and 1995. The policy failed badly in both instances.

The history of the dollar from 1967 to 1998, expressed in the trade-weighted dollar index, is shown in Figure 7.2. A number of points are annotated on the figure:

Figure 7.2 **TRADE-WEIGHTED DOLLAR INDEX (SEE TEXT FOR EXPLANATION OF POINTS A–F.)**

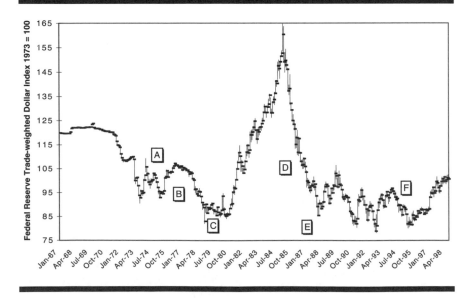

A. Post–oil shock dollar demand

B. Monetary expansion and inflation under the administration of President Jimmy Carter

C. Appointment of Paul Volcker as Federal Reserve chairman. The Dollar begins huge rally under combination of Volcker's tight money policy and fiscal stimulation of tax cuts by President Ronald Reagan.

D. September 1985 Plaza Accord to drive down U.S. dollar further via lower U.S. interest rates. U.S. equity prices double in 2 years, then crash in October 1987 as fears grow of runaway dollar collapse that would need to be stemmed by higher short-term interest rates.

E. February 1987 Louvre Accord to support the value of the dollar

F. Attempt by the Clinton administration to redress U.S.–Japan bilateral trade deficit by revaluation of the yen in the midst of the ongoing Japanese recession

ONE EQUATION WITH THREE UNKNOWNS

The fourth and final source of defeat for the policy of floating exchange rates came from a source now readily obvious but never discussed at the time—the disconnection between currency trading and the current account balance. Prior to the advent of the floating exchange rate regime in the early 1970s, currency trading was only a marginally respectable business. There were no organized futures markets for financial instruments; the currency contracts introduced by the Chicago Mercantile Exchange in 1972 were the first financial futures contracts of any kind anywhere. Banks facilitated foreign exchange transactions as part and parcel of their normal trade financing business alongside letters of credit, warehouse receipts, and banker's acceptances, and there was some arbitrage between short-term debt instruments denominated in different currencies. However, open speculation against the fixed exchange rate of an established government was not a genteel business.

Once markets began to trade currencies freely, they quickly discovered that there was no need to have any underlying physical trade flow. If we wished to speculate on the imminent appreciation of another currency, say the Swiss franc, against the U.S. dollar, all we would have to do would be:

1. Borrow dollars at prevailing U.S. interest rates
2. Sell these dollars
3. Buy francs at the current spot rate
4. Lend francs at prevailing Swiss rates

These four steps are embodied in Equation 7.1. This one equation has three variables, the current spot exchange rate, the U.S. interest rate, and the Swiss interest rate. To solve this equation, we must fix either two of these three variables or one variable and the relation between the remaining two.

$$Future \equiv \cfrac{1}{Spot \cdot \cfrac{1 + R_{us} \cdot \cfrac{d}{360}}{1 + R_{for} \cdot \cfrac{d}{360}}} \tag{7.1}$$

Once traders were freed from the constraint of underlying trade flows and once they realized the possibilities implied by Equation 7.1, currency trading mushroomed into the biggest business in the world: Any purchase of a currency meant that one was lending in that currency, which placed downward pressure on interest rates denominated in that currency, which lowered its attractiveness, which lowered its spot rate, which opened up a new set of arbitrage possibilities. This never-ending cycle of trading opportunities, combined with the advent of real-time global trading networks, allowed the interbank foreign exchange market to operate on a nearly seamless 24-hour-per-day schedule.

How did all of this exciting, nonstop action affect the original object of the game, restoring current account balances and allowing for the most efficient allocation of resources across different economies? Not much. Once importers and exporters became aware of the risks involved in their currency exposures, which oftentimes dwarfed their basic profit margins, they wisely began to hedge themselves so that trade flows could continue regardless of subsequent currency fluctuations. Of course, these hedging actions changed the nature of the perceived risk via the mechanism of rational expectations discussed in Chapter 6.

SLOUCHING TOWARD ARMAGEDDON

Another unintended consequence of floating exchange rates has been the decreasing effectiveness of monetary policy as an instrument of national economic policy. This can be seen by incorporating Fisher's Law, which states that a nominal interest rate at any maturity is composed of the real interest rate, designated as R^*, plus the expected rate of inflation, designated as ε, into Equation 7.1 to produce Equation 7.2. Since there can be only one real interest rate worldwide at any given maturity to preclude arbitrage opportunities, then R^*_{us} and R^*_{for} must be equal. The changes in relative currency valuations, therefore, must arise from different inflationary expectations in the two economies.

$$Future \equiv \cfrac{1}{Spot \cdot \cfrac{1+(R^*_{us}+\varepsilon_{us})\cdot \dfrac{d}{360}}{1+(R^*_{for}+\varepsilon_{for})\cdot \dfrac{d}{360}}} \tag{7.2}$$

If the theory of rational expectations is correct, then expected changes in monetary policy will have no effect on real interest rates or on output and employment, but these changes will have an effect on inflationary expectations and, by extension, on the shape of the yield curve. The changes in inflationary expectations then have an effect on exchange rates, and per Table 7.1, these effects on exchange rates have profound macroeconomic impacts—not always the ones intended by the central bank.

An interesting confirmation of this interest rate expectation model comes from the EuroTension Index (ETI) developed in Chapter 6. We can fit predictive regression models to the price changes for both the Eurodollar and Euromark futures based on the ETI values; we have already seen the utility of the ETI as a trading indicator for the Eurodollar. The two regression fits are similar:

$$\Delta ED = 1.595 \cdot ETI_{t-1} + 11.779 \cdot \Delta ETI, \ R^2 = .275$$
$$\Delta EM = 1.622 \cdot ETI_{t-1} + 14.544 \cdot \Delta ETI, \ R^2 = .331 \tag{7.3}$$

If the time spans to expiration in Equation 7.2 are adjusted and if the real interest rates, R^*, are equal in the two markets, then the next day's Deutsche mark future must be a function of the current spot rate adjusted by the two different sets of inflationary expectations. These inflationary expectations can be represented by the two relationships in Equation 7.3; therefore, given a current spot rate, the next day's Deutsche mark future should be:

$$DM_{t1} = \cfrac{1}{Spot \cdot \cfrac{f(ETI^{ed},\Delta ETI^{ed})}{f(ETI^{em},\Delta ETI^{em})}} \tag{7.4}$$

The functions referred to in Equation 7.4 are the regression equations in Equation 7.3. The fitted values from Equation 7.4 match the actual closing values of the next day's Deutsche mark future in a linear fashion, as shown in Figure 7.3.

A classic example of markets' defeating the best intentions of the central banks occurred in the early 1990s. The United States was facing a recession triggered by the 1990 tax increase, the savings and loan bailout, and the Persian Gulf War. The administration of President George Bush had no idea how to stimulate the economy other than to plead with the Federal Reserve for lower interest rates. Even though the Federal Reserve obliged by lowering short-term interest rates on several occasions, the bond market was less accommodating, as seen in Figure 7.4. As the Federal Reserve flooded the market with liquidity, the yield curve steepened. Since capital investment decisions are made on the basis of longer-term interest rates, the monetary stimulus was ineffective.

The effects on exchange rates were significant, however. At the same time the Federal Reserve was driving short-term interest rates lower in the United States, the Bundesbank was tightening monetary policy in Germany to combat the inflationary effects associated with German reunification, principally the decision to exchange the former

Figure 7.3 **NEXT-DAY DEUTSCHE MARK FUTURES AS A FUNCTION OF EURODOLLAR AND EUROMARK EUROTENSION INDEX (ETI)**

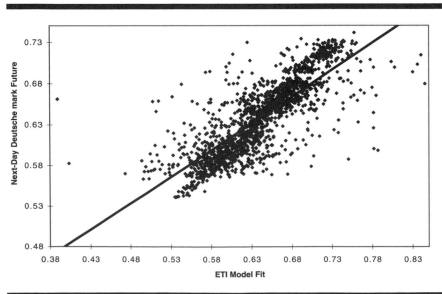

Figure 7.4 **THREE-MONTH TREASURY BILL YIELDS AND SPREAD TO 10-YEAR TREASURY NOTE YIELDS**

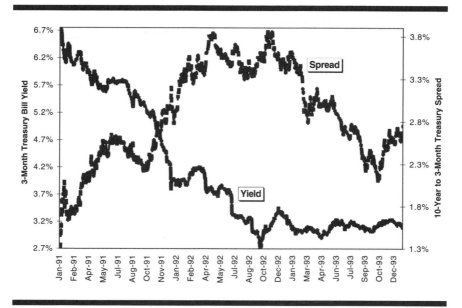

East German ostmark on a one-for-one basis with the West German Deutsche mark. As a result, the yield spread between the United States and Germany grew, the German yield curve inverted, and the dollar sank in value against the mark, as seen in Figure 7.5.

The hoped-for effects of monetary policy in each country were filtered through the system of macroeconomic effects listed in Table 7.1, and the final results of the policies were not what either bank or government desired. The tight monetary policy of the Bundesbank forced other European central banks to raise their interest rates in an attempt to stay within the bounds of the European exchange rate mechanism. In September 1992, speculators attacked some of the weaker currencies in Europe, notably the British pound, on the theory that the central banks could not raise interest rates indefinitely. The speculation was successful, and it has been estimated that European central banks lost close to $60 billion of their taxpayers' money playing a game in which they personally had no risk.

The litany of currency-related fiascoes since the advent of the floating exchange rate system reads like a world atlas. The European fiasco of 1992 was followed by the sharp revaluation of the yen between 1993 and 1995, by the collapse of the Mexican peso in Decem-

Figure 7.5 **U.S.–GERMAN INTEREST RATE SPREADS AND EXCHANGE RATE**

ber 1994, and by the collapse of the south Asian currencies in 1997. The advent of the Euro will surely have its own problems; the attempt to have a single currency over a number of different political systems is just as revolutionary as the decision to let currencies float in the early 1970s was.

THROUGH NO FAULT OF OUR OWN

The temptation always exists to find someone to blame for such a sorry state of affairs. One of the interesting aftereffects of the 1997 collapse of the south Asian currencies was a very loud and very public attack on currency traders by Malaysian Prime Minister Mahathir bin Muhammad. His attack was based on the true statement that the volume of currency transactions now exceeded the volume of underlying trade by a factor of 20 and that smaller currencies such as the Malaysian ringgit could be overwhelmed in a speculative attack that would leave huge macroeconomic damage in its wake.

Dr. Muhammad failed to note, however, several critical items. The first is that free markets unwittingly are disciplining devices. It does not matter whether the object of the discipline is a corporation whose management is failing the shareholders or a nation whose government is failing its citizens; markets will sell assets expected to underperform their alternatives on a risk-adjusted basis. If a government or central bank expands its money supply faster than the underlying demand for that currency increases, then the expected rate of inflation will increase and the currency will become less valuable. Should any speculator or group of speculators attempt to push a currency below its market-clearing value for any length of time, they will fail, as arbitrageurs will step in and lend in the undervalued currency.

The opposite holds true for the governments and central banks involved. A government can decide to debauch the value of its currency to satisfy some or all of the policy goals listed in Table 7.1 for depreciated currencies. The United States, which as the world's key reserve currency for the last half of the twentieth century has enjoyed the right of seignorage, or the ability to spend its currency first before the rest of the world realizes its depreciation, has embarked on this policy several times, most notably between 1985 and 1987. The IMF, which has been enamored of policy mixes involving a combination of fiscal austerity and currency devaluation as a way of correcting trade imbalances, has advocated currency devaluation to many nations, most recently and notably the south Asian nations in 1997. A government adopting these policies does so at the explicit risk of causing a combination of inflation, higher interest rates, and a runaway depreciation of its currency; the cruelest irony is that it seldom corrects the original trade imbalance.

The policy errors can accumulate on the other side as well. Too frequently, governments decide to go toe-to-toe with the currency markets and adopt a policy of higher interest rates to "defend" their currency, as if there were some matter of national honor at stake. The consequences of such currency defense policies are often disastrous. The best example of this was the global stock market crashes of October 1987; the United States had sent mixed signals to the markets regarding whether it would use competitive devaluation as a tool of rectifying its trade imbalance. As investors feared that the value of their dollar-denominated assets would erode either through a continued devaluation or through increasing short-term interest rates, they chose to liquidate their assets. Figure 7.6 illustrates how Eurodollar rates had to keep rising through 1986 as the dollar index weakened. After the February 1987 Louvre Accord, the dollar index stabilized, but at the cost of a continued rise in interest rates. The mounting trade deficit in August and September 1987 convinced markets that yields would have to keep on rising, and this led, quite directly, to the October crash.

Figure 7.6 **CURRENCY DEFENSE AND ITS CONSEQUENCES: THE 1987 EXPERIENCE. S&P 500 = STANDARD AND POOR'S 500**

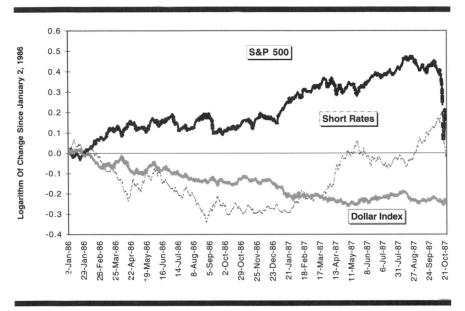

The litany of policy errors committed by governments and central banks in the floating exchange rate system is really quite tragic. The 1997 south Asian debacle had different origins than did the 1994 Mexican debacle, which in turn had different origins from the 1992 European debacle, which was really quite different from the 1987 European debacle, and so on. Only one thing remained in common between these experiences and others not enumerated: The markets will let you fix a currency level anywhere you want to accommodate the policy mix desired from Table 7.1, or the markets will let you fix your own short-term interest rate levels anywhere you want to accommodate whatever goals of monetary policy desired, but the markets will not—cannot, given the imperatives dictated by Equation 7.1—let you fix both.

John Maynard Keynes mused that we are all slaves to defunct economists. The present regime—and we must emphasize the word *present*, since no regime has ever been permanent—makes us all slaves to one equation with three unknowns, an equation that cannot be solved without turning the internal variables into constants. The experience with this system since the mid-1970s should be instructive to all: Try though we might, we cannot solve this equation via official policies. Even when these policies are well designed, the ability of markets to adapt their expectations in a rational fashion defeats their intent. Badly designed policies produce disasters, some of which are short lived, like the 1987 stock crash, and some of which are longer lived, like the inflation of the 1970s. In all instances, we are bound to fail in the initial intent of the floating exchange rate system, which was to have an automatic trade adjustment system, since the financial transactions can be disconnected from the physical transactions totally.

Given the colossal investment in the present system and the number of parties who have stakes in its outcome, how will we extricate ourselves from it and move on to something else? It is not encouraging to note that mercantilism rose from the disaster of the Thirty Years' War, that the British pound standard rose from the Napoleonic Wars, that the dollar–pound standard arose from World War I, the dollar standard from World War II, and the present system from the Vietnam War. There can be no accident in such a consistent pedigree, and therefore there can be no optimism regarding the future agent of change.

The curious inability of the global economy ever to solve the seemingly mundane problem of trade imbalances has never diminished our own hubris in regard to our ability to design an international monetary system. Maybe the problem cannot be solved, and that, the inevitable consequence of a world where we live both separately and together, is the modern version of the original sin.

PART II

TOWARD THE DYNAMIC OPTION SELECTION SYSTEM

8

But Not the Obligation

All great ideas are simple, either by themselves or in combination. Just as all of chemistry is based on a handful of elements, all of modern finance is based on a call option, a put option, and a zero-coupon bond. All cash market positions, all derivatives no matter how exotic, all insurance claims, and all valuation of future claims can be broken down into these three elements.

We will approach options from two points of reference familiar to nearly all readers, regardless of their background in finance, lending, and insurance. These references, which will be integrated into the characteristics of markets as discussed in Part I of this book, will then serve as bases for development of our trading and investment strategies.

BASIC TERMINOLOGY

Although this is not a text devoted to the mechanics of option modeling, it is necessary to ensure that we are working from a common vocabulary. Since we will be devoting most of our attention to options on futures, we will refer to the underlying asset as a future, and not as a stock, bond, or forward in most cases. The following definitions are pertinent:

- **Strike:** The price at which an option will be exercised
- **Expiration:** The date by which (American exercise) or on which (European exercise) an option must be exercised
- **Long call:** The right—but not the obligation—to purchase an underlying asset at a fixed strike price on or by (American exercise) or on (European exercise) a designated expiration date

- **Long put:** The right—but not the obligation—to sell an underlying asset at a fixed strike price on or by (American exercise) or on (European exercise) a designated expiration date
- **Short call:** The obligation to deliver an underlying asset at a fixed strike price on or by (American exercise) or on (European exercise) a designated expiration date
- **Short put:** The obligation to purchase an underlying asset at a fixed strike price on or by (American exercise) or on (European exercise) a designated expiration date
- **Premium:** The market value of an option at any point in time
- **Intrinsic value:** What an option would be worth at expiration at the current price. For a call option, this is the maximum of *(future − strike, 0)*. For a put option, this is the maximum of *(strike − future, 0)*
- **Time premium:** Premium minus intrinsic value
- **Volatility:** Market-determined measure of price uncertainty
- **In the money (ITM):** When the intrinsic value of an option is greater than 0. For a long call option, this means future > strike, and for a long put option, this means strike > future
- **Out of the money (OTM):** When the intrinsic value of an option is 0. For a long call option, this means future < strike, and for a long put option, this means strike < future
- **At the money (ATM):** A nebulous definition of when the underlying asset is simply closer to this strike than to any other

PROFIT PROFILES AND INSTRUMENT SYNTHESIS

The profit profiles of long and short option positions, both puts and calls, flow directly from their definitions. These are illustrated in Table 8.1 with the data for treasury bond futures at the close of business on Friday, August 14, 1998.

A long call option becomes more valuable as the price of the underlying asset rises. The profit profile exchanges a known cost, the option's premium, for a combination of limited losses at lower prices and open-ended gains at higher prices, as shown in Figure 8.1. A long put option becomes more valuable as the price of the underlying asset falls. The profit profile exchanges a known cost, the option's premium, for a combination of limited losses at higher prices and open-ended gains at lower prices, as shown in Figure 8.2. A short call option

Table 8.1 **PROFIT PROFILE DATA**

Aspect	Value
Future	124.03125
December 124[a] call	1.93750
December 124 put	1.90625
Days to expiration	99
Volatility	7.538%
Treasury bill rate	4.800%

[a] Right to buy the December future at 124 for the call, and right to sell the December future at 124 for the put.

becomes a greater liability as the price of the underlying asset rises. The profit profile exchanges a known gain, the option's premium, for a combination of unlimited losses at higher prices and limited gains at lower prices, as shown in Figure 8.3. A short put option becomes a greater liability as the price of the underlying asset falls. The profit profile exchanges a known gain, the option's premium, for a combination of unlimited losses at lower prices and limited gains at higher prices, as shown in Figure 8.4.

Figure 8.1 **PROFIT PROFILE OF A LONG AT-THE-MONEY CALL OPTION**

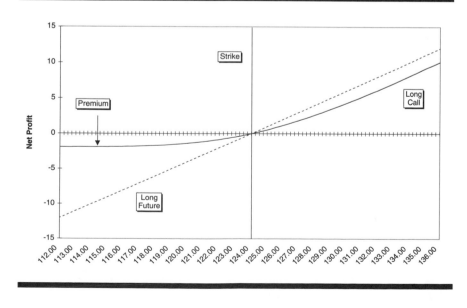

Figure 8.2 **PROFIT PROFILE OF A LONG AT-THE-MONEY PUT OPTION**

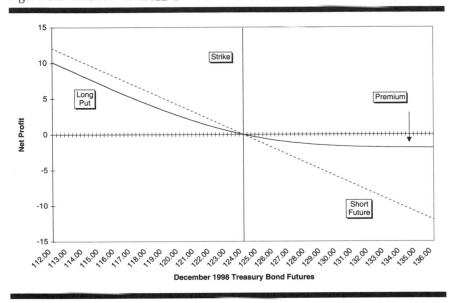

Figure 8.3 **PROFIT PROFILE OF A SHORT AT-THE-MONEY CALL OPTION**

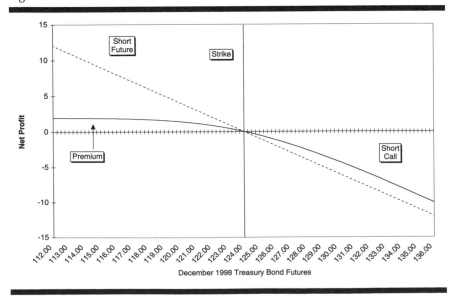

Figure 8.4 **PROFIT PROFILE OF A SHORT AT-THE-MONEY PUT OPTION**

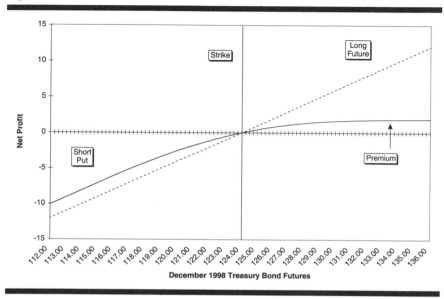

In each of Figures 8.1 through 8.4, the profit profile of the under-lying instrument was included, a long future for the long call and short put graphs, and a short future for the long put and short call graphs. This was done to serve as a visual guide to the presence of each of the options in the underlying instrument; the presence of these options allows us to develop the synthesis relationships listed below. Also included in the list is the put–call parity relationship, which states that the difference between the price of a call option and the price of a put option, of the same expiration and strike, is the present value of the difference between the underlying asset and the strike. Put–call parity links the three elements of finance, the call option, the put option, and the zero-coupon bond. The synthesis relationships are as follows:

- Long future = long call + short put
- Short future = long put + short call
- Long call = long future + long put
- Long put = short future + long call
- Short call = short future + short put
- Short put = long future + short call
- $[\text{Call} - \text{put}] = [\text{future} - \text{strike}]e^{-rt}$

Since we will return to many of these synthetic relationships later, each is illustrated below. Moreover, it is important to realize just how inescapable these options are; many corporate traders are either prohibited directly from trading all options or from selling options as a matter of corporate risk management. All futures, forwards, and cash market positions can be reconstructed via option synthesis, however, and unless a given corporation has been able to repeal the reflexive property of equality, all such transactions contain an embedded short option. It is far better to understand these relationships than to fear them.

In Figure 8.5, we can combine the dotted line of the long call option position moving to the northeast with the solid line of the short put option position moving to the southwest, and we re-create the linear profit profile of a long futures position. In Figure 8.6, we can combine the dotted line of the long put option position moving to the northwest with the solid line of the short call option position moving to the southeast, and we re-create the linear profit profile of a short futures position. In Figure 8.7, we can combine the dotted line of the long futures position moving from southwest to northeast with the solid line of the long put option position moving to the northwest, and we re-create the profit profile of a long synthetic call option moving to the northeast, shown in a dashed line. In Figure 8.8, we can

Figure 8.5 **PROFIT PROFILE OF A SYNTHETIC LONG FUTURE**

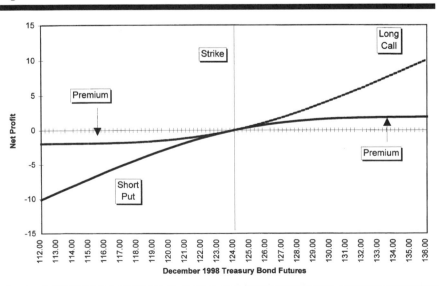

Figure 8.6 **PROFIT PROFILE OF A SYNTHETIC SHORT FUTURE**

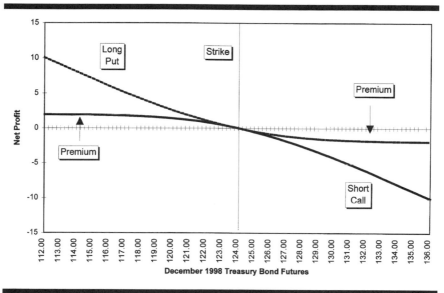

Figure 8.7 **PROFIT PROFILE OF A LONG SYNTHETIC CALL**

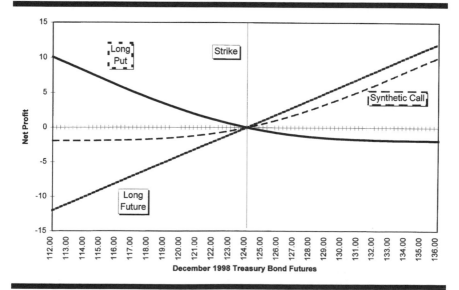

Figure 8.8 **PROFIT PROFILE OF A LONG SYNTHETIC PUT**

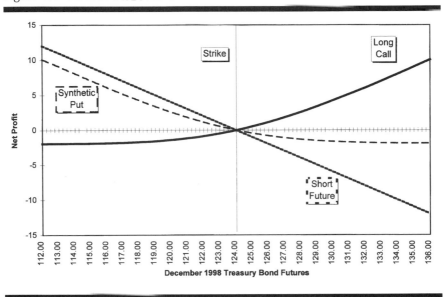

December 1998 Treasury Bond Futures

combine the dotted line of the short futures position moving from northwest to southeast with the solid line of the long call option position moving to the northeast, and we re-create the profit profile of a long synthetic put option moving to the northwest, shown in a dashed line. In Figure 8.9, we can combine the dotted line of the short futures position moving from northwest to southeast with the solid line of the short put option position moving to the southwest, and we re-create the profit profile of a short call option moving to the southeast, shown in a dashed line. Finally, in Figure 8.10, we can combine the dotted line of the long futures position moving from southwest to northeast with the solid line of the short call option position moving to the southeast, and we re-create the profit profile of a short put option moving to the southwest, shown in a dashed line.

BORROWING AND LENDING

The original Black–Scholes models for pricing call options and put options, respectively, are shown in Equation 8.1 and 8.2, where N represents the normal probability density function; r, the risk-free interest rate; σ, the volatility of the underlying asset; and $\sqrt{t}$, the year fraction remaining until expiration.

Figure 8.9 **PROFIT PROFILE OF A SHORT SYNTHETIC CALL**

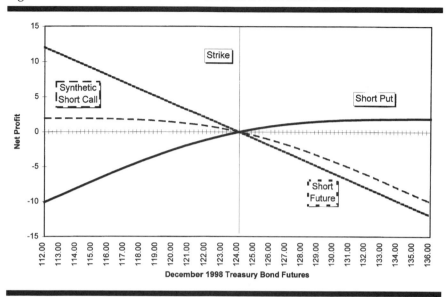

Figure 8.10 **PROFIT PROFILE OF A SHORT SYNTHETIC PUT**

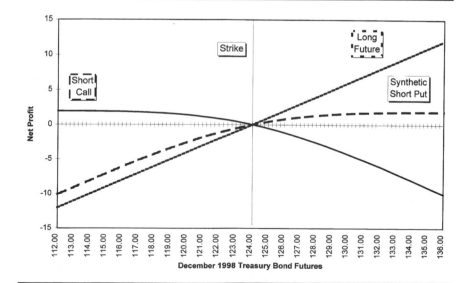

$$Call = Future \cdot N(x) - Strike \cdot r^{-1} \cdot N(x - \sigma\sqrt{t}), where$$

$$x \equiv \frac{\log(\frac{Future}{Strike \cdot r^{-1}})}{\sigma\sqrt{t}} + \frac{1}{2}\sigma\sqrt{t} \tag{8.1}$$

$$Put = Strike \cdot r^{-1} \cdot N(y + \sigma\sqrt{t}) - Future \cdot N(y), where$$

$$y \equiv \frac{\log(\frac{Future}{Strike \cdot r^{-1}})}{\sigma\sqrt{t}} - \frac{1}{2}\sigma\sqrt{t} \tag{8.2}$$

The premise behind these models is fairly straightforward: that the value of an option represents the difference between the amount borrowed to finance the purchase of an asset—*Strike · r⁻¹ · N (x − σ √t)* in the case of the call option—and the amount invested in the asset—*Future · N(x)* in the case of the call option.

The result is that option buyers are always borrowing money to invest in an asset that may or may not turn out to be worth anything. In this respect, it is no different than a standard business debt decision in which, say, a manufacturer borrows money to finance new plant and equipment. The borrower is trading the known cost of his borrowing against the potential for open-ended returns on his investment equity. The writer of the option, on the other hand, is lending money and can only hope to get repaid on his loan. The lender is faced with an entrepreneurial opportunity cost: He could have assumed the risk himself in exchange for equity.

Even though this relation between option purchases and borrowing has been discussed in the option literature from the start, students find it counterintuitive; the association between funds flowing out and lending money is far more comfortable. One device for absorbing this lesson is this: "If I can lose money solely as a function of time, this is equivalent to paying interest, and therefore I am borrowing money." The opposite is true as well, and it is equally difficult for students: All short option positions involve lending money. Here, the learning device must become "If I can make money solely as a function of time, this is equivalent to receiving interest, and therefore I am lending money."

We can illustrate these principles using the data from Table 8.1. The intrinsic value of the December 124 call option is *[124.03125 − 124]*, or .03125. This is all that the option will be worth at expiration in a static world. Our time premium is *[1.9375 − .03125]*, or 1.90625. Our static case borrowing cost on an annualized basis, therefore, is:

$$\left[1 + \frac{1.90625}{124.03125}\right]^{\frac{365}{99}} - 1, \text{ or } 5.78\% \tag{8.3}$$

Of course, the actual borrowing cost will depend on the realized value of the call option at the point of exercise. Since options on treasury bond futures are of an American exercise, we can depict the potential annualized borrowing cost across the dimensions of price and time over the last month of the option's life, with volatility held constant. A negative borrowing cost implies a positive return on the purchase of the call option, as shown in Figure 8.11.

It is critical to emphasize the assumption here of constant volatility. The actual borrowing cost or return on investment will be influenced by the time premium of the option. Time premium is a function of three different factors. The first is time, or, more properly, the square root of the year fraction remaining to expiration. The second is volatility, or the market's price for uncertainty. The third is the prevailing risk-free interest rate. We can build direct analogies between time premium and normal lending by noting that anything capable of increasing the value of a loan—higher interest rates, a longer time to maturity, and a lower credit quality or volatility—will also increase

Figure 8.11 **ANNUALIZED BORROWING COST OF A CALL OPTION OVER PRICE AND TIME**

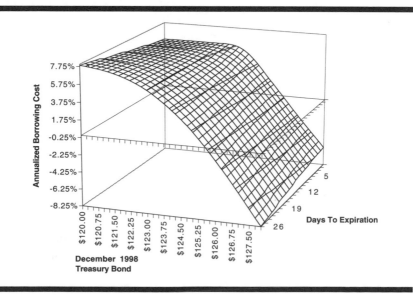

the value of a long option position. However, the value of a loan generally is unbounded: If we increase the rate of interest, the value of the loan will increase along a known compound interest curve, with the only potential bound being an increase in default risk. If we increase the maturity of the loan, the value will increase along the same compound interest curve.

Option values, unlike loan values, have bounds. No matter how high volatility goes, no matter how long the holding period, or no matter how high the interest rate, no one will pay more for the right to buy the asset than the price of the asset itself, and no one will pay more for the right to sell that asset than the present value of the strike price.

The interplay of the three components of time premium as these bounds are approached are critical for understanding option behavior. As an aside, we will see that the components of time premium have a relationship not unlike the four forces of nature—the strong and weak nuclear forces, electromagnetism, and gravity. Volatility is like the nuclear forces; it is extremely powerful over short-dated options, but its effects decrease with time. The risk-free interest rate is more akin to gravity; it has almost no effect over short-dated options, but it is the principal determinant of longer-dated option values.

INTEREST RATES

First, let us take a look at interest rates. All else held equal, an increase in interest rates will increase the value of a long call option, but as rates approach infinity, the value of the call option will approach the value of the underlying asset, and the price of the put option will approach the present value of the strike. We will illustrate the case of the call option. The sensitivity of a call option's price to interest rates is designated with the Greek letter ρ (rho), and is defined as:

$$\rho \equiv t \cdot Strike - (t+1) \cdot N(x - \sigma\sqrt{t}) > 0 \tag{8.4}$$

In Figure 8.12, the data from Table 8.1 are used to illustrate the effects of time and interest rates on the price of the December 124 call. With all else held constant, the risk-free interest rate is moved around fairly dramatically, from 1% to 35%, and yet the effect of interest rates is minimal compared with the effect of time.

Figure 8.12 **VALUE OF AN AT-THE-MONEY CALL AS A FUNCTION OF TIME AND INTEREST RATES**

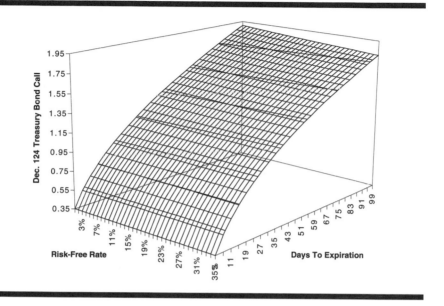

TIME

Next, we can take a look at the influence of time, which is a unique variable in the world of trading in the sense that it moves only in one direction and it does so at a known rate. Although this may sound somewhat silly, please consider that all other variables in the option model—the price of the underlying asset, volatility, and interest rates—move in both directions and in uncertain paths. The bound for a call option of the price of the underlying asset and the bound for a put option of the present value of the strike apply as the time remaining approaches infinity. Time decay is more rapid in the ATM environment than it is in either the ITM or OTM environments, and therefore it is sensitive to the *log(future/strike)* relationship. Time decay proceeds more slowly at initiation in more volatile markets, but its convergence to zero is more rapid in these environments. The sensitivity of the price of a call option to time is designated with the Greek letter θ (theta), and is defined as:

$$\theta \equiv (\frac{Future}{2} \cdot \sqrt{t} \cdot N(x) + Strike^{r-1})) N(x - \sigma \sqrt{t}) > 0 \qquad (8.5)$$

Two views of time decay are provided here. The first, shown in Figure 8.13, holds volatility constant and depicts the value of our December 124 treasury bond call across the dimensions of price and time remaining to expiration. The slope of the call option value surface becomes far more angular as expiration approaches across the entire price spectrum. At expiration, the curve becomes a linear angle as the value of the option collapses to its intrinsic value. At longer times remaining to expiration, the surface is more linear at both deep ITM and far OTM situations, but the region near the 124 strike is curved. This is a visual representation of the influence of the *log(future/strike)* on time decay.

The second representation, shown in Figure 8.14, is the relationship between time and volatility. This is depicted with the price of the December treasury bond future held constant at 124.03125. Time decay proceeds more slowly at initiation in high volatility but must accelerate as expiration approaches. Two factors that always increase the value of a loan, greater time to maturity and higher volatility/risk, combine to push the price of the call higher in the back corner of the graph. Time decay proceeds at a more constant rate in low-volatility environments.

Figure 8.13 **VALUE OF AN AT-THE-MONEY CALL AS A FUNCTION OF TIME AND PRICE**

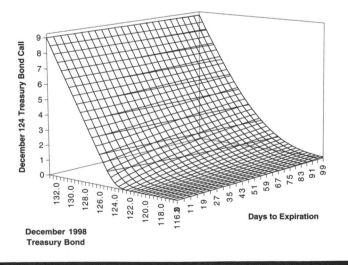

December 1998
Treasury Bond

Figure 8.14 **VALUE OF AN AT-THE-MONEY CALL AS A FUNCTION OF TIME AND VOLATILITY**

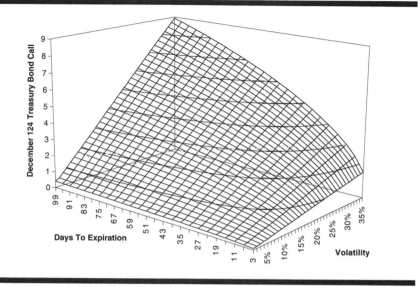

VOLATILITY

Implied volatility is the market's price of uncertainty; this differs considerably from the relative frequency measure or historical measures such as the high-low-close volatility shown in Equation 2.9. Indeed, we have used the differences between implied and historical volatility in developing the excess volatility component of the Market Tension Index (MTI) and EuroTension Index (ETI), as shown in Equation 5.1.

That the two measures can be different by significant amounts should not be surprising. Consider how a life insurance company can construct an actuarial table of mortality rates; an applicant is screened for age, weight, medical conditions, work environment, and personal habits and vices, and then the insurer looks up a mortality probability in a table of morbid accuracy. Now consider how an insurance quote needs to be assembled for an unusual and unprecedented risk. Let's say that an energy firm decides to ship liquefied natural gas in a nuclear-powered submarine from the Alaska North Slope under the polar ice cap to northern Norway. The energy firm will solicit insurance quotes from a number of firms, all of which have to make the best estimate they can of this unusual risk. The energy firm will of course choose the lowest offering rate. This is exactly how an options market sets implied volatility. The market must digest normal price variance along with scheduled high-impact events, such as government reports, along with random events. Then the market must ascertain both the probability of the occurrence of market-moving events along with the reactions of the market itself to those events. To predict volatility, therefore, one must predict both the occurrence of random events and the reaction of other traders to those events. It is submitted that this is quite simply impossible.

It must be mentioned in passing that volatility is the only element of the option pricing model not known exactly at initiation. The price of the underlying asset, the strike price, time remaining to expiration, and the risk-free interest rate are all known exactly.

The relation between implied and 21-day close-to-close volatility in the treasury bond future market is shown in Figure 8.15. The relation is not particularly linear, and there is a small group of implied high-volatility days occurring in the Persian Gulf War that are not matched by high historical volatility.

The sensitivity of the price of a call option with respect to volatility is designated as vega, which is not a Greek letter at all but rather the commemoration of a truly forgettable attempt by General Motors to build a small car in the early 1970s; there is no option derivative designated as the Pinto, however. Vega is defined as:

Figure 8.15 **IMPLIED AND HISTORICAL TREASURY BOND VOLATILITY**

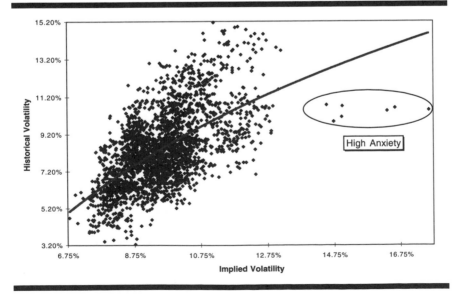

$$Vega \equiv Future \cdot \sqrt{t} \cdot N'(x) > 0 \tag{8.6}$$

We have seen already the interaction of volatility with time. The interaction with price is shown in Figure 8.16 with the full 99 days remaining to expiration.

STRIKE

The decision of which strike price to employ is critical. First, we should note that strike cannot be changed in an exchange-traded option but that there are exotic over-the-counter (OTC) options where not only can the strike change but the buyer gets to choose after the fact whether the option is a call or a put. As the strike of a call option approaches zero, the value of the call option approaches the value of the underlying asset, and as the strike approaches infinity, the value of the call option approaches zero. This relationship is illustrated in Figure 8.17, which depicts the behavior of a call option using the data in Table 8.1 over a wide range of strikes.

Figure 8.16 **VALUE OF AN AT-THE-MONEY CALL AS A FUNCTION OF PRICE AND VOLATILITY**

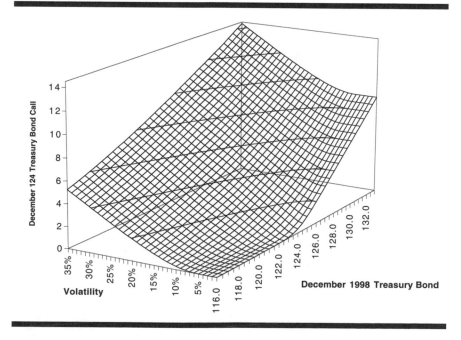

Figure 8.17 **VALUE OF AN AT-THE-MONEY CALL OPTION AS A FUNCTION OF PRICE AND STRIKE**

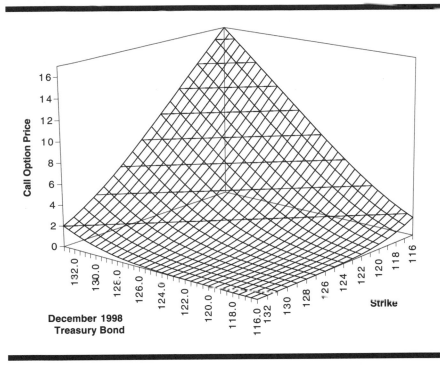

The sensitivity of a call option's price to the strike is designated with the Greek letter Ψ (psi) and is defined as $N(x) > 0$. This normal distribution relationship accounts for the tradeoffs between using an ITM strike and an OTM strike and is related to the risk-seeking and risk-averting behavior discussed in Chapter 1. The more that an option is OTM, the less risk will be involved in the domain of losses. This is risk-averse behavior on the part of the purchaser, especially one with a short position elsewhere: The buyer now has a synthetic put at the OTM strike. In addition, the purchase of an OTM strike places the buyer in the position of making large percentage gains on the initial investment, and this behavior is risk seeking in the same manner as the purchase of a lottery ticket. The purchase of an ITM option, which offers more direct and more immediate gains, but at a greater initial cost, does not seem particularly attractive in comparison.

We can illustrate this tradeoff by depicting the expected returns on a series of given strikes. Instead of using the treasury bond data in Table 8.1, we can use the options on the Standard & Poor's (S&P) 500 futures, which, by virtue of the market's extreme range at the late August 1998 time of this writing, has a wide range of actively traded strikes. Table 8.2 lists the September 1998 option strikes and their volatilities.

First, several things stand out immediately from Table 8.2. A volatility curve normally follows a generalized "smile" shape, with the low point occurring near the ATM strike, 1,085 in this case, and with volatility rising in both the ATM and OTM regions, as shown in Figure 8.18. However, August 21, 1998, was a day of extreme financial disruption on a worldwide scale, with Russian banks threatening to

Table 8.2 **STANDARD & POOR'S 500 OPTION PRICES, AUGUST 21, 1998**

Strike	Call Price ($)	Call Volatility (%)	Put Price ($)	Put Volatility (%)
1,020	81.2	33.32	14.7	33.36
1,025	77.0	32.72	15.5	32.78
1,030	72.9	32.17	16.4	32.25
1,035	69.1	31.86	17.3	31.66
1,040	64.9	31.09	18.3	31.11
1,045	61.1	30.65	19.3	30.49
1,050	57.0	29.86	20.4	29.91
1,055	53.3	29.37	21.5	29.26
1,060	49.4	28.64	22.7	28.63
1,065	45.7	28.00	24.0	28.02
1,070	42.1	27.38	25.4	27.41
1,075	38.6	26.75	26.9	26.80
1,080	35.4	26.29	28.6	26.27
1,085	32.2	25.74	30.4	25.73
1,090	29.3	25.33	32.5	25.34
1,095	26.4	24.81	34.6	24.84
1,100	23.7	24.35	26.8	15.94
1,105	21.2	23.94	39.3	23.91
1,110	18.8	23.49	41.9	23.48
1,115	16.6	23.09	44.7	23.10
1,120	14.6	22.74	47.6	22.67
1,125	12.7	22.34	50.7	22.29
1,130	11.0	21.98	54.0	21.95
1,135	9.5	21.69	57.5	21.68
1,140	8.1	21.35	61.1	21.36
1,145	6.9	21.08	64.8	21.00
1,150	5.8	20.77	68.7	20.71
1,155	4.8	20.43	72.7	20.39
1,160	3.9	20.05	76.8	20.03

Underlying: 1,086.8; time: 29 days.

Figure 8.18 **VOLATILITY CURVE OF OPTIONS FOR STANDARD & POOR'S 500. ATM = AT-THE-MONEY**

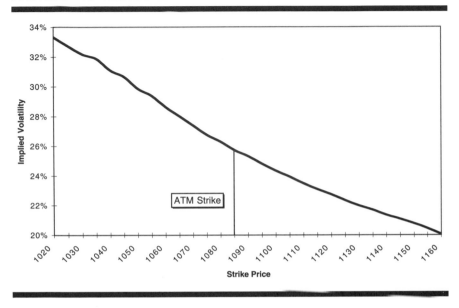

default on their loans and Venezuela threatening to devalue its currency. (Historians, if no one else, may find the financial incapacity of Russia on the thirtieth anniversary of its invasion of the former Czechoslovakia deliciously ironic.)

Volatility on that day took a linear path, one that continued falling at OTM strikes. The single interpretation of this is that put sellers are demanding a large price premium for the privilege of buying a put, and by the put–call parity theorem shown in the list of synthesis relationships above, the price of the call must rise as well.

Now we can take each call at each strike and construct an expected return surface for the next day, 26 days of time remaining, using the range formula shown in Equation 2.6 for each strike and at each volatility. Each cumulative probability shown in the graph is converted into its inverse of the normal distribution, or Z-value, which is then plugged into Equation 2.6 at the strike's implied volatility and at the square root of 26/365 as the year fraction. The value of the call option at that strike is then calculated, netted of its initial cost, and then multiplied by the probability to achieve an expected return, as shown in Figure 8.19. The results indicate a higher return for the ITM strikes at higher prices than the 1,086.8 seen at initiation, but at the cost of a potential loss of the initial option premium. The opposite

Figure 8.19 **ABSOLUTE EXPECTED RETURN PER STRIKE**

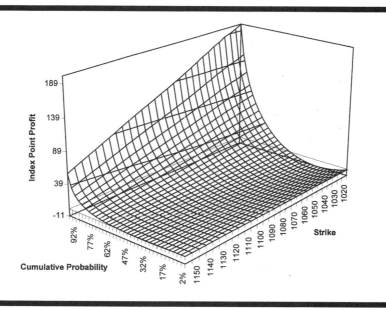

is true for the OTM strikes: low loss of premium but lower absolute participation in moves higher.

We can convert the display in Figure 8.19 to a return-on-capital view. This is achieved simply by dividing the net return by the initial premium paid, as shown in Figure 8.20.

It is now easy to visualize the appeal of OTM options: lower initial cost and the potential for a several-fold increase in value on the initial investment. We shall see in Chapter 10 in our discussion of the Dynamic Option Selection System that this is actually a risk-averse stance in the domain of profits and a risk-seeking stance in the domain of losses, which takes us back to our original discussion of investor psychology in Chapter 1. Selection of an ITM strike restores some risk seeking to the domain of profits and risk aversion to the domain of losses, especially for hedged positions.

DELTA AND GAMMA

Option-based hedging requires an understanding of delta, or the first derivative of the option pricing model with respect to the underlying asset's price. Delta provides us with a snapshot, an

Figure 8.20   **MULTIPLE OF INITIAL INVESTMENT RECEIVED ON CALL OPTIONS**

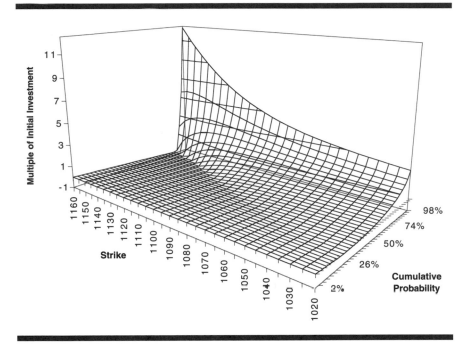

instantaneous estimate, of how we should expect an option's price to move with respect to changes in the underlying asset's price. As a result, the delta of an option is referred to frequently as its hedge ratio, since it determines the number of options required to offset an underlying exposure:

$$\text{Number of Options} = \frac{\text{Underlying Exposure}}{\Delta} \qquad (8.7)$$

Since the price of an option cannot fall below zero or exceed either the price of the underlying asset in the case of a call option or the present value of the strike price in the case of a put option, we know that delta must be bounded on both sides. In the case of a call option, the lower bound is zero, the limit that an OTM option will reach as expiration approaches, and the upper bound is 1, the limit that an ITM option will reach as expiration approaches. In the case of a put option, the upper bound is zero for OTM options as expiration approaches, whereas the lower bound is –1, the limit that an ITM option will reach as expiration approaches.

The delta of a long future or any other underlying asset is 1; it always changes as a linear function of its own price movement. The delta of a short future or any other underlying asset is –1 by the same logic. The bounds for delta are illustrated in Figure 8.21 for both call options and put options, using the data from Table 8.1.

The two delta curves run parallel to each other. The shape of the curves is identical to the cumulative normal probability curve of Figure 2.7, and the equation for producing the curves is the same as Equation 3.2. The rate of change of delta is most rapid in the ATM regions for both puts and calls, and the rate of change in both ITM and OTM regions starts to approach zero as the price of the underlying asset moves further away from the strike.

If the delta describes the cumulative normal distribution curve, then its first derivative should describe the standard normal distribution, and it does. This derivative, the rate of change for delta, is referred to as gamma and is overlaid on the delta curves in Figure 8.22. It is the

Figure 8.21 **DELTA OF AT-THE-MONEY OPTIONS**

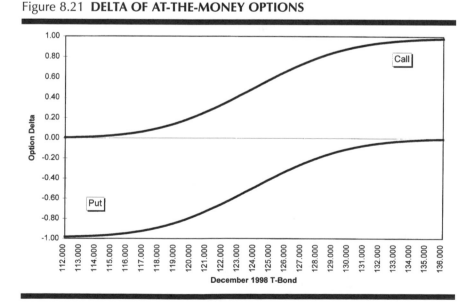

Figure 8.22 **DELTA AND GAMMA OF AT-THE-MONEY OPTIONS**

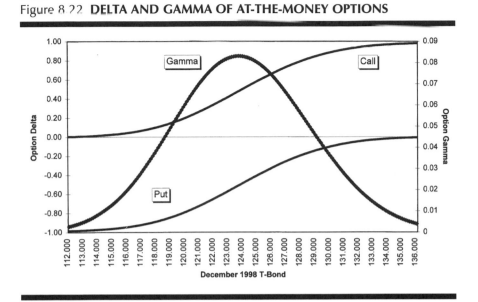

December 1998 T-Bond

same curve we saw in Figure 2.6. The equation for a call option's gamma is:

$$\Gamma \equiv \frac{1}{Future * \sigma * \sqrt{t}} N'(x) \tag{8.8}$$

Since the delta of a put option and a call option parallel each other, both rising to the bounds of 1 and zero, respectively, as the price of the underlying asset rises, the gamma of a long option position is always positive. Since any long option position has a finite risk—the value of the premium paid—having any long option position is therefore equivalent to owning insurance. Any short option position has negative gamma, and having it is equivalent to writing insurance. Hedging, which is risk transference with the goal of risk minimization, can be achieved only through a gamma-positive position.

A quick glance at both the delta and gamma curves should confirm that both derivatives behave in a decidedly nonlinear manner. This nonlinearity increases when we examine delta and gamma with respect to other option pricing variables, especially time and volatility.

First, let's extend the general concept of price sensitivity to one higher level. The third derivative of the option price with respect to the underlying asset's price is referred to as speed. In a rapidly moving market, the delta of a position changes quite swiftly, especially as OTM options cross over into ITM options; recall the region of rapid ascent of delta near the ATM strike. This change in delta is buffered by higher volatility and exacerbated by lower volatility. The speed of our December 124 treasury bond call is depicted in Figure 8.23.

The buffering effect of volatility on delta suggests that option-based hedges are more effective when initiated in a low-volatility environment; not only is the delta more responsive to movements in the underlying asset but the long option will be in a position to benefit from any subsequent increase in volatility.

The responsiveness of delta is also a function of the time remaining to expiration. Since delta must collapse to a terminal value of zero at expiration for OTM options and either 1 or –1 for ITM calls and puts, respectively, the movement of delta to these terminal values must accelerate as expiration approaches. This first derivative of delta with respect to time is called charm and is depicted in Figure 8.24.

Figure 8.23 **SPEED OF AN AT-THE-MONEY CALL OPTION**

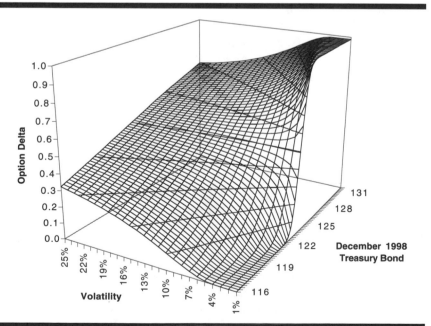

Figure 8.24 **CHARM OF AN AT-THE-MONEY CALL OPTION**

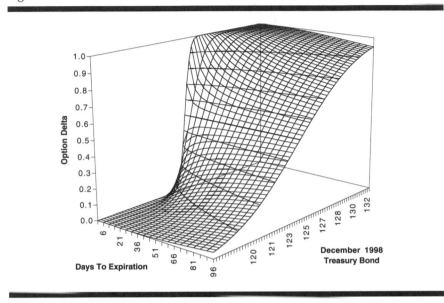

Just as higher volatility buffers the movement of delta, so does additional time remaining to expiration. Both variables increase the time premium of an option, and since time premium must converge to zero by expiration, at which point delta will have its terminal value of either zero for OTM values or 1 or –1 for call options and put options, respectively, the movement of delta will necessarily become more extreme as both time remaining to expiration and volatility approach zero. This can be seen in Figure 8.25.

The instability of delta in low-volatility, low-time environments makes the management of these trades exceedingly difficult. Since gamma is the first derivative of delta, it stands to reason that gamma is even more unstable than delta in these environments. The first derivative of gamma with respect to time is referred to as color. Just as we did in the case of delta, we can examine the color of our December 124 treasury bond future call option with respect to both price and volatility. This is depicted in Figure 8.26.

Each cross-section in time of Figure 8.26 depicts a normal distribution's bell curve, with each succeeding cross-section becoming more peaked as expiration approaches. As was the case for charm, we should expect that lower volatility will increase the rate of change for gamma as well; our expectation is confirmed in Figure 8.27.

Figure 8.25 **CHARM OF AN AT-THE-MONEY CALL**

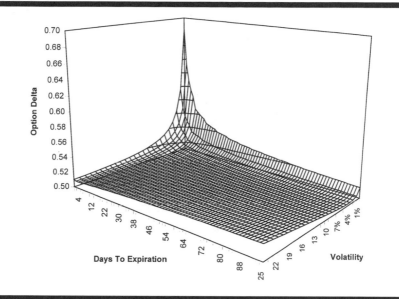

Figure 8.26 **COLOR OF AN AT-THE-MONEY CALL: TIME**

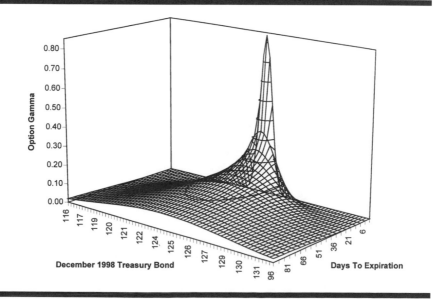

Figure 8.2 / **COLOR OF AN AT-THE-MONEY CALL: VOLATILITY**

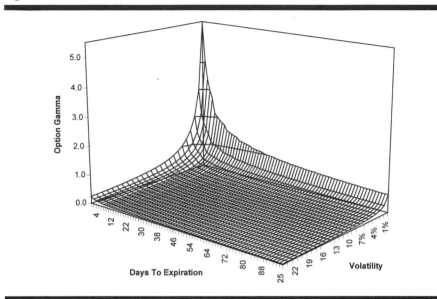

The aspects of option behavior discussed here will be applied to the construction of option spreads, which will be our last avenue of inquiry before we combine the aspects of futures markets with option mechanics into the Dynamic Option Selection System.

9

Choose Your Weapons

The most sought-after epitaph for any trader should be "He maximized his return while minimizing his risk." Indeed, such an accolade should be the prerequisite for burial in the northwest corner of the cemetery, a place from which one could overlook the efficient frontier for eternity.

DESIRED ATTRIBUTES OF OPTION POSITIONS

It should stand to reason that each and every component of one's trading strategies should meet the same test. We can discuss most of the attributes we want in the intuitive terms of loans and insurance discussed in Chapter 8. All references in the discussion below will be to options; this is based on the principle that all financial assets can be decomposed into some combination of a call option, a put option, and a zero-coupon bond. In this light, futures and cash market positions are merely special cases of option spreads, as seen in the synthesis relationships outlined in Chapter 8. We will approach trading problems from the standpoint of the hedger, someone who is looking to convert an economic exposure into a synthetic option, unless stated otherwise, and therefore we will need to account for cash market gains and losses as well as option position gains and losses. The desired strategy components are as follows:

1. Be a buyer of insurance; maintain positive gamma.
2. Make the calendar work for you; minimize time decay exposure.
3. Make accidents work in your favor.

4. Minimize capital commitments.

5. Leverage potential gains.

6. Sell forward months in carry markets.

7. Buy forward months in backwardated markets.

8. Minimize net borrowing and maximize net lending.

There are several tradeoffs involved in satisfying these attributes, most of which have been discussed by this point. The most important is the tradeoff between the maintenance of positive gamma and the minimization of time decay. We can maximize gamma by staying near the at-the-money (ATM) strike, as seen in Figure 8.22, but this exposes us to the maximum rate of time decay, as seen in Figure 8.13. Another important tradeoff is the one between leveraging potential gains and minimizing net borrowing. The realized net borrowing of an option can be determined only after the fact, as we saw in Figure 8.11, but we know beforehand the leverage of strike, seen in Figure 8.17, and the expected return surface, as seen in Figure 8.19. An out-of-the-money (OTM) option obviously offers a far greater return if a low-probability move occurs, but it is also a far more likely net loser. In this sense, an OTM option takes on the very same attributes of a lottery ticket that we discussed in Chapter 1. The opposite tradeoff occurs when an in-the-money (ITM) option is purchased: The percentage gains will be much smaller and the net borrowing will be less relative to the intrinsic value of the option, but we are not minimizing capital commitments.

The second, sixth, and seventh in the list above will be discussed in passing in Chapter 10 as we discuss the mechanics of option spreads. The very nature of time decay for options, which declines as $\sqrt{t}$, means there is an expected advantage, all else held equal, to selling an option with shorter maturity against a long option with longer maturity. The mechanics of backwardation and contango, discussed in Chapter 4, provide us with net borrowing and lending opportunities by buying and selling at different points along the forward curve in the futures market at the cost of a known set of risks, and we will incorporate these effects into calendar spreads in Chapter 10.

CONTINUOUS INSURANCE AND THE HEDGE PRINCIPLES

The concept of making accidents work for you presents some interesting trade-offs as well. If we return to our insurance analogy, we should recognize that the best possible outcome for any insurance premium paid is that it is a deadweight loss: If at the end of the year your house has not burned down, you are better off than if it had and you collected a large payoff from your insurance company. Although few of us ever would hold otherwise, it is interesting to see how often traders feel duped by paying an option premium, not having an adverse event occur, and then losing the option premium in all or in part. It is also interesting, as noted in Chapter 1, how we are perfectly willing to overinsure for mundane and predictable expenses, such as routine medical payments. We should seek insurance during times of calm when the risks are perceived to be lower; this provides us the opportunity to purchase volatility at a lower level than during the midst of a crisis. Extreme cases of this are seen in equity markets after a crash, in currency markets after a threatened devaluation, in grain markets during a drought, or in energy markets during turmoil in oil-producing regions: Volatility surges, raising the net borrowing cost and lowering the expected return on the long option. This is part of human nature; one suspects that most umbrellas are purchased by price-indifferent buyers during afternoon rainstorms.

An absolutely critical distinction should be kept in mind. It is true that in an efficient and fairly priced option market, each option's price and therefore volatility takes into account the likelihood that price movements will reach a certain level; indeed, much of Chapter 2 was devoted to the mechanics of calculating these levels. This is static analysis for a dynamic and chaotic world. No option price can take into account the future path of underlying prices and volatilities. However, unless we assume that between the initiation of a trade and its completion the world will be perfectly static, we know that the markets will be offering us opportunities to manage our option-based hedges during this period so as to maximize the net return. At the risk of sounding trite, we can say that every day is a new day in the markets, presenting us with new risks and opportunities. Each position needs to be reevaluated continuously; options and option spreads are the very antithesis of the buy-and-hold philosophy.

Options offer something that futures, forwards, and cash market positions cannot—the ability to change their underlying exposure—and it is critical that we take advantage of this attribute. If we were to hedge our cash market exposure to corn with call options, and the price of corn were to move higher, we would find that the total delta of our option hedge has increased. This leaves us with delta in excess of our desired exposure and, more importantly, creates the risk that the monetary value of this excess delta will disappear. In addition, our total net market exposure, zero delta at the initiation of the hedge, is now a positive number. We need to sell this excess delta back to the market to defray the costs of insurance. We have now arrived at the two critical premises of option-based hedging:

- The total delta of the hedge must be less than or equal to the delta of the cash market risk.
- The management of the position, especially the sale of this excess delta and the restructuring of the position as required, is the only way to reduce the overall cost of insurance and/or the initial net borrowing involved in the position.

Adherence to these two principles is what allows us to place ourselves in a position to have our combined cash market and option-based hedge position outperform the base case expectation of a standard hedge. This outperformance is not certain and cannot be made certain; only the subsequent path of price and volatility over time can determine the final outcome. Management of positions according to these principles will be discussed in more detail in Chapter 11.

STRIKE SELECTIONS

The key to satisfying the conflicting goals described above is proper strike selection for a set of trading components that we can then combine into concise trading strategies. Table 9.1 lists and enumerates these components, each of which is discussed in turn and is referred to by its number.

Strike 1: The Long Call for Bullish Purposes

Just as we based the examples in Chapter 8 on a snapshot of treasury bond data, we will base the discussion here on a snapshot of corn

Table 9.1 **TRADING STRATEGY COMPONENTS**

Call	Put
1. Strike to buy for bullish purposes	2. Strike to buy for bearish purposes
3. Strike to sell in bull spread	4. Strike to sell in bear spread
5. ITM straddle strike	6. ITM straddle strike
7. OTM strike for covering long future	8. OTM strike for covering short future

ITM = in-the-money; OTM = out-of-the-money.

futures and options at the close of business on September 1, 1998. On this day, the December 1998 contract closed at a price of $2.03 per bushel, with 81 trading days left to the expiration of the December options on November 20, 1998. The closing price and derivative data for the December call and put options are presented in Table 9.2.

Which call option for strike 1 best satisfies the characteristics we listed earlier as desirable option positions? Let's describe the problem first. When we purchase an option for the purposes of offsetting an underlying risk, we are most interested in the option's delta, the hedge ratio defined in Equation 8.7. The more delta we buy per option, the more each option will move to protect the underlying asset, and the fewer options will be needed. However, we will need to risk more capital because of the greater initial cost of ITM options, and this starts to defeat the whole concept of using options instead of futures as a hedge instrument. If we purchase a larger number of OTM options, each option will move far less in response to the underlying asset, and so despite their lower cost, they will be an ineffective hedge for all except the most extreme price movements.

Table 9.2 **DECEMBER 1998 CORN OPTION DATA, SEPTEMBER 1, 1998**

Strike ($)	Premium ($)	Delta	Gamma	Theta	Vega	Volatility (%)
Calls						
1.60	0.430	0.958	0.264	(0.000)	0.001	28.34
1.70	0.335	0.919	0.527	(0.000)	0.001	26.94
1.80	0.247	0.846	0.922	(0.000)	0.002	25.62
1.90	0.168	0.730	1.390	(0.000)	0.003	24.28
2.00	0.103	0.570	1.750	(0.001)	0.004	23.17
2.10	0.056	0.391	1.768	(0.001)	0.004	22.54
2.20	0.030	0.243	1.418	(0.000)	0.003	22.96
2.30	0.018	0.151	0.998	(0.000)	0.002	24.48
2.40	0.009	0.084	0.649	(0.000)	0.001	24.88
Puts						
1.600	0.004	(0.032)	0.264	(0.000)	0.001	28.34
1.700	0.009	(0.071)	0.527	(0.000)	0.001	26.94
1.800	0.019	(0.144)	0.922	(0.000)	0.002	25.62
1.900	0.040	(0.262)	1.375	(0.000)	0.003	24.67
2.000	0.073	(0.420)	1.756	(0.001)	0.004	23.09
2.100	0.126	(0.598)	1.755	(0.000)	0.004	22.73
2.200	0.198	(0.750)	1.426	(0.000)	0.003	22.69
2.300	0.283	(0.851)	0.988	(0.000)	0.002	23.42
2.400	0.373	(0.923)	0.589	(0.000)	0.001	22.94

This last point is often counterintuitive to hedgers, many of whom still think of their option purchases in terms of lottery tickets: low cost and high payoff. We can illustrate the expected net returns on each of our corn call options in Table 9.3. For each strike, we need to buy *1/delta* number of options, which gives us a total option cost shown in column 5. The cash market gain and loss for a corn buyer is shown as the difference between the initial price and $2.03 in column 6. We can use Equation 2.7 to calculate the number of standard deviations away each strike price will be after the 81 days remaining to expiration and calculate the probability that the futures price will be greater than the strike price at that date. Settlement at the strike price is always the worst case in any option-based hedge, since the cash market losses are not offset by any gain on the option, and this number is displayed in column 10 as the expected return.

Although the more risk averse among us might argue that the worst case is the only case that ever matters, we already have submitted in Chapter 3 that no business ever prospered by insuring away 100% of its risk. Minimizing the worst case by buying the deepest ITM option returns us to the dilemma of hedging's being merely a conversion of external market risk to internal trading decision risk because a deep-in-the-money (DITM) option approaches a future in its behavior over a wide range of prices, including the entire spectrum of adverse cash market moves.

The option hedge principles can be illustrated easily at this point. We can take the initial option positions for corn on September 1 and,

Table 9.3 **EXPECTED HEDGE RETURNS FOR STRIKE 1**

Strike ($)	Price ($)	Delta	1/Delta	Option Cost ($)	Cash Gain ($)	Volatility (%)	Z-Value	Probability of Futures Price > Strike Price (%)	Expected Return ($)
1.60	0.43	0.96	1.04	0.45	0.43	28.34	−1.78	96.27	0.00
1.70	0.34	0.92	1.09	0.36	0.33	26.94	−1.40	91.89	0.00
1.80	0.25	0.85	1.18	0.29	0.23	25.62	−1.00	84.05	−0.00
1.90	0.17	0.73	1.37	0.23	0.13	24.28	−0.58	71.86	−0.00
2.00	0.10	0.57	1.75	0.18	0.03	23.17	−0.14	55.42	−0.00
2.10	0.06	0.39	2.56	0.14	−0.07	22.54	0.32	37.48	−0.00
2.20	0.03	0.24	4.12	0.12	−0.17	22.96	0.74	22.86	−0.00
2.30	0.02	0.15	6.62	0.12	−0.27	24.48	1.08	13.95	−0.00
2.40	0.01	0.08	11.84	0.10	−0.37	24.88	1.43	7.65	−0.00

all else held equal, examine how the hedge would look on September 4 if the price of December corn had risen from $2.03 to $2.20. As seen in Table 9.4, the total delta of each option position at each strike increases, with the increases being especially pronounced for the initially OTM strikes. Each strike now has excess delta available for resale back to the market, with the total excess increasing with the strike. The total option position gain is greatest at these strikes, but our total net sales of excess delta are greatest at the slightly OTM strikes.

Although the purchase of a DITM call option might appeal to our desire to minimize the worst case, the purchase of OTM options, which offer us the potential to expose a smaller amount of capital at initiation and then to recoup a large percentage of that sum in price moves favorable to the option position, might appeal to our desire to treat options as lottery tickets.

The resolution of this tradeoff is offered by the options themselves, and we describe it like this: We want to buy the most delta possible so that we may have the most favorable worst case for our hedge; we want this delta to expand as rapidly as possible in price movements favorable to the option so that we may sell it back to the market; and we want this option to retain as much of its value as possible in price movements unfavorable to the option so that we will retain as much time value as possible for as long as possible. The optimal strike that satisfies these three desires for our strike 1, produced by a proprietary algorithm, is $1.90, which is the first ITM strike for the call option, as shown in Figure 9.1.

Table 9.4 **ACTIONS ON SEPTEMBER 4, 1998, FOR STRIKE 1**

Strike ($)	Price ($)	Delta	Total Delta	Excess Delta	Cash Gain ($)	Option Gain ($)	Net Gain ($)	Net Sales ($)	Sale/Total Cost %
1.60	0.60	0.98	1.03	0.03	−0.17	0.18	0.01	0.02	3.63
1.70	0.50	0.97	1.06	0.06	−0.17	0.18	0.01	0.03	8.24
1.80	0.40	0.95	1.12	0.12	−0.17	0.18	0.01	0.05	17.01
1.90	0.31	0.90	1.24	0.24	−0.17	0.19	0.02	0.07	32.02
2.00	0.22	0.82	1.44	0.44	−0.17	0.21	0.04	0.10	53.72
2.10	0.15	0.68	1.75	0.75	−0.17	0.23	0.06	0.11	76.45
2.20	0.09	0.52	2.13	1.13	−0.17	0.26	0.09	0.10	84.03
2.30	0.06	0.36	2.41	1.41	−0.17	0.27	0.10	0.08	71.67
2.40	0.03	0.24	2.84	1.84	−0.17	0.30	0.13	0.06	60.23

Figure 9.1 **STRIKE SELECTION FOR BULLISH CALL OPTION**

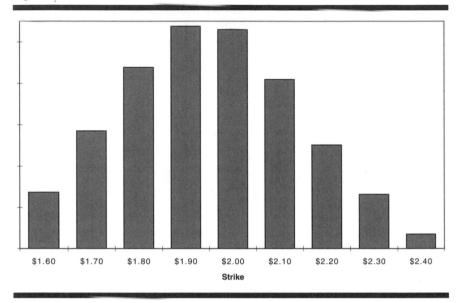

Strike 2: The Long Put for Bearish Purposes

The considerations motivating the strike selection for strike 2 are, unsurprisingly, the opposite of those for strike 1. Table 9.5 depicts how the highest expected return along the worst-case line occurs at

Table 9.5 **EXPECTED HEDGE RETURNS FOR STRIKE 2**

Strike ($)	Price ($)	Delta	−1/Delta	Option Cost ($)	Cash Gain ($)	Volatility (%)	Z-Value	Probability of Futures Price < Strike Price (%)	Expected Return ($)
1.60	0.00	−0.03	31.37	0.11	−0.43	28.34	−1.78	3.73	−0.02
1.70	0.01	−0.07	14.04	0.12	−0.33	26.94	−1.40	8.11	−0.04
1.80	0.02	−0.14	6.95	0.13	−0.23	25.62	−1.00	15.95	−0.06
1.90	0.04	−0.26	3.81	0.15	−0.13	24.67	−0.58	28.14	−0.08
2.00	0.07	−0.42	2.38	0.17	−0.03	23.09	−0.14	44.58	−0.09
2.10	0.13	−0.60	1.67	0.21	0.07	22.73	0.32	62.52	−0.05
2.20	0.20	−0.75	1.33	0.26	0.17	22.69	0.74	77.14	−0.02
2.30	0.28	−0.85	1.18	0.33	0.27	23.42	1.08	86.05	−0.01
2.40	0.37	−0.92	1.08	0.40	0.37	22.94	1.43	92.35	0.00

the DITM strikes for a corn seller protecting himself with put options. Once again, this information alone might lead us to believe that we would benefit from converting our put option purchases into something akin to short futures.

Once we convert the static analysis into initiation into a dynamic price path by dropping the price of corn down to $1.87, the opposite conclusion jumps out just as it did for strike 1. Our OTM option gains are quite large, and we get to buy a large amount of excess put delta back from the market. In absolute dollar terms, the largest sales occur at the ATM strike of $2.00, as shown in Table 9.6.

Once again, the resolution of this trade-off is offered by the options themselves. We can summarize the resolution this way. We want to buy the most delta possible so that we may have the most favorable worst case for our hedge; we want this delta to expand as rapidly as possible in price movements favorable to the option so that we may buy it back from the market; and we want this option to retain as much of its value as possible in price movements unfavorable to the option so that we will retain as much time value as possible for as long as possible. The optimal strike that satisfies these three desires for our strike 2, produced by a proprietary algorithm, is $2.20, which is the second ITM strike for the put option, as shown in Figure 9.2.

Strike 3: The Short Call for a Bull Spread

We now come to some of the more interesting applications, all of which are illustrated in Chapter 10, and once again it is helpful to

Table 9.6 **ACTIONS ON SEPTEMBER 4, 1998, FOR STRIKE 2**

Strike ($)	Price ($)	Delta	Total Delta	Excess Delta	Cash Gain ($)	Option Gain ($)	Net Gain ($)	Net Sales ($)	Sale/Total Cost %
1.60	0.01	−0.10	−3.25	−2.25	−0.16	0.29	0.13	0.03	25.97
1.70	0.03	−0.20	−2.84	−1.84	−0.16	0.27	0.11	0.05	42.73
1.80	0.06	−0.35	−2.42	−1.42	−0.16	0.25	0.09	0.08	59.31
1.90	0.10	−0.53	−2.01	−1.01	−0.16	0.23	0.07	0.10	66.71
2.00	0.16	−0.71	−1.69	−0.69	−0.16	0.21	0.05	0.11	64.85
2.10	0.24	−0.85	−1.41	−0.41	−0.16	0.19	0.03	0.10	47.42
2.20	0.33	−0.92	−1.23	−0.23	−0.16	0.18	0.02	0.08	29.23
2.30	0.43	−0.96	−1.13	−0.13	−0.16	0.17	0.01	0.05	16.51
2.40	0.53	−0.98	−1.06	−0.06	−0.16	0.17	0.01	0.03	8.03

Figure 9.2 **STRIKE SELECTION FOR BEARISH PUT OPTION**

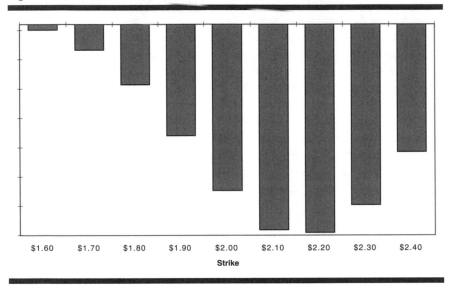

define what we would like to see in our strike—strike 3. Since we will, by definition, be in a bull spread—long an ITM call option and short an OTM call option—we do not have to worry about open-ended liabilities at higher prices for the position itself. Ideally, we would like to sell this call option right at a resistance level, or the highest price level we would expect to see for whatever reason. We are trading off premium received against the likelihood that the buyer will wish to exercise this call option.

Table 9.7 illustrates the net expected returns at the OTM strikes for a spread involving strike 1, our long $1.90 call option, and potential

Table 9.7 **EXPECTED HEDGE RETURNS: STRIKE 1 – STRIKE 3**

Strike ($)	Price ($)	Delta	1/Delta	Option Cost ($)	Cash Gain ($)	Volatility (%)	Z-Value	Probability of Futures Price > Strike Price (%)	Expected Return ($)
2.10	0.11	0.34	2.95	0.33	–0.07	22.54	0.32	37.48	0.07
2.20	0.14	0.49	2.05	0.28	–0.17	22.96	0.74	22.86	0.04
2.30	0.15	0.58	1.73	0.26	–0.27	24.48	1.08	13.95	0.02
2.40	0.16	0.65	1.55	0.25	–0.37	24.88	1.43	7.65	0.01

strike 3s. We can subtract the premium of strike 3 from strike 1 to get a net cost for the spread, and we can subtract the option deltas as well to get a net delta. Since the net delta of a spread involving a strike 3 closer to the ATM strike is lower, we need to purchase more of them, and this involves a higher initial outlay. The expected return for strike 3 at expiration, which is the gain on the $1.90 call plus the premium received on strike 3 minus the loss on the cash market position, all multiplied by the probability of reaching strike 3, is shown. This is not the worst-case outcome; at higher prices, the loss on the cash market position will be greater than the gains on the bull call option spread, so there is no definite worst case. We shall see in Chapter 10 that bull call spreads rarely come into solution in the Dynamic Option Selection System for this reason. Moreover, as we can see in Table 9.8, a jump from $2.03 to $2.20 in 3 days will not produce the opportunities to sell excess delta except at the very highest strike, $2.40.

The logic dictated by the numbers in Tables 9.7 and 9.8 can be confirmed intuitively. If a hedger is confronting an open-ended price risk—higher corn prices in this instance—he should keep an open-ended hedge position as well. Any short call option position adds to the initial risk of being exposed to higher prices, but if any call option is to be sold, it might as well be the most OTM available. This is confirmed by our proprietary algorithm for strike 3, which selects $2.40 for the value of strike 3, as shown in Figure 9.3.

Strike 4: The Short Put for a Bear Spread

Just as strike 2 was the logical opposite of strike 1, the same applies to the relation between strike 4 and strike 3. Our desired attributes for strike 4 include selling a put option near an identifiable support level, or the lowest price level we would expect to see for whatever reason. We do not have to worry about open-ended liabilities on the position

Table 9.8 **ACTIONS ON SEPTEMBER 4, 1998: STRIKE 1 – STRIKE 3**

Strike ($)	Price ($)	Delta	Total Delta	Excess Delta	Cash Gain ($)	Option Gain ($)	Net Gain ($)	Net Sales ($)	Sale/Total Cost %
2.10	0.15	0.22	0.64	—	−0.17	0.11	−0.06	—	—
2.20	0.20	0.36	0.75	—	−0.17	0.14	−0.03	—	—
2.30	0.25	0.52	0.90	—	−0.17	0.17	0.00	—	—
2.40	0.28	0.67	1.04	0.04	−0.17	0.18	0.01	0.01	4.37

Figure 9.3 **STRIKE SELECTION FOR SHORT CALL OPTION IN BULL SPREAD**

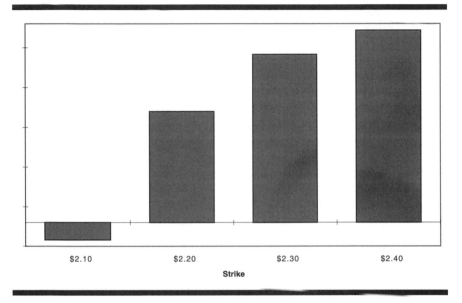

by itself because we will be long an ITM put option against this short OTM put option. As before, we are trading off premium received against the likelihood that the buyer will wish to exercise this put option.

The same relationship seen for strike 3 appears to apply here as well, and for the same reasons. Table 9.9 illustrates the net expected returns at the OTM strikes for a spread involving strike 2, our long

Table 9.9 **EXPECTED HEDGE RETURNS: STRIKE 2 – STRIKE 4**

Strike ($)	Price ($)	Delta	1/Delta	Option Cost ($)	Cash Gain ($)	Volatility (%)	Z-Value	Probability of Futures Price < Strike Price (%)	Expected Return ($)
1.90	0.16	−0.49	2.05	0.32	0.03	24.67	−0.57	28.45	0.11
1.80	0.18	−0.61	1.65	0.29	0.13	25.62	−1.00	15.95	0.09
1.70	0.19	−0.68	1.47	0.28	0.23	26.94	−1.40	8.11	0.06
1.60	0.19	−0.72	1.39	0.27	0.33	28.34	−1.78	3.73	0.03

$2.20 put option, and potential strike 4s. We can subtract the premium of strike 4 from strike 2 to get a net cost for the spread, and we can subtract the option deltas as well to get a net delta. Since the net delta of a spread involving a strike 4 closer to the ATM strike is higher, we need to purchase more of them, and this involves a higher initial outlay. The expected return at strike 4 at expiration, which is the gain on the $2.20 put plus the premium received on strike 4 minus the loss on the cash market position, all multiplied by the probability of reaching strike 4, is shown. As was the case for strike 3, this is not the worst-case outcome; at lower prices, the loss on the cash market position will be greater than the gains on the bear put option spread, so there is no definite worst case.

Once again, we can confirm the logic dictated by the numbers in Tables 9.9 and 9.10 intuitively. If a hedger is confronting an open-ended price risk—lower corn prices in this instance—he should keep an open-ended hedge position as well. Any short put option position adds to the initial risk of being exposed to lower prices, but if any put option is to be sold, it might as well be the most OTM available. This is confirmed by our proprietary algorithm for strike 4, which selects $1.60 for the value of strike 4, as shown in Figure 9.4.

Strike 5: The Bullish In-The-Money Straddle

The combined purchase of a call option and a put option at the same strike is referred to as a straddle, possibly in derisive homage to its apparent indecision. However, this is an unfair characterization, since a properly emplaced straddle can be a very aggressive directional trading tool.

Let's take the first case of the corn buyer who needs to acquire protection from higher corn prices, and let's posit that volatility is lower than the present reading over 23% for the ATM strike. In addi-

---

Table 9.10 **ACTIONS ON SEPTEMBER 4, 1998: STRIKE 2 – STRIKE 4**

Strike ($)	Price ($)	Delta	Total Delta	Excess Delta	Cash Gain ($)	Option Gain ($)	Net Gain ($)	Net Sales ($)	Sale/Total Cost %
1.90	0.23	−0.36	−0.75	—	−0.16	0.15	−0.01	—	—
1.80	0.28	−0.55	−0.90	—	−0.16	0.17	0.01	—	—
1.70	0.31	−0.72	−1.06	−0.06	−0.16	0.18	0.02	0.02	7.02
1.60	0.33	−0.86	−1.19	−0.19	−0.16	0.19	0.03	0.06	23.18

Figure 9.4 **STRIKE SELECTION FOR SHORT PUT OPTION IN A BEARISH SPREAD**

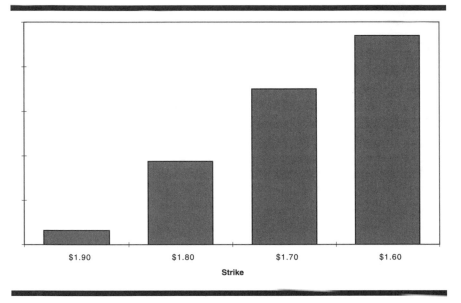

tion, let's assume that the corn market has been in a prolonged trading range because of the lack of solid information about the forthcoming crop. Our buyer may be perfectly correct in assuming that any subsequent move out of this range will be powerful and abrupt should value change, as illustrated in Figure 2.5. A bullish ITM straddle, one consisting of both a long ITM call option and a long OTM put option, will have a lower net delta than will a simple bullish call such as our selection in strike 1, and therefore we will need to purchase more of these positions. Should the market move higher, the delta of the long ITM call option will expand far more rapidly than the delta of the long OTM put option will rise, and this will present powerful opportunities for recouping the initial outlay on the hedge. Of course, the principal drawback of the straddle position is its higher initial outlay for the two long options and the absolute certainty that at least one of these options will expire worthless. Table 9.11 illustrates the profiles of the ITM straddles at initiation.

The expected return at the given straddle strike is indeed a worst-case measure; the cash market gain is offset by a complete loss of the combined option premium. Just as was the case for strike 1, the best expected return occurs at the deepest ITM strike available, the $1.60. Unless the world remains a static place, however, we should not

Table 9.11 **EXPECTED HEDGE RETURNS FOR STRIKE 5 STRADDLE**

Strike ($)	Net Price ($)	Net Delta	1/Delta	Option Cost ($)	Cash Gain ($)	Volatility (%)	Z-Value	Probability of Futures Price < Strike Price (%)	Expected Return ($)
1.9	0.21	0.47	2.14	0.44	0.13	24.67	−0.57	28.45	−0.09
1.8	0.27	0.70	1.42	0.38	0.23	25.62	−1.00	15.95	−0.02
1.7	0.34	0.85	1.18	0.41	0.33	26.94	−1.40	8.11	−0.01
1.6	0.43	0.93	1.08	0.47	0.43	28.34	−1.78	3.73	0.00

expect to see a complete loss of the option premium. Once again, we will increase the price to $2.20 per bushel on September 4, 1998, to see, in Table 9.12, how our hedge position would be managed.

The dichotomy between which strike has the greatest management potential and which has the worst worst-case potential is striking. The first ITM strike, $1.90, which had a positive delta of only 0.47 at initiation and which presented us with an intrinsic value of only $0.13, will explode in delta with an early price movement. It should be noted in passing that its put option component would explode in value should prices fall, which would present us with the unusual opportunity to witness gains on both the short cash market position and the initially long hedge position, something that is categorically impossible to do with any futures-based hedge.

The trade-off between how much capital we wish to expose to the ravages of time decay in a static market and how much potential we wish for position management opportunities is solved by our proprietary algorithm, and is presented in Figure 9.5. The resolution is overwhelmingly in favor of the first ITM strike.

Table 9.12 **ACTIONS ON SEPTEMBER 4, 1998 FOR STRIKE 5 STRADDLE**

Strike ($)	Price ($)	Delta	Total Delta	Excess Delta	Cash Gain ($)	Option Gain ($)	Net Gain ($)	Net Sales ($)	Sale/Total Cost %
1.90	0.33	0.78	1.66	0.66	−0.17	0.25	0.08	0.22	48.75
1.80	0.40	0.91	1.30	0.30	−0.17	0.20	0.03	0.12	31.87
1.70	0.50	0.97	1.14	0.14	−0.17	0.19	0.02	0.07	17.86
1.60	0.60	0.99	1.07	0.07	−0.17	0.18	0.01	0.04	8.55

Figure 9.5 **STRIKE SELECTION FOR BULLISH IN-THE-MONEY STRADDLE**

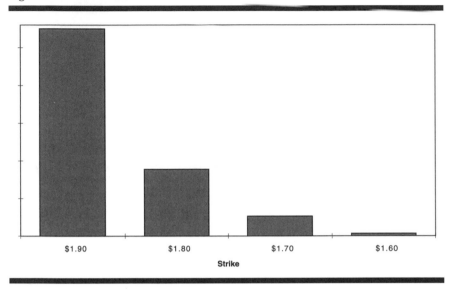

Strike

Strike 6: The Bearish In-The-Money Straddle

As has been the case in our previous strike selection pairs, the selection of a strike for a long straddle involving an ITM put option is the mirror image of the call option process. Once again, we are exposed to the same compelling logic of highly leveraged gains in the event of a price move in favor of the hedge, downward in this case, balanced against the trade-off of the high initial cost of the position and the possibility of losing all of the initial outlay to time decay. Table 9.13 presents our usual analysis of the position at initiation.

Table 9.13 **EXPECTED HEDGE RETURNS FOR STRIKE 6 STRADDLE**

Strike ($)	Net Price ($)	Net Delta	−1/Delta	Option Cost ($)	Cash Gain ($)	Volatility (%)	Z-Value	Probability of Futures Price > Strike Price (%)	Expected Return ($)
2.10	0.18	−0.21	4.84	0.88	0.07	22.73	0.32	37.58	−0.23
2.20	0.23	−0.51	1.97	0.45	0.17	22.69	0.75	22.59	−0.04
2.30	0.30	−0.70	1.43	0.43	0.27	23.42	1.13	12.88	−0.01
2.40	0.38	−0.84	1.19	0.45	0.37	22.94	1.55	6.06	0.00

Once again, we are faced with the worst-case scenario's being dictated by exposure to time decay at the first ITM strike of $2.10. However, we are also presented with the same opportunity as before to move toward the ATM strike and to be in a position to capture early price movements favorable to the hedge, as illustrated in Table 9.14.

A relatively minor price movement presents us with the opportunity to buy back some of the excess put delta at all strikes, but the leverage and recovery of initial costs clearly is greater at the first ITM strike of $2.10, as confirmed in Figure 9.6. Just as the strike 5 straddle gave us the opportunity to make money on both the short cash market position and bullish option straddle, the short option position provides us with an opportunity to do the exact opposite: make money on both a long cash market position and on the bearish option straddle should the long OTM call option increase in value more quickly than does the long ITM put option.

Strike 7: The Out-Of-The-Money Strike For Covering A Long Future

A covered future is one with an OTM option of the same risk sold against it. Thus, a long future can be covered by selling a call option against it, which converts the long future into a short ITM put option at that strike, as illustrated in Figure 8.10. A short future can be covered by selling a put option against it, which converts the short future into a short ITM call option at that strike, as illustrated in Figure 8.9. As a result, we can restate the strike selection problem as the need to choose at which strike we would want a short ITM put for bullish purposes.

This application is obviously a high-risk affair taken by itself; we are exchanging the limited profit potential of a short put option for the risk of the present value of the strike less the option premium received. Even if we add a short cash market risk back to the long covered future, we get the open-ended risk of the short call option, yet these trades are wildly popular and, as most retail-oriented brokers

Table 9.14 **ACTIONS ON SEPTEMBER 4, 1998: STRIKE 6 STRADDLE**

Strike ($)	Price ($)	Delta	Total Delta	Excess Delta	Cash Gain ($)	Option Gain ($)	Net Gain ($)	Net Sales ($)	Sale/Total Cost %
2.10	0.28	−0.58	−2.82	−1.82	−0.16	0.48	0.32	0.51	57.77
2.20	0.35	−0.78	−1.53	−0.53	−0.16	0.24	0.08	0.19	41.64
2.30	0.43	−0.90	−1.29	−0.29	−0.16	0.19	0.03	0.12	29.00
2.40	0.53	−0.96	−1.14	−0.14	−0.16	0.18	0.02	0.08	16.55

Figure 9.6 **STRIKE SELECTION FOR BEARISH IN-THE-MONEY STRADDLE**

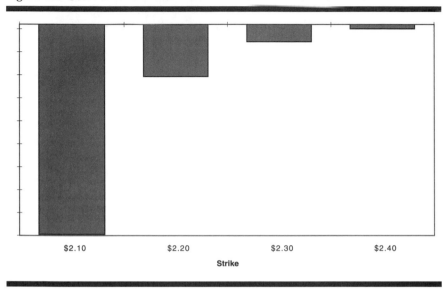

know, are quite easy to sell to customers at nearly all levels of sophistication. Table 9.15 presents the expected return analysis for each
OTM call option strike; the option cost is stated as a negative number
to reflect the initial collection, as opposed to payment, of premium.

The highest expected return occurs at the most OTM strike, which
is equivalent to saying that a long position is best effected through a
short DITM put option. The sale of a strike near the ATM level presents us with insufficient compensation for the risks assumed. The
sale of the most OTM call option also presents us with the best opportunities to sell excess delta back to the market in higher price environments, as shown in Table 9.16. The intuitively compelling argument

Table 9.15 **EXPECTED HEDGE RETURNS FOR STRIKE 7 COVERED FUTURE**

Strike ($)	Net Price ($)	Net Delta	1/Delta	Option Cost ($)	Cash Gain ($)	Volatility (%)	Z-Value	Probability of Futures Price > Strike Price (%)	Expected Return ($)
2.10	−0.06	0.61	1.64	−0.09	−0.07	22.54	0.32	37.48	−0.03
2.20	−0.03	0.76	1.32	−0.04	−0.17	22.96	0.74	22.86	−0.01
2.30	−0.02	0.85	1.18	−0.02	−0.27	24.48	1.08	13.95	0.00
2.40	−0.01	0.92	1.09	−0.01	−0.37	24.88	1.43	7.65	0.00

Table 9.16 **ACTIONS ON SEPTEMBER 4, 1998: STRIKE 7 COVERED FUTURE**

Strike ($)	Price ($)	Delta	Total Delta	Excess Delta	Cash Gain ($)	Covered Future Gain ($)	Net Gain ($)	Net Sales ($)	Sale/Total Cost %
2.10	−0.15	0.85	1.40	0.40	−0.17	0.02	−0.15	0.01	9.33
2.20	−0.09	0.91	1.20	0.20	−0.17	0.09	−0.08	0.02	44.09
2.30	−0.06	0.94	1.11	0.11	−0.17	0.12	−0.05	0.01	64.18
2.40	−0.03	0.97	1.06	0.06	−0.17	0.14	−0.03	0.01	82.36

for selling this strike is confirmed by the proprietary algorithm for its selection, as shown in Figure 9.7.

Strike 8: The Out-of-the-Money Strike for Covering a Short Future

Covering a short future with a short put option leaves us with a synthetic short call option. The same logic that pertained to the selection of strike 7 applies here: The most efficient short call option for hedging a long cash market position will be the most OTM strike possible. This is illustrated in Table 9.17, the expected return on this strategy

Figure 9.7 **STRIKE SELECTION FOR LONG COVERED FUTURE**

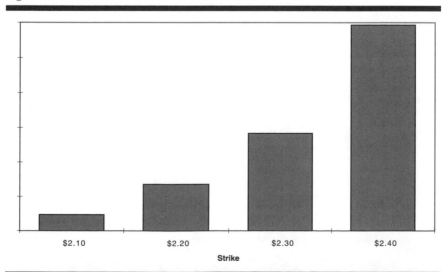

| $2.10 | $2.20 | $2.30 | $2.40 |

Strike

Table 9.17 **EXPECTED HEDGE RETURNS FOR STRIKE 8 COVERED FUTURE**

Strike ($)	Net Price ($)	Net Delta	−1/Delta	Option Cost ($)	Cash Gain ($)	Volatility (%)	Z-Value	Probability of Futures Price < Strike Price (%)	Expected Return ($)
1.90	−0.04	−0.74	1.36	−0.05	−0.13	24.67	−0.57	28.45	−0.02
1.80	−0.02	−0.86	1.17	−0.02	−0.23	25.62	−1.00	15.95	0.00
1.70	−0.01	−0.93	1.08	−0.01	−0.33	26.94	−1.40	8.11	0.00
1.60	0.00	−0.97	1.03	0.00	−0.43	28.34	−1.78	3.73	0.00

across strikes. The highest expected return, rounded to $0.00 at two decimal places, occurs at the $1.60 strike. The delta of this synthetic short call is close to its −1.00 limit and would have provided us with the best opportunities to take advantage of our posited short-term drop in prices, as shown in Table 9.18, had the total delta of the covered short future fallen below −1.00. The verbal argument for the selection of the $1.60 strike is confirmed by the proprietary algorithm for its selection, as depicted in Figure 9.8.

Summary of Strike Selections

Table 9.19 presents our selected strikes. The algorithms that produce these strike selections are unusually stable and are influenced by four factors: the *log(future/strike)* relationship, time remaining to expiration, absolute levels of volatility, and the shape of the volatility curve over

Table 9.18 **ACTIONS ON SEPTEMBER 4, 1998: STRIKE 8 COVERED FUTURE**

Strike ($)	Price ($)	Delta	Total Delta	Excess Delta	Cash Gain ($)	Covered Future Gain ($)	Net Gain ($)	Net Sales ($)	Sale/Total Cost %
1.90	−0.10	−0.47	−0.64	—	−0.16	0.08	−0.08	—	—
1.80	−0.06	−0.65	−0.76	—	−0.16	0.12	−0.04	—	—
1.70	−0.03	−0.80	−0.86	—	−0.16	0.14	−0.02	—	—
1.60	−0.01	−0.90	−0.93	—	−0.16	0.15	−0.01	—	—

Figure 9.8 **STRIKE SELECTION FOR SHORT COVERED FUTURE**

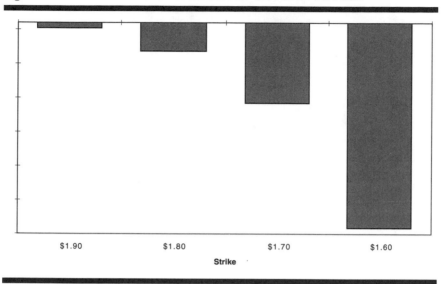

Table 9.19 **SELECTED TRADING STRATEGY COMPONENTS**

Call	Put
Strike 1: $1.90	Strike 2: $2.20
Strike 3: $2.40	Strike 4: $1.60
Strike 5: $1.90	Strike 6: $2.10
Strike 7: $2.40	Strike 8: $1.60

strike, or smile. These strikes are selected separately for each month along the forward curve of the underlying future market. These strikes, along with the ATM strike, can be combined into final strategies in the Dynamic Option Selection System, and that is our next task.

10

So Many Positions, So Little Time

We have, to this point, examined market mechanics and psychology, the nature of risk, carrying costs and the shape of the forward curve, aspects of option pricing, and strike selection. We are now ready to integrate all of this information into option-based hedges.

Since all our positions are designed to create a synthetic index that we can use to hedge an opposite risk, we observe a simple constraint here: All positions must have a total delta at initiation equivalent to this underlying exposure. This eliminates the so-called precision trades designed to capture small differences over time; these trades include "boxes," "butterflies," and "condors." In practice, we limit our universe of direction positions here to those with only one or two components: Simplicity is a virtue in trading, a precept often honored in the breach.

We can assemble positions across calendar months. In the corn options file we started examining in Chapter 9, we selected strikes for December 1998 expiration, but the file contains information on the March 1999 and May 1999 expirations as well. The same set of strikes were selected for these months as were for the December expiration. If we focus on the March 1999 expiration, we can assemble positions solely within March, and between both December and March and March and May. The December-to-March spreads are referred to here as backward calendar spreads, and the March-to-May spreads are referred to here simply as calendar spreads. The key data for the 3 months are shown in Table 10.1.

Table 10.1   **SITUATION ON SEPTEMBER 1, 1998**

	December	March	May
Price	$2.0300	$2.1525	$2.2275
Days to expiration	81	172	235
At-the-money volatility	23.17%	22.63%	21.26%

A total of 44 different spreads are assembled in this chapter for evaluation in March for both bullish and bearish positions. These are listed separately in alphabetical order in Table 10.2 for the bullish positions and, much later in this chapter, in Table 10.3 for the bearish positions. In both cases, the underlying exposure is defined as 1 million bushels of corn, or 200 futures contracts. Each position is discussed in turn in terms of class of trade with a reference back to the trade number in the table. A graph of each position's profit and loss characteristics with 30 days remaining on the life of the shortest-dated option in the spread, both for itself and for the total hedge position, is provided. All graphs are based on all-else-held-equal considerations for volatility, interest rates, and intermonth spreads.

The positions as assembled are a snapshot of the Dynamic Option Selection System run at the close of business on September 1, 1998. As a consequence of the prevailing market conditions, several of the positions presented obviously will be out of solution for a variety of reasons, including cost, number of contracts required, and negative gamma. These trades are presented and discussed nevertheless for the sake of a complete analysis of all alternatives.

The depiction of the net hedge position—the cash market gains and losses plus the option position loss and gain—is the most important datum in the graphs. Each hedge position must—and this is an absolute must—have a zone of underperformance, a place along the price spectrum where there are net losses. Otherwise, we would be creating a financial perpetual-motion machine; there simply is no way to eliminate or control risk without paying a net cost. The most common price zone for this underperformance is the static price case: The worst that happens is that nothing happens. Although this is the mode of our lognormal price distribution, experienced traders and bumper-sticker slogan authors alike know that over time, "things happen." Our goal is to trade a known zone of limited losses in a static environment for net gains in a dynamic environment. This forms the basis for the applications discussed in Chapter 11.

The criteria for comparing and selecting a final position are discussed without releasing proprietary details at the end of this chapter.

THE LONG POSITIONS

Table 10.2 presents the 44 different long hedges considered for buying the equivalent of 1 million bushels of March 1999 corn. These trades

Table 10.2. **EQUIVALENT OF LONG 200 MARCH CORN FUTURES**

Designation	Buy Quantity and Selection	Strike ($)	Sell Quantity and Selection	Strike ($)
1. ATM put/OTM call	302 strike 3 calls	2.60	302 ATM puts	2.20
2. ATM synthetic future	200 ATM calls	2.20	200 ATM puts	2.20
3. Backward calendar call spread	498 strike 1 calls	2.00	200 December strike 1 calls	1.90
4. Backward calendar ATM put/OTM call	333 December strike 3 calls	2.40	333 ATM puts	2.20
5. Backward calendar ATM synthetic future	200 ATM calls	2.20	200 December ATM puts	2.00
6. Backward calendar bull call	525 ATM calls	2.20	525 December strike 3 calls	2.40
7. Backward calendar bull put	489 December ATM puts	2.00	489 strike 7 puts	2.60
8. Backward calendar call frontspread	466 ATM calls	2.20	200 December strike 3 calls	2.40
9. Backward calendar covered future	328 futures	2.10	328 December strike 7 calls	2.10
10. Backward calendar long straddle 1	626 strike 5 calls and December strike 5 puts	2.10 1.90		
11. Backward calendar long straddle 2	601 December strike 5 calls and strike 5 puts	1.90 2.10		
12. Backward calendar OTM put/OTM call 1	491 strike 3 calls	2.60	491 December strike 4 puts	1.90
13. Backward calendar OTM put/OTM call 2	415 December strike 3 calls	2.40	415 strike 4 puts	2.10
14. Backward calendar put backspread	200 December ATM puts	2.00	342 strike 3 puts	2.60
15. Backward calendar short straddle 1		2.30 2.10	816 strike 6 calls and December strike 6 puts	2.30 2.10
16. Backward calendar short straddle 2		2.10 2.30	851 December strike 6 calls and strike 6 puts	2.10 2.30
17. Backward calendar synthetic call	271 December strike 1 puts and futures	1.90		

(continues)

Table 10.2 **CONTINUED**

Designation	Buy Quantity and Selection	Strike ($)	Sell Quantity and Selection	Strike ($)
18. Bull call	624 ATM calls	2.20	624 strike 3 calls	2.60
19. Bull put	641 ATM puts	2.20	641 strike 6 puts	2.60
20. Calendar call spread	445 strike 1 calls	2.00	200 May strike 1 calls	2.20
21. Calendar ATM put/OTM call	269 May strike 1 calls	2.60	269 ATM puts	2.20
22. Calendar ATM SLF	200 ATM calls	2.20	200 May ATM puts	2.20
23. Calendar bull call	833 ATM calls	2.20	833 May strike 3 calls	2.60
24. Calendar bull put	495 May ATM puts	2.20	495 strike 7 puts	2.60
25. Calendar call frontspread	527 ATM calls	2.20	200 May strike 3 calls	2.60
26. Calendar covered future	363 futures	2.30	363 May strike 7 calls	2.30
27. Calendar long straddle 1	771 strike 5 calls and May strike 5 puts	2.10 2.10		
28. Calendar long straddle 2	827 May strike 5 calls and strike 5 puts	2.10 2.10		
29. Calendar OTM put/OTM call 1	428 strike 3 calls	2.60	428 May strike 4 puts	2.10
30. Calendar OTM put/OTM call 2	321 May strike 3 calls	2.60	321 strike 4 puts	2.10
31. Calendar put backspread	200 May ATM puts	2.20	344 strike 7 puts	2.60
32. Calendar short straddle 1		2.30 2.30	1,167 strike 6 calls and May strike 6 puts	2.30
33. Calendar short straddle 2		2.30 2.30	1,126 May strike 6 calls and strike 6 puts	2.30 2.30
34. Calendar synthetic call	348 May strike 1 puts and futures	2.20		
35. Call	288 strike 1 calls	2.00		
36. Call frontspread	492 ATM calls	2.20	200 strike 3 calls	2.60
37. Covered future	309 futures	2.30	309 strike 7 calls	2.30
38. Long straddle	1,082 strike 5 calls and strike 5 puts	2.10		
39. OTM put/ATM call	232 ATM calls	2.20	232 strike 4 puts	2.10
40. OTM put/OTM call	369 strike 3 calls	2.60	369 strike 4 puts	2.10
41. Put		2.40	280 strike 2 puts	2.40
42. Put backspread	200 ATM puts	2.20	366 strike 3 puts	2.60
43. Short straddle		2.30 2.30	731 strike 6 calls and strike 6 puts	2.30 2.30
44. Synthetic call	280 strike 1 puts and futures	2.00		

ATM = at-the-money; OTM = out-of-the-money

are broken down into the classes of calls and call spreads, puts and put spreads, put–call combinations, and straddles for further discussion. Intermonth spreads are discussed separately from March-only positions.

Calls and Call Spreads

Out of respect for simplicity, we should begin with trade 35, which consists of buying 288 March $2.00 call options at $0.21375 apiece, as shown in Figure 10.1. This position confers unlimited gain potential in return for the premium paid and is easy to initiate, liquidate, and manage over the life of the trade. In the absence of a position selection algorithm, one would emplace this position in a low-volatility, low-price environment, such as at the end of a long period of price consolidation near a major support level. One's price outlook should be quite bullish and unconstrained by fears of overhead selling nearby, and the intermonth curve should not be in a position of either strong backwardation or contango.

Trade 44, the synthetic $2.00 call consisting of buying 280 March $2.00 puts at $0.065 and buying 280 March futures at $2.1525, will behave in an parallel manner to trade 35 and should be emplaced with the same overall outlook, as shown in Figure 10.2. The lower cap-

Figure 10.1 **PROFILE FOR 288 MARCH $2.00 CALL OPTIONS**

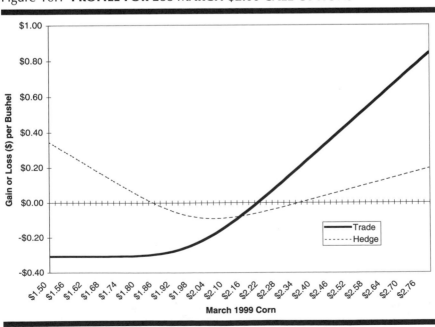

Figure 10.2   **PROFILE FOR 280 MARCH $2.00 SYNTHETIC CALL OPTIONS**

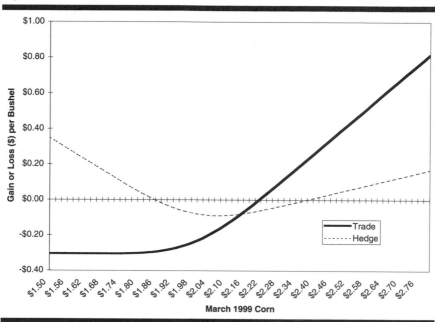

ital outlay for the put options appeals to many traders even though it means segregating additional funds for margin financing.

Trade 18, the bull call spread consisting of buying 624 $2.20 calls at $0.11 and selling 624 $2.60 calls at $0.025, does not have open-ended gain potential by virtue of the short $2.60 call option. Its large leverage at modest price gains and its larger capital cost indicate that it should be emplaced when the trader expects a substantial and quick price movement that will hit an early resistance point; this is a rather defined outlook. Volatility should have a pronounced smile, with the $2.60 volatility priced well above the $2.20 volatility, as shown in Figure 10.3. The bull call spread is enormously successful when all of these prior assumptions about market behavior prove to be correct, but this is placing an inordinate burden on one's self as a trader.

Trade 36, the call frontspread, consists of buying 492 $2.20 calls at $0.11 and selling 200 $2.60 calls at $0.025, as shown in Figure 10.4. It is a close relative of the bull call spread. The small number of contracts involved, especially for the long ATM call, reduces the capital outlay at initiation, but this also reduces the enormous leverage enjoyed by the bull call spread in an early market rally. The small number of short $2.60 calls provides greater upside potential should the market approach or exceed the $2.60 strike.

Figure 10.3 **PROFILE FOR 624 MARCH $2.20 TO $2.60 BULL CALL SPREADS**

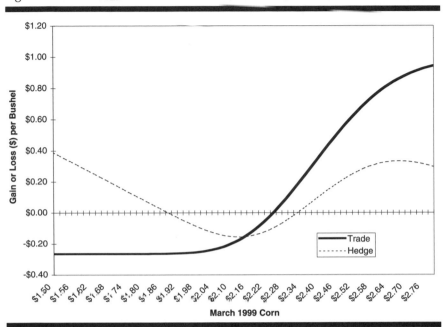

Figure 10.4 **PROFILE FOR 492 MARCH $2.20 TO 200 MARCH $2.60 CALL FRONTSPREAD**

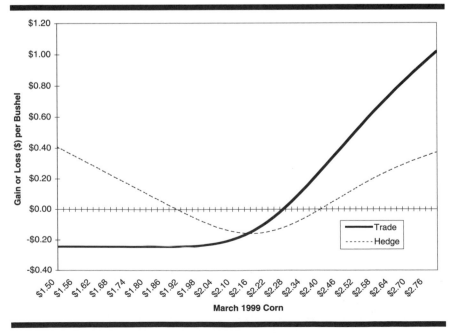

Intermonth Calls and Call Spreads

We can now move on to spreads involving the intermonth spread. The spread between December and March futures of $0.1225 is less than the full carry level at a 5.0% cost of capital and $0.048/bushel/month storage cost of $0.169375. The annualized convenience yield of 9.56% is sufficiently high to discourage inventory building in corn and indicates an incentive to postpone purchases for as late as possible. The risk that a buyer faces for making such a decision is that the spot month price will rise relative to the nearby month price. The buyer should remain floating on his purchase commitments for March but may wish to hedge his exposure to higher prices in December. The buyer will naturally benefit from both lower prices overall and from a deeper carry level.

The spread between March and May of $0.055 is far less than the full carry level of $0.1143, and the convenience yield is far higher, an annualized 18.86%. The same hedge incentives that apply for the December-to-March spread apply for the March-to-May spread. The calendar spreads discussed below address this specific risk for March by placing the long hedge in March and defraying its costs by taking an offsetting action in May. The backward calendar spreads discussed below address the opposite risk by placing the long hedge in March and defraying its costs by taking an offsetting action in December.

Trade 34, a calendar synthetic call consisting of buying 348 May $2.20 puts at $0.1325 and buying 348 March futures, is a clear bet both on higher prices for corn overall and on a move toward backwardation in corn. Although a move toward a deeper carry at lower prices is a clear risk, the downside is relatively confined because a full carry level is only $0.06 deeper than the current intermonth spread, as shown in Figure 10.5.

Trade 20, a calendar call spread consisting of buying 445 March $2.00 calls at $0.21375 and selling 200 May $2.20 calls at $0.16, is a trade that would take advantage of both higher prices and greater backwardation in corn; the earlier this move occurs, the more the trade benefits, as shown in Figure 10.6.

Trade 23, a calendar bull call spread consisting of buying 833 March $2.20 calls at $0.11 and selling 833 May $2.60 calls at $0.05, is an extremely leveraged trade that will benefit enormously from an early increase in prices and from a move toward backwardation in corn. Offsetting the benefits of this leverage are the higher initial capital costs of the trade, its resulting greater exposure to time decay if the market is quiet or declines during its early phase, and the declining efficiency of the hedge as the short call strike is approached, as shown in Figure 10.7.

Figure 10.5 **PROFILE FOR 348 MAY $2.20 PUT TO MARCH FUTURE SPREADS**

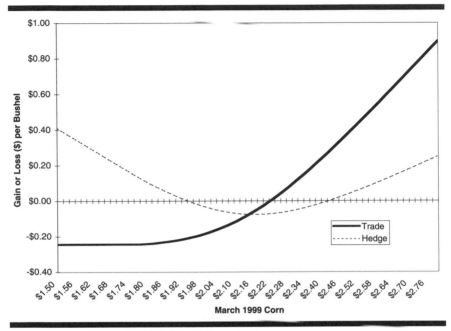

Figure 10.6 **PROFILE FOR 445 MARCH $2.00 TO 200 MARCH SPREADS**

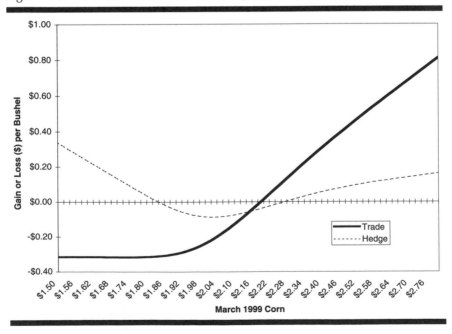

Figure 10.7 **PROFILE FOR 833 MARCH $2.20 TO MAY $2.60 BULL CALL SPREADS**

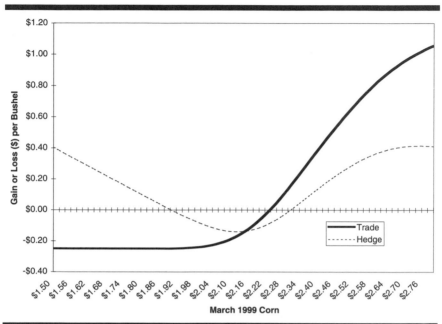

Trade 25, a calendar call frontspread consisting of buying 527 March $2.20 calls at $0.11 and selling 200 May $2.60 calls at $0.05, is a close relative of trade 23. It still retains a large degree of leverage in large early moves upward and has the additional benefit of not being as restricted at higher price levels should the short $2.60 strike be approached, as shown in Figure 10.8. The smaller trade size reduces the initial capital outlay involved and makes the position more manageable as well.

Trade 3, consisting of buying 498 March $2.00 calls at $0.21375 and selling 200 December $1.90 calls at $0.1675, is our first backward calendar trade for a long position, as shown in Figure 10.9. Our market view now shifts to that of much greater defensiveness and an increased carrying level in the markets; although the calendar call spreads discussed above benefit from early and active price movement, these spreads will benefit more from later price movement.

Trade 17, a backward calendar synthetic call, consists of buying 271 December $1.90 puts at $0.04 and buying 271 March futures at $2.1525, as shown in Figure 10.10. The best outcome for this trade would be the unusual combination of higher March prices and lower December prices, and with the spread not too far away from full carry,

Figure 10.8 **PROFILE FOR 527 MARCH $2.20 TO 200 MAY $2.60 CALL FRONTSPREAD**

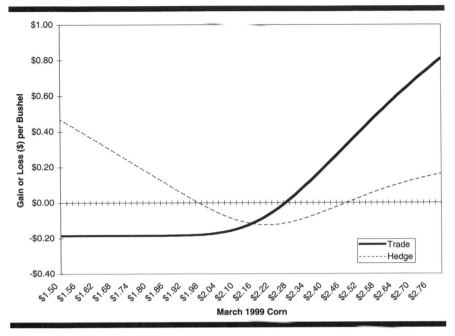

Figure 10.9 **PROFILE FOR 498 MARCH $2.00 TO 200 DECEMBER $1.90 CALL SPREADS**

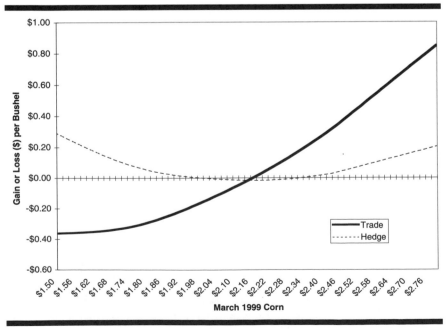

Figure 10.10 **PROFILE FOR 271 DECEMBER $1.90 TO MARCH SYNTHETIC CALLS**

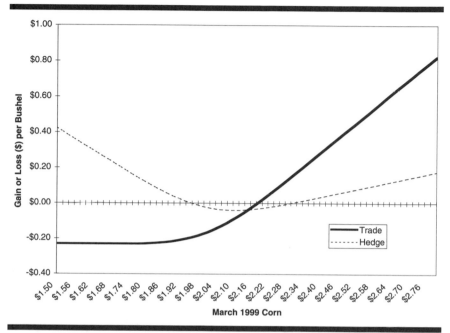

this is not likely. However, this type of trade could be useful in a back-wardated market where the backwardation is reaching its historical highs, as we discussed in Chapter 4.

Trade 6 is a backward calendar bull call spread consisting of buying 525 March $2.20 calls at $0.11 and selling 525 December $2.40 calls at $0.0875, as shown in Figure 10.11. Once again, this trade benefits most from the unusual combination of a deepening carry in a higher price environment, so it would not be particularly useful in this situation; it would best be employed when the market is near peak backwardation. As is the case with the other bull call spreads we have examined, trade 6 is highly leveraged toward a strong move higher at the cost of a high initial capital outlay.

Trade 8, a backward calendar call frontspread, consists of buying 466 March $2.20 calls at $0.11 and selling 200 December $2.40 calls at $0.00875, as shown in Figure 10.12. This trade depends on a strong early rise in March corn prices and, like all the other spreads in this class, on no further increase in backwardation. This trade enjoys a major advantage over trade 6 at higher price levels because of the smaller number of short December $2.40 calls.

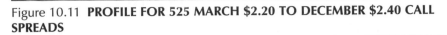

Figure 10.11 **PROFILE FOR 525 MARCH $2.20 TO DECEMBER $2.40 CALL SPREADS**

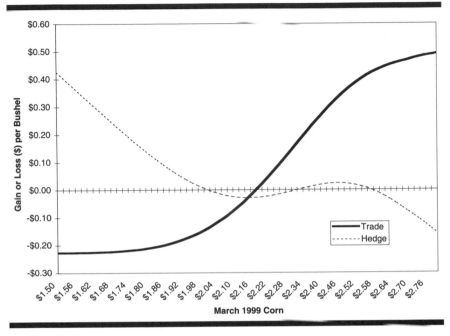

Figure 10.12 **PROFILE FOR 466 MARCH $2.20 TO 200 DECEMBER $2.40 CALL SPREADS**

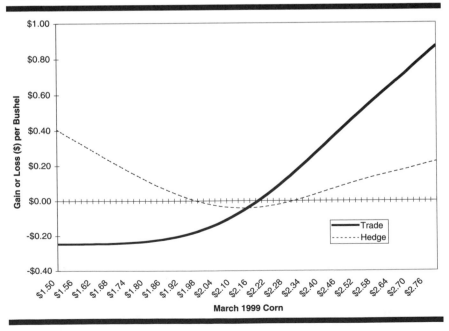

Puts and Put Spreads

The use of puts and put spreads to implement a long position often is greeted skeptically. After all, one of our stated goals for our option hedges is to maintain a positive gamma for our position, and any short put option—which by itself is a necessary and embedded component of any long cash market or futures position—has, by definition, a negative gamma. We will see, however, that put spreads can be quite efficient and quite attractive in this role.

Trade 41, which consists of selling 280 $2.40 puts at $0.3725, is a surprisingly efficient trade within a wide range—nearly $1.70 on the downside and just over $2.60 on the upside, as shown in Figure 10.13. However, the gamma on the trade is always negative, and as a result, it trades a limited profit for open-ended losses on both sides.

Trade 37 is a synthetic short put option, as described in Figure 8.10, consisting of 309 long March futures and 309 short March $2.30 call options sold at $0.2175, as shown in Figure 10.14. This trade, too, is surprisingly efficient over a wide range of prices, from nearly $1.50 to $2.70. However, its gamma is always negative as well, and it does a poor job of protecting the corn buyer in a rising market.

Trade 19, a bull put spread consisting of selling 641 $2.60 puts at $0.465 and buying 641 $2.20 puts at $0.1525, is a strongly efficient trade from many respects, as shown in Figure 10.15. First, the long $2.20 put option provides a limit to the downside of the trade, whereas the greater than 3 : 1 leverage afforded by the short $2.60 put option provides an accelerated gain in price gains up to that strike, but the trade loses efficiency rapidly as the $2.60 strike is approached. The trade benefits from initiation at lower volatility levels so as to minimize the cost of the long $2.20 put. We want the price gains to occur early on in the life of the trade to maximize the value of the $2.20 put when we manage the position.

Trade 42, a short put backspread consisting of buying 200 of the March $2.20 puts at $0.1525 and selling 366 March $2.60 puts at $0.465, is a more aggressive trade than the simple bull put spread because it has fewer long put options for downside protection. Like trade 41, the short $2.20 put, this trade suffers from negative gamma, and as a result, its hedge efficiency is mediocre at best, as shown in Figure 10.16.

Intermonth Put Spreads

The same considerations of intermonth spreads and convenience yields we discussed in the section on intermonth call spreads apply

Figure 10.13 **PROFILE FOR 280 SHORT MARCH $2.40 PUT OPTIONS**

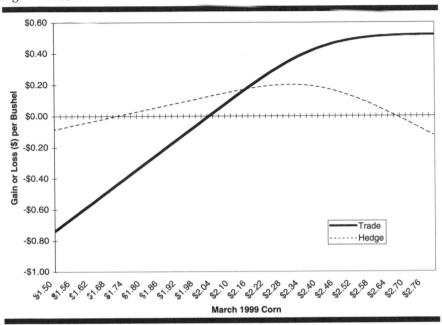

Figure 10.14 **PROFILE FOR 309 MARCH $2.30 SHORT SYNTHETIC PUT OPTIONS**

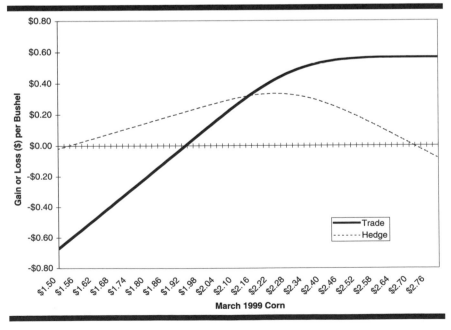

Figure 10.15 **PROFILE FOR 641 MARCH $2.20 TO $2.60 BULL PUT SPREADS**

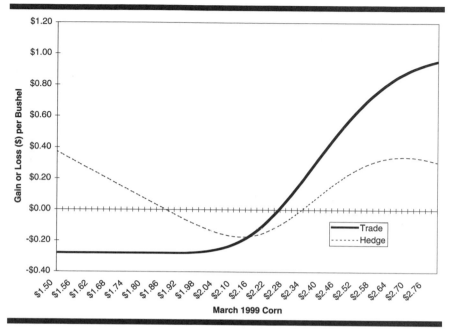

Figure 10.16 **PROFILE FOR 200 MARCH $2.20 TO 366 MARCH $2.60 PUT BACKSPREAD**

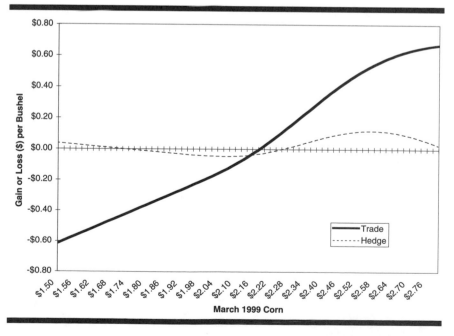

for the intermonth put spreads. With the corn market in a carry, the bias favors selling a put option in December and buying a put option in March rather than the other way around.

Trade 24, a calendar bull put consisting of buying 495 May $2.20 put options at $0.1325 and selling 495 March $2.60 puts at $0.465, takes full advantage of the carry in the corn market. The trade's hedge profile is highly efficient up until the short $2.60 strike is approached, as shown in Figure 10.17. As was true with the direct bull put spread, lower volatility at initiation benefits the trade.

Trade 31, a calendar put backspread, consists of buying 200 May $2.20 puts at $0.1325 and selling 344 March $2.60 puts at $0.465, as shown in Figure 10.18. It is a much more aggressive position than trade 24 because it has uncovered short in-the-money (ITM) puts. Its gamma is negative over much of the price spectrum, and as a result, it is an inefficient hedge position.

The final trade discussed in this category, trade 26, is an interesting hybrid, the calendar covered future consisting of 363 long March futures at $2.1525 and 363 May $2.30 calls sold at $0.19, as shown in Figure 10.19. By the synthesis relationships discussed in Chapter 8, this is equivalent to selling a March $2.30 put at $0.2175, buying a March $2.30

Figure 10.17 **PROFILE FOR 495 MAY $2.20 TO MARCH $2.60 BULL PUT SPREADS**

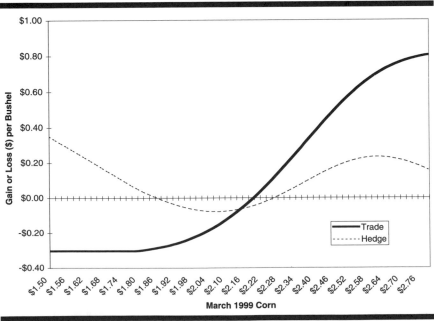

Figure 10.18 **PROFILE FOR 200 MARCH $2.20 TO 344 MAY $2.60 PUT BACKSPREAD**

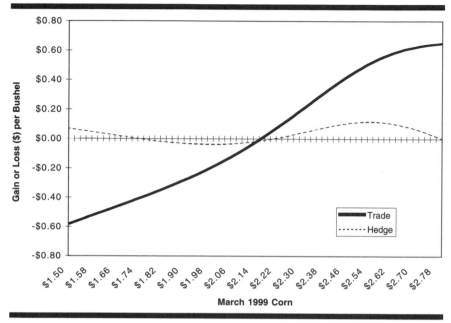

Figure 10.19 **PROFILE FOR 363 MARCH FUTURES TO MAY $2.30 COVERED FUTURES**

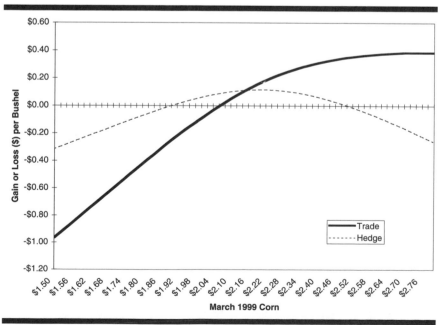

call at $0.0725, and selling the May $2.30 call at $0.12. The trade has only a modest range of efficiency if the March-to-May spread stays at present levels but would benefit from a move toward backwardation.

Given the carrying structure of the corn market, we should not expect the backward calendar put spreads, those involving selling December puts and buying March puts, to be as efficient as the calendar bull put spread. Trade 7, which consists of buying 489 December $2.00 puts at $0.0725 and selling 489 March $2.60 puts at $0.465, places us in the position of selling December corn and buying March corn when the market is already approaching a full carry level, and it exposes us to the more rapid time decay of the December $2.00 put as well. In spite of these disadvantages, the lower initial capital outlay for the December $2.00 put and its more rapid price appreciation allow for great hedge efficiency at lower prices levels and acceptable hedge efficiency at higher price levels up to the approach of the $2.60 strike, as shown in Figure 10.20.

Trade 14 is a backward calendar put backspread consisting of buying 200 December $2.00 puts at $0.0725 and selling 342 March $2.60 puts at $0.465, as shown in Figure 10.21. The combination of negative gamma from the short $2.60 puts, the greater time decay on the long

Figure 10.20 **PROFILE FOR 489 DECEMBER $2.00 TO MARCH $2.60 PUT SPREADS**

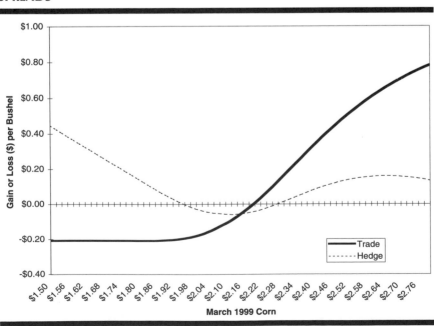

March 1999 Corn

Figure 10.21 **PROFILE FOR 200 DECEMBER $2.00 TO 342 MARCH $2.60 PUT BACKSPREAD**

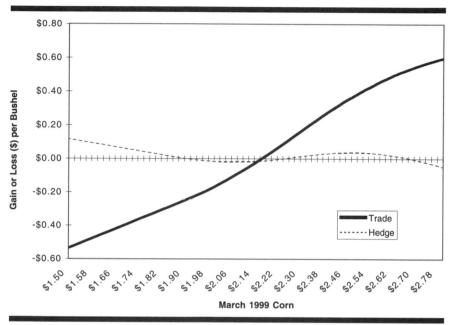

$2.00 put, and the carry structure of the corn market are too much for this trade to bear; it is only weakly efficient across a very narrow segment of the price spectrum.

The final trade in this category, trade 9, is a backward calendar covered future consisting of 328 long March futures at $2.1525 and 328 short December $2.10 calls sold at $0.05625, as shown in Figure 10.22. Just as we did for trade 26, we can decompose this trade into a short March $2.10 put sold at $0.10125, a long March $2.10 call bought at $0.15375, and the short December $2.10 call. The trade is efficient over only a tiny portion of the price spectrum and would benefit only from the unusual combination of much higher corn prices combined with a deepening carry level.

Synthetic Futures and Put–Call Combinations

Students and new traders generally are introduced to the entire concept of hedging and risk management through the application of an offsetting futures position, as shown in the classic diagram of Figure 3.1. Indeed, for all the problems associated with risk transference using this method, it is still an excellent standard for comparison: If an

Figure 10.22 **PROFILE FOR 328 MARCH FUTURES TO DECEMBER $2.10 COVERED FUTURES**

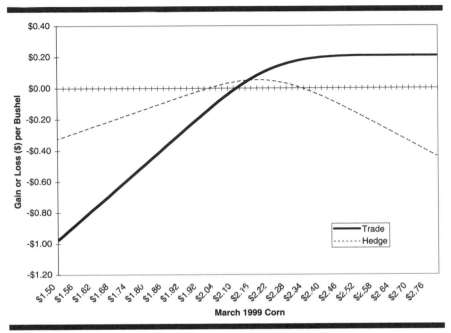

March 1999 Corn

option-based hedge does not provide stochastically superior hedge results to the naive application of futures, then why bother? We can regard all futures contracts as special cases of option spreads, as shown in Figures 8.5 and 8.6, in which the month and strike of the put–call spreads are the same. We can and will make the performance of this synthetic future the base case for rating the performance of all other hedge instruments.

Accordingly, we will dispense with the depiction of trade 2, the synthetic long future (SLF), and move on to other same-month put–call spreads. Trade 1 maintains selling the March $2.20 put at $0.1525 but buys a $2.60 call at $0.025 instead of a $2.20 call at $0.11, as shown in Figure 10.23. A quantity of 302 of each strike are traded. The resulting hedge profile is inefficient at both higher and lower prices, and the trade itself has an open-ended liability at lower prices in exchange for its open-ended profitability at higher prices. Overall, this trade suffers from too much downside exposure relative to upside potential.

We can reverse the order of this combination in trade 39, which consists of buying 232 March $2.20 calls at $0.1525 and selling 232 March $2.10 puts at $0.10125, as shown in Figure 10.24. However, this

Figure 10.23 **PROFILE FOR 302 MARCH $2.20 PUT TO $2.60 CALL SPREADS**

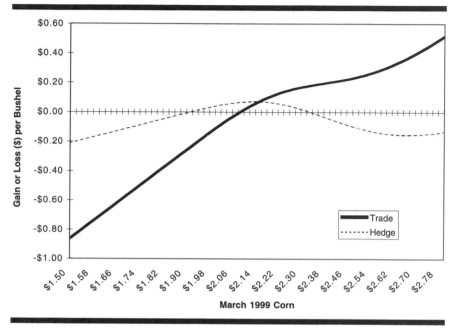

Figure 10.24 **PROFILE FOR 232 MARCH $2.20 CALL TO $2.10 PUT SPREADS**

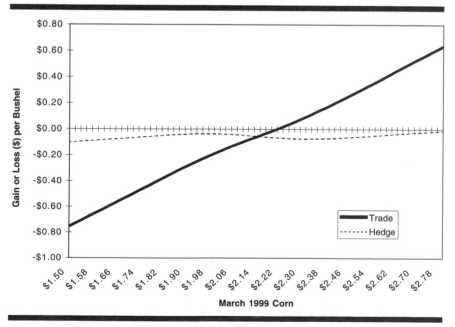

does not solve the imbalance problem of too much downside exposure relative to upside potential, and the resulting hedge profile is remarkable in that it is always negative by the time the trade has 30 days left.

Trade 40 consists of buying 369 March $2.60 calls at $0.025 and selling 369 March $2.10 puts at $0.10125, as shown in Figure 10.25. This is a very aggressive trade that requires a large move higher to be made quickly; a more protracted advance does little for the value of the long $2.60 call, and the presence of the short put option makes any move lower dangerous for the overall position.

None of the above trades in this class have a very good hedge profile; nevertheless, these tend to be popular trades, probably because the short put option defrays the cost of the long call option. As we have done before, we can look backward and forward over time to take advantage of the opportunities afforded by the shape of the forward curve and the different rates of time decay between months.

The simplest variation on the intermonth put–call combination is the calendar at-the-money (ATM) synthetic future, trade 22. This trade consists of buying 200 March $2.20 calls at $0.11 and selling 200 May $2.20 puts at $0.1325, as shown in Figure 10.26. This trade obviously

Figure 10.25 **PROFILE FOR 369 MARCH $2.60 CALL TO $2.10 PUT SPREADS**

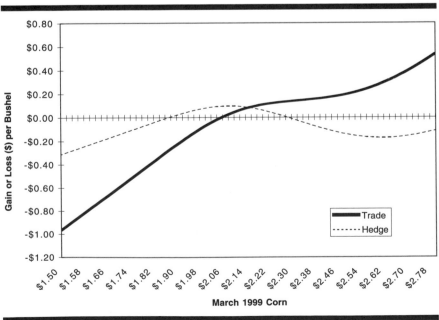

March 1999 Corn

Figure 10.26 **PROFILE FOR 200 MARCH $2.20 CALL TO MAY $2.20 PUT SPREADS**

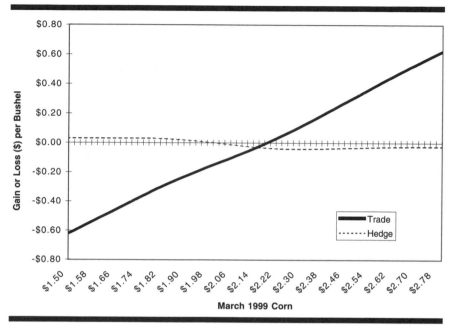

benefits from any move toward backwardation in the corn market, and although its bias is still toward early gains in the corn market, it is less time sensitive than are most of the other positions we have examined. Given the ATM status of both components, it should come as no surprise that the hedge profile is virtually flat; there is some gain at lower price levels and some loss at higher price levels, but there is little efficiency gain from this position.

Trade 21, which consists of buying 269 May $2.60 calls at $0.05 and selling 269 March $2.20 puts at $0.1525, is a far more aggressive long position than trade 22, as shown in Figure 10.27. It virtually requires a quick move higher and would benefit from a move toward backwardation. Otherwise, the trade is efficient across only a small portion of the price spectrum.

Trade 30 consists of buying 321 May $2.60 calls at $0.05 and selling 321 March $2.10 puts at $0.10125, as shown in Figure 10.28. The lower put strike does little to improve the efficiency of the trade; whatever gain may arise from the lower strike is lost to the lower credit at initiation.

Trade 29 consists of buying 428 March $2.60 calls at $0.025 and selling 428 May $2.10 puts at $0.0875, as shown in Figure 10.29. Once

Figure 10.27 PROFILE FOR 269 MAY $2.60 CALL TO MARCH $2.20 PUT SPREADS

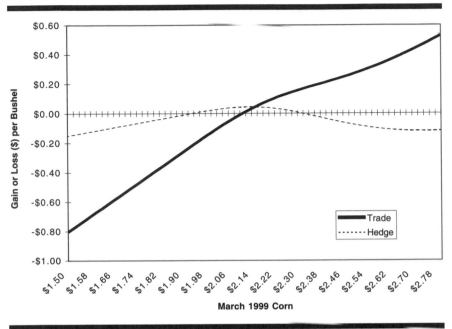

Figure 10.28 PROFILE FOR 321 MAY $2.60 CALL TO MARCH $2.10 PUT SPREADS

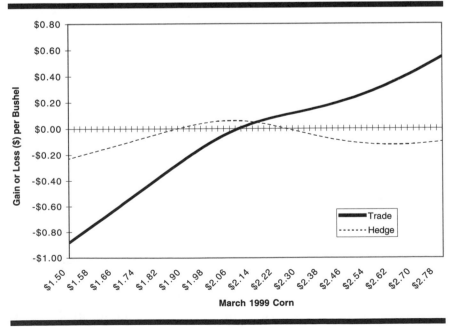

Figure 10.29 **PROFILE FOR 428 MARCH $2.60 CALL TO MAY $2.10 PUT SPREADS**

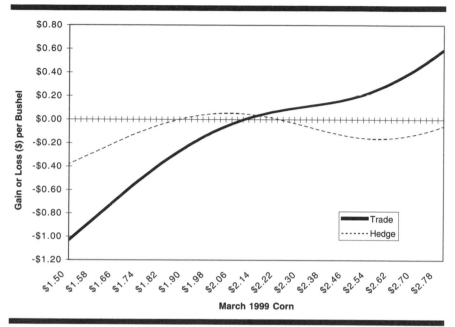

again, the efficiency of the trade is quite poor; the short $2.10 put in May provides too little in the way of a net credit to support the trade in higher prices but exposes the seller quickly to the effects of lower prices. The long $2.60 call in March comes into play at too high a level to afford significant protection from higher prices for the buyer.

None of the calendar split-strike futures, combinations of puts and calls between March and May, have attractive hedge efficiency. We now can turn to the backward calendar split strike futures, those combinations of puts and calls between March and December. The first, trade 5, is the backward calendar synthetic future consisting of buying 200 March $2.20 calls at $0.11 and selling 200 December $2.00 puts at $0.0725, as shown in Figure 10.30. The trade's efficiency is confined to a narrow zone of lower prices, but it could become a net winner at higher prices if the carry between December and March narrows.

Trade 4, which consists of buying 333 December $2.40 calls at $0.00875 and selling 333 March $2.20 puts at $0.1525, is a more aggressive bet on the narrowing of the December-to-March carry in a rising market, as shown in Figure 10.31. The long $2.40 call does not come into play quickly enough to become an efficient hedge instrument at

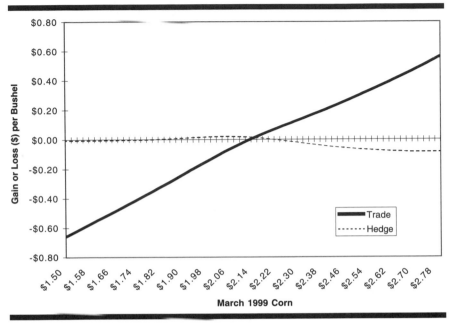

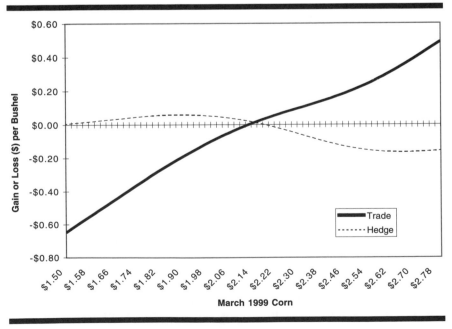

higher prices. The smaller number of contracts involved in this trade allow the hedge to maintain a modest degree of efficiency at lower prices.

Trade 13, which consists of buying 415 December $2.40 calls at $0.00875 and selling 415 March $2.10 puts at $0.10125, increases the overall exposure level by increasing the number of contracts involved in the trade, as shown in Figure 10.32. This increases the efficiency of the hedge at higher price levels, but at the cost of degraded performance in lower price environments.

Trade 12, which consists of 491 March $2.60 calls at $0.025 and selling 491 December $1.90 puts at $0.04, deploys the short put option in the discounted month and therefore is less exposed to any deepening of the carry level, as shown in Figure 10.33. However, the hedge is exposed badly to lower price levels overall and lacks any compensating gains at higher price levels.

The backward calendar spreads are no more attractive for the present structure of the corn market than are the calendar spreads. Once again, this does not seem to detract from the popularity of these trades; this is no doubt due to the reduction in the overall cost of the long option by the short option. These trades also form the basis for many

Figure 10.32 **PROFILE FOR 415 DECEMBER $2.40 CALL TO MARCH $2.10 PUT SPREADS**

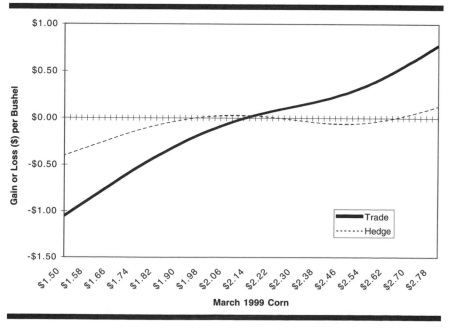

Figure 10.33 **PROFILE FOR 495 MARCH $2.60 CALL TO DECEMBER $1.90 PUT SPREADS**

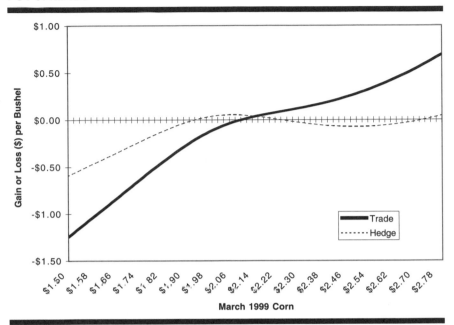

types of swaps, including the ever-popular "costless collar." An experienced observer might conclude that they cost less because they are worth less.

Straddles

We come now to the final class of trade used to hedge a short cash commitment, the put–call combination in which both instruments are either bought or sold together. As we noted in Chapter 9, these trades tend to get overlooked because of either the high initial costs involved in a long straddle or the open-ended liabilities involved with the short straddle. However, they can be surprisingly effective hedge instruments.

Trade 38, which consists of buying 1,082 March $2.10 calls at $0.15375 and 1,082 March $2.10 puts at $0.10125, is a highly leveraged trade that should be emplaced only during periods of historically low volatility, as shown in Figure 10.34. Everything about this trade is out-sized, from the number of contracts to its exposure to time decay to the gain potential at both higher and lower prices. Once a trade like this is on, the market simply must move and move violently.

Figure 10.34 **PROFILE FOR 1,082 MARCH $2.10 STRADDLES**

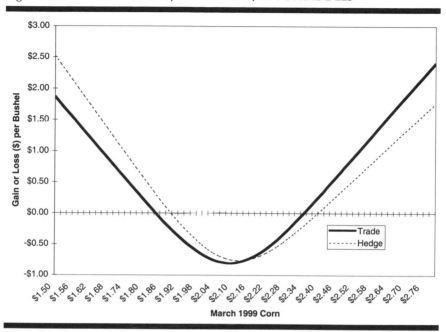

March 1999 Corn

Trade 43, which consists of selling 731 March $2.30 calls at $0.0725 and 731 March $2.30 puts at $0.2175, sits at the opposite end of the risk spectrum. Here, the danger is that the market will move and move violently. This trade should be emplaced when volatility is historically high. The trade is less leveraged than is trade 38, but it will produce some outsized negative results if the market moves strongly in either direction, as shown in Figure 10.35.

A calendar straddle, one involving buying a call option in one month and buying a put option in another, presents us with an opportunity to make a direct bet on the forward curve simultaneously with ones on volatility and price direction. Trade 27 consists of buying 771 March $2.10 calls at $0.15375 and 771 May $2.10 puts at $0.0875. This trade has lower leverage than does trade 38, and hence lower time decay, but it also has a shallower zone of loss, as shown in Figure 10.36.

Trade 28, which consists of buying 827 May $2.10 calls at $0.215 and buying 827 March $2.10 puts at $0.10125, reverses the position of the long call option and long put option, as shown in Figure 10.37. The trade is still exposed to the same desire for higher volatility and price movement, but it is now a bet on a deepening carry between March and May as well. This trade has greater leverage than does trade 27,

Figure 10.35 **PROFILE FOR 731 SHORT MARCH $2.30 STRADDLES**

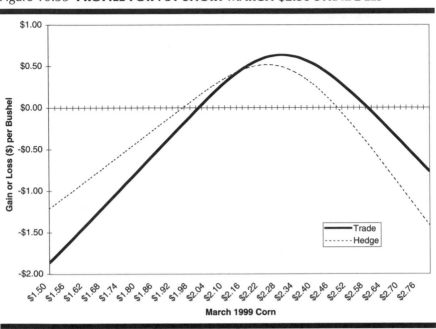

Figure 10.36 **PROFILE FOR 771 MARCH $2.10 CALL TO MAY $2.10 PUT STRADDLES**

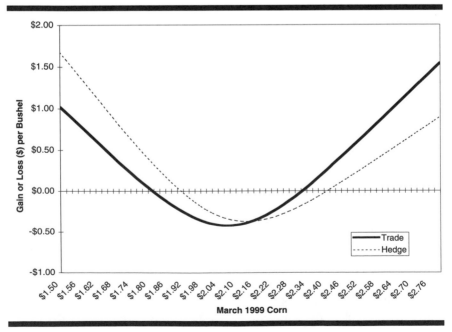

Figure 10.37 **PROFILE FOR 827 MAY $2.10 CALL TO MARCH $2.10 PUT STRADDLES**

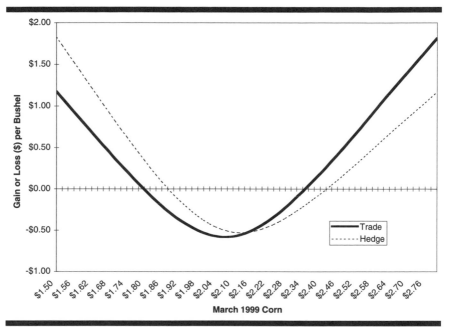

and therefore greater exposure to time decay and a slightly deeper loss profile, but it still retains great hedge efficiency should the corn market become active.

Trade 32 is a short calendar straddle which consists of selling 1,167 March $2.30 calls at $0.0725 and selling 1,167 May $2.30 puts at $0.19, as shown in Figure 10.38. The desired outcome for this highly lever-aged trade is lower volatility and a move toward greater carry in the corn market. However, the open-ended liabilities in either price direc-tion are too large relative to the defined gain for the trade to be useful as a hedge instrument.

Trade 33, which consists of selling 1,126 March $2.30 puts at $0.2175 and 1,126 May $2.30 calls at $0.12, benefits from a move toward backwardation in the corn market and lower volatility as prices rise. It is almost as leveraged as trade 32, and once again, its large open-ended liabilities at both price directions should pre-clude its serious consideration as a hedge instrument, as shown in Figure 10.39.

The backward calendar straddles involve smaller initial capital outlays for the long spreads and smaller initial credits for the short spreads. The lower time remaining on the December options relative

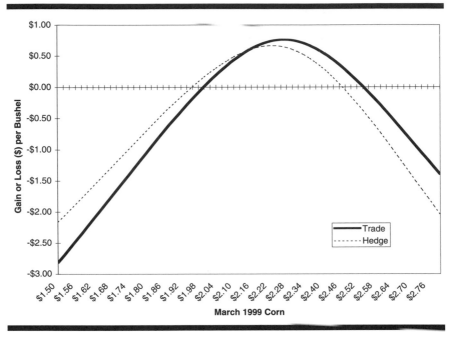

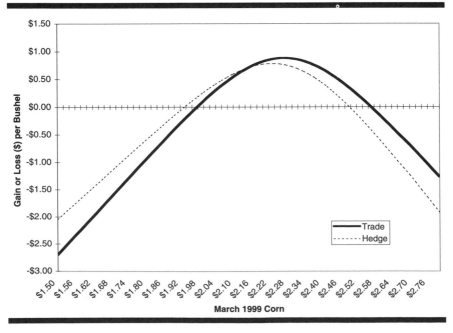

to the May options tends to move the option deltas closer to unity and away from zero; this serves to reduce the number of spreads required for a given exposure and thus reduces the leverage of the trades.

Trade 10 consists of buying 626 March $2.10 calls at $0.15375 and 626 December $1.90 puts at $0.04, as shown in Figure 10.40. The trade will benefit from higher prices, higher volatility, and an increase in the carrying level between December and March. Even without these factors changing from the base case, the trade exhibits enormous hedge efficiency, especially at the lower price levels.

Trade 11, which consists of buying 601 March $2.10 puts at $0.10125 and 601 December $1.90 calls at $0.1675, enjoys the advantage of buying December while it is in a deep carry to March. As a result, it has a more balanced profile than does trade 10, and its hedge efficiency is strong across most of the price spectrum, as shown in Figure 10.41.

If the two long backward calendar straddles are strongly efficient, one would expect their short counterparts to be inefficient. Trade 15 consists of selling 816 March $2.30 calls at $0.2175 and 816 December $2.10 puts at $0.12625, as shown in Figure 10.42. This trade will bene-

Figure 10.40 **PROFILE FOR 626 MARCH $2.10 CALL TO DECEMBER $1.90 PUT STRADDLES**

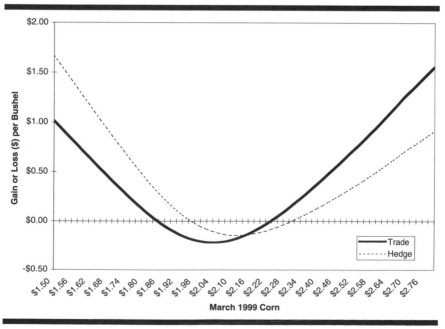

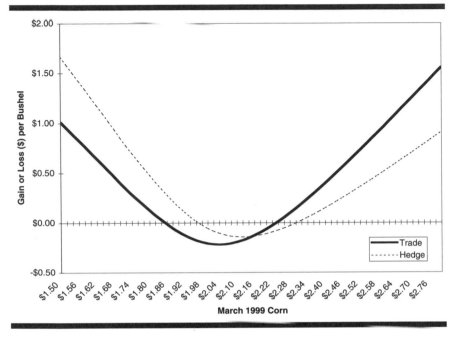

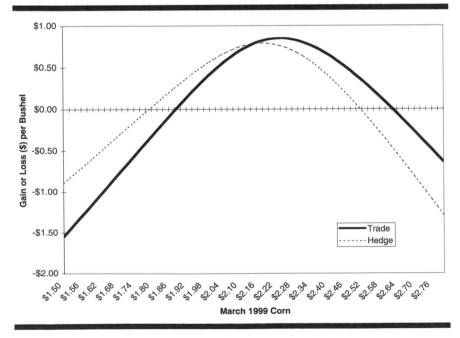

fit from lower volatility and a narrowing of the carry between December and March. Although the trade has open-ended liabilities on either side, it remains efficient over a surprisingly wide band of the price spectrum.

The final trade in this class, and the final trade for our entire range of long hedges, is trade 16, which consists of selling 851 December $2.10 calls at $0.05625 and 851 March $2.30 puts at $0.2175, as shown in Figure 10.43.

THE SHORT POSITIONS

Table 10.3 presents the 44 different short hedges considered for selling the equivalent of 1 million bushels of March 1999 corn. As was done for the long hedges, these trades are broken down into the classes of puts and put spreads, calls and call spreads, put–call combinations, and straddles for further discussion. Intermonth spreads are discussed separately from March-only positions.

Figure 10.43 **PROFILE FOR 851 SHORT MARCH $2.30 PUT TO DECEMBER $2.10 CALL STRADDLES**

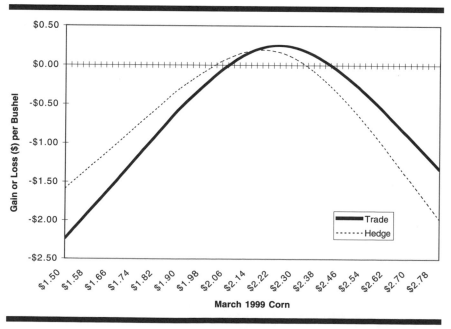

Table 10.3. **EQUIVALENT OF SHORT 200 MARCH CORN FUTURES**

Designation	Buy Quantity and Selection	Strike ($)	Sell Quantity and Selection	Strike ($)
1. ATM call/OTM put	232 strike 4 puts	2.10	232 ATM calls	2.20
2. ATM synthetic future	200 ATM puts	2.20	200 ATM calls	2.20
3. Backward calendar put frontspread	285 ATM puts	2.20	200 December strike 4 puts	1.90
4. Backward calendar put spread	491 strike 2 puts	2.40	200 December strike 2 puts	2.20
5. Backward calendar ATM call/OTM put	275 December strike 4 puts	1.90	275 ATM calls	2.20
6. Backward calendar ATM SSF	200 ATM puts	2.20	200 December ATM calls	2.20
7. Backward calendar bear call	1,764 strike 8 calls	2.10	1,764 December ATM calls	2.00
8. Backward calendar bear put	786 ATM puts	2.20	786 December strike 4 puts	1.90
9. Backward calendar call backspread	200 December ATM calls	2.00	540 strike 8 calls	2.10
10. Backward calendar covered future			271 December strike 4 puts and future	1.90
11. Backward calendar long straddle	816 strike 6 calls and 816 December strike 6 puts	2.30 2.10		
12. Backward calendar long straddle 2	851 December strike 6 calls and 851 strike 6 puts	2.10 2.30		
13. Backward calendar OTM call/OTM put 1	415 strike 4 puts	2.10	415 December strike 3 calls	2.40
14. Backward calendar OTM call/OTM put 2	491 December strike 4 puts	1.90	491 strike 3 calls	2.60
15. Backward calendar short straddle 1			1,168 March strike 5 calls and December strike 5 puts	1.90 2.10
16. Backward calendar short straddle 2			601 December strike 5 calls and March strike 5 puts	1.90 2.10
17. Backward calendar synthetic put	264 December strike 2 puts and futures	2.20		
18. Bear call	1,712 strike 8 calls	2.20	1,712 ATM calls	2.10
19. Bear put	1,670 ATM puts	2.20	1,670 strike 4 puts	2.10
20. Calendar put frontspread	262 ATM puts	2.20	200 May strike 4 puts	2.10
21. Calendar put spread	452 strike 2 puts	2.40	200 May strike 2 puts	2.50
22. Calendar ATM call/OTM put	254 May strike 4 puts	2.10	254 ATM calls	2.20
23. Calendar ATM SSF	200 ATM puts	2.20	200 May ATM calls	2.20
24. Calendar bear call	5,731 May ATM calls	2.20	5,731 strike 8 calls	2.10

(continues)

TABLE 10.3 CONTINUED

Designation	Buy Quantity and Selection	Strike ($)	Sell Quantity and Selection	Strike ($)
25. Calendar bear put	1,029 ATM puts	2.20	1,029 May strike 4 puts	2.10
26. Calendar call backspread	200 May ATM calls	2.20	532 strike 8 calls	2.10
27. Calendar covered future		2.10	295 May strike 4 puts and futures	2.10
28. Calendar long straddle 1	1,167 strike 6 calls and May strike 6 puts	2.30 2.30		
29. Calendar long straddle 2	1,126 May strike 6 calls and strike 6 puts	2.30 2.30		
30. Calendar OTM call/OTM put 1	321 strike 4 puts	2.10	321 May strike 3 calls	2.60
31. Calendar OTM call/OTM put 2	428 May strike 4 puts	2.10	428 strike 3 calls	2.60
32. Calendar short straddle 1		2.10 2.10	771 May strike 5 puts and strike 5 calls	2.10 2.10
33. Calendar short straddle 2		2.10 2.10	827 May strike 5 calls and March strike 5 puts	2.10 2.10
34. Calendar synthetic put	281 May strike 2 calls and futures	2.50		
35. Call		2.00	288 strike 1 calls	2.00
36. Call backspread	200 ATM calls	2.20	504 strike 8 calls	2.10
37. Covered future		2.10	332 strike 4 puts and futures	2.10
38. Long straddle	731 strike 6 calls and strike 6 puts	2.30 2.30		
39. OTM call/ATM put	302 ATM puts	2.20	302 strike 3 calls	2.60
40. OTM call/OTM put	369 strike 4 puts	2.10	369 strike 3 calls	2.60
41. Put	280 strike 2 puts	2.40		
42. Put frontspread	233 ATM puts	2.20	200 strike 4 puts	2.10
43. Short straddle		2.10 2.10	1,082 strike 5 calls and strike 5 puts	2.10 2.10
44. Synthetic put	272 strike 2 calls	2.40	272 futures	

ATM = at-the-money; OTM = out-of-the-money

Puts and Put Spreads

Once again, we begin with the simplest trade. Trade 41 consists of buying 280 March $2.40 puts at $0.29375, as shown in Figure 10.44. This trade has the advantages of providing downside protection to the present value of the strike and of allowing for gains to accrue at higher price levels. It is simple to execute, manage, and liquidate, and

Figure 10.44 **PROFILE FOR 280 MARCH $2.40 PUT OPTIONS**

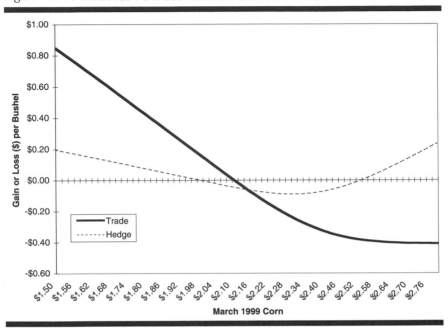

it will benefit directly from any increase in volatility. Most important, the hedge is quite efficient over a wide range of prices.

Trade 44, a synthetic put, consists of buying 272 March $2.40 calls at $0.05125 and selling 272 March futures at $2.1525, as shown in Figure 10.45. Its behavior will be parallel to that of the natural put. Its lower initial capital outlay appeals to many traders, although additional funds will have to be segregated for margin purposes.

Trade 19, a bear put spread, consists of buying 1,670 March $2.20 puts at $0.1525 and selling 1,670 March $2.10 puts at $0.10125, as shown in Figure 10.46. The large number of contracts involved results from the proximity of the strikes, which reduces the delta of the spread. Since the gains are limited on the downside, hedge efficiency falls in a linear manner at lower prices; the opposite is true at higher prices, where hedge efficiency rises in a linear manner.

Trade 42 uses the same two strikes, but changes the structure of the trade to a frontspread consisting of buying 233 March $2.20 puts at $0.1525 and selling 200 March $2.10 puts at $0.10125, as shown in Figure 10.47. The small capital outlay at initiation and the proximity of the strikes give the trade near linear efficiency at higher prices—and near linear losses at lower prices.

Figure 10.45 **PROFILE FOR 272 MARCH $2.40 SYNTHETIC PUTS**

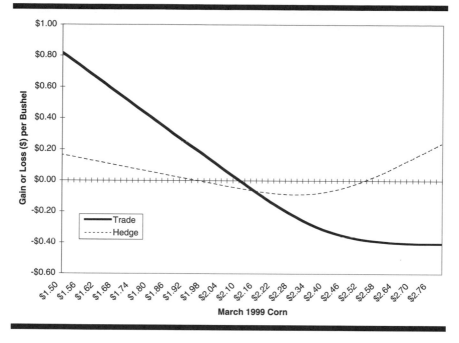

Figure 10.46 **PROFILE FOR 1,670 MARCH $2.20 TO MARCH $2.10 PUT SPREADS**

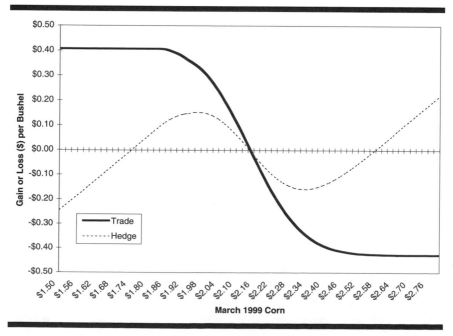

Figure 10.47 **PROFILE FOR 233 MARCH $2.20 TO 200 MARCH $2.10 PUT FRONTSPREAD**

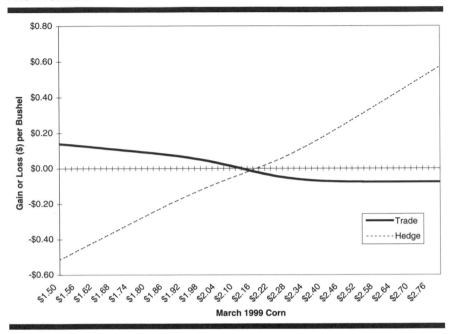

Intermonth Puts and Put Spreads

The same observations regarding the shape of the forward curve for corn made earlier apply here, only in reverse. Although we could buy December and sell March, for example, with the knowledge that we were near a full carry level, we should now be wary of selling December and buying March for the same reason.

Trade 34 is a calendar synthetic put consisting of buying 281 May $2.50 calls at $0.0675 and selling 281 March futures at $2.1525, as shown in Figure 10.48. This trade would benefit from a move toward a deeper carry between March and May. The low initial capital cost of the trade allows for good hedge efficiency at lower prices, whereas the time value retained by the May $2.60 call affords protection at higher prices. The trade has a rather wide range of hedge inefficiency at a static price environment.

Trade 21 is a calendar put spread consisting of buying 452 March $2.40 puts at $0.29375 and selling 200 May $2.50 puts at $0.335, as shown in Figure 10.49. Once again, this trade will benefit from a deepening of the carry level between March and May. The large credit received for the short May $2.50 put makes the hedge efficient at

Figure 10.48 **PROFILE FOR 281 MAY $2.50 TO MARCH FUTURE SYNTHETIC PUTS**

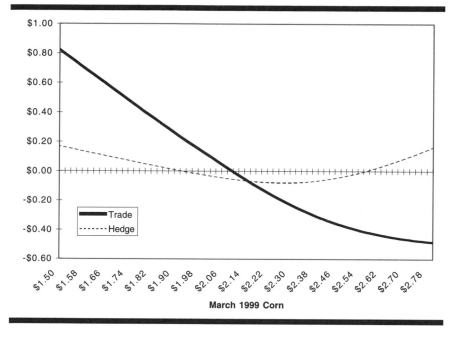

Figure 10.49 **PROFILE FOR 452 MARCH $2.50 TO 200 MAY $2.50 PUT SPREADS**

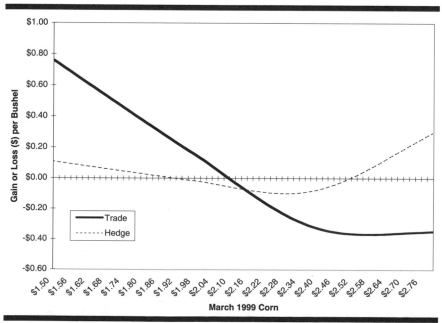

higher prices, whereas the excess of March $2.40 puts provides efficiency at lower prices.

Trade 25 is a calendar bear put consisting of buying 1,029 March $2.20 puts at $0.1525 and selling 1,029 May $2.10 puts at $0.0875, as shown in Figure 10.50. The proximity of the strikes leads to near linear efficiency at higher prices and near linear inefficiency at lower prices. The large number of contracts involved, even with the small initial debit per contract, leads to significant exposure to time decay, especially at modestly higher prices. The trade would benefit from a deepening of the March-to-May carry.

Trade 20, a calendar put frontspread, consists of buying 262 March $2.20 puts at $0.1525 and selling 200 May $2.10 puts at $0.0875, as shown in Figure 10.51. The smaller number of contracts involved in this trade and the proximity of the strikes gives it near linear efficiency at higher prices and near linear inefficiency at lower prices.

We can move now to the backward calendar put positions, those involving a combination of December and March instruments. Trade 4 is a backward calendar put spread consisting of buying 491 March $2.40 puts at $0.29375 and selling 200 December $2.20 puts at $0.1975,

Figure 10.50 **PROFILE FOR 1,029 MARCH $2.20 TO MAY $2.10 PUT SPREADS**

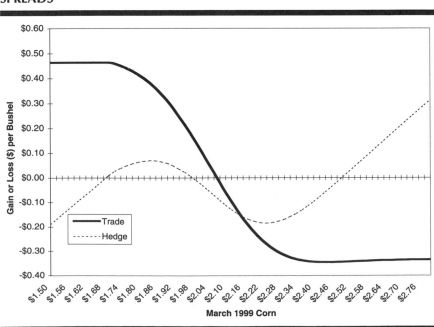

Figure 10.51 **PROFILE FOR 262 MARCH $2.20 TO 200 MAY $2.10 PUT SPREADS**

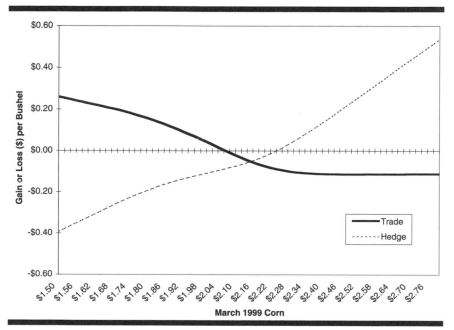

as shown in Figure 10.52. The large credit received for the December $2.20 put makes this an efficient trade at higher price levels, whereas the excess of March $2.40 puts makes the trade efficient at lower price levels. Any narrowing of the carry between December and March will benefit the trade as well.

Trade 17 is a backward calendar synthetic put consisting of 264 December $2.20 calls at $0.03 and selling 264 March futures at $2.1525, as shown in Figure 10.53. The low capital outlay for the $2.20 calls gives this trade very strong hedge efficiency at lower prices, and the small number of contracts involved allows for hedge gains at higher prices as well. Any narrowing of the carry between December and March will benefit the trade.

Trade 8 is a backward calendar bear put consisting of buying 786 March $2.20 puts at $0.1525 and selling 764 December $1.90 puts at $0.04, as shown in Figure 10.54. The short $1.90 put limits the trade's gain at lower prices and therefore makes the hedge very inefficient in this region while it is simultaneously very efficient in the higher price region. Once again, the trade will benefit from a deepening of the December-to-March carry.

Figure 10.52 **PROFILE FOR 491 MARCH $2.40 TO DECEMBER $2.20 PUT SPREADS**

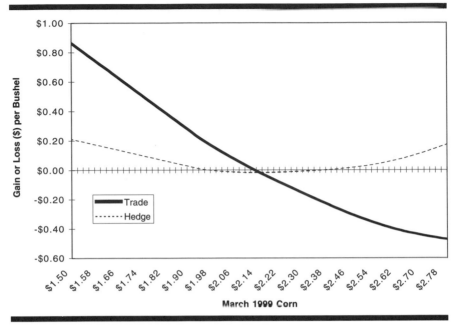

Figure 10.53 **PROFILE FOR 264 DECEMBER $2.20 TO MARCH FUTURE SYNTHETIC PUTS**

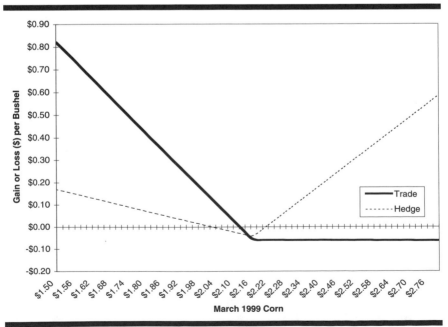

Figure 10.54 **PROFILE FOR 786 MARCH $2.20 TO DECEMBER $1.90 PUT SPREADS**

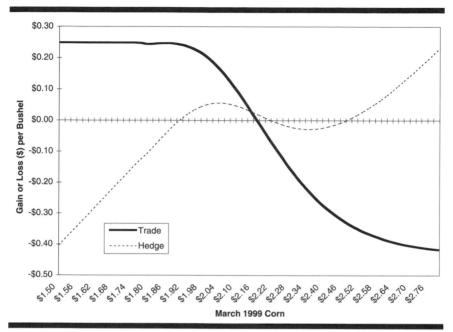

Trade 3 is a backward calendar put frontspread consisting of buying 285 March $2.20 puts at $0.1525 and selling 200 December $1.90 puts at $0.04, as shown in Figure 10.55. The short December $1.90 puts make the trade inefficient at lower price levels. Once the net debit for the long March $2.20 puts is absorbed, the trade becomes highly efficient at higher price levels, however.

Calls and Call Spreads

The use of call options to emplace a short hedge is just as appropriate as the use of put options to emplace a long hedge, and for the same reasons and with the same caveats. A short call option is embedded within every short cash market or futures position; complete elimination of this option can be both expensive and unnecessary to the completion of our trading goals. However, retention of the short call option limits upside gains and injects the element of negative gamma into the trade.

Trade 35, selling 288 March $2.00 calls at $0.21375, is the simplest trade in this class, as shown in Figure 10.56. The trade has poor hedge

Figure 10.55 **PROFILE FOR 285 MARCH $2.20 TO 200 DECEMBER $1.90 PUT SPREADS**

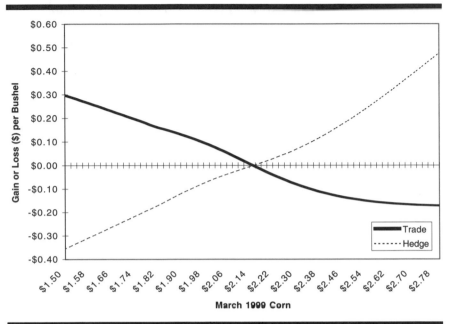

Figure 10.56 **PROFILE FOR 288 SHORT MARCH $2.00 CALLS**

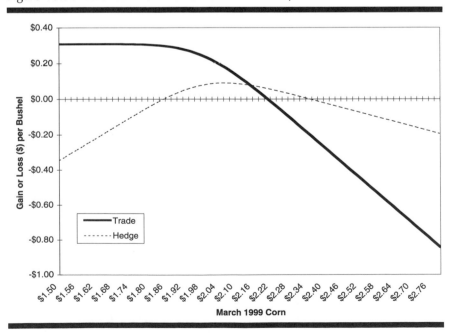

efficiency at both higher and lower price levels. Even in the static price case, the hedge efficiency is rather poor, since the initial premium received is not very large and certainly does not compensate for the continuous negative gamma of this trade.

Trade 37 is a synthetic short call consisting of selling 332 March $2.10 puts at $0.10125 and selling 332 March futures at $2.1525, as shown in Figure 10.57. The general profile does not differ significantly from that of trade 35; it is merely selling a greater quantity of a higher strike call and thus has an even worse gamma position than does trade 35. Its trade efficiency is positive for only a small zone of static prices.

Trade 18 is a bear call spread consisting of selling 1,712 March $2.10 calls at $0.15375 and buying 1,712 March $2.20 calls at $0.11, as shown in Figure 10.58. The trade's unwieldy size results from the proximity of the strikes and the resulting small delta. The trade has near linear efficiency at higher prices and near linear inefficiency at lower prices, with only a small zone of efficiency at modestly lower prices.

Trade 36 is a call backspread consisting of selling 504 March $2.10 calls at $0.15735 and buying 200 March $2.20 calls at $0.11, as shown in Figure 10.59. The excess of short $2.10 calls allows for a much more

Figure 10.57 **PROFILE FOR 332 MARCH $2.10 SYNTHETIC CALLS**

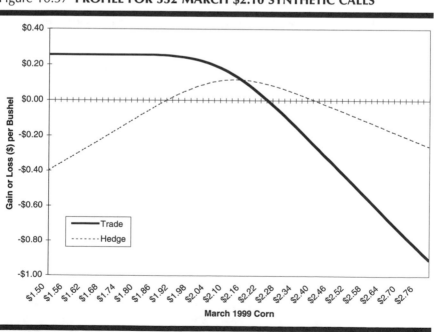

March 1999 Corn

Figure 10.58 **PROFILE FOR 1,712 MARCH $2.20 TO $2.10 CALL SPREADS**

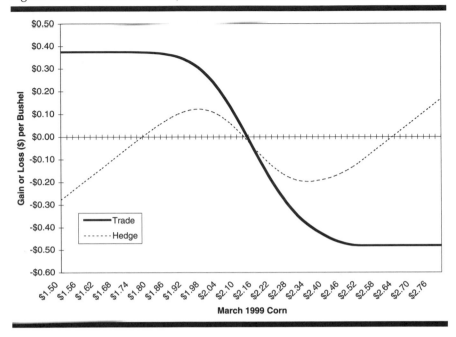

Figure 10.59 **PROFILE FOR 200 MARCH $2.20 TO 504 $2.10 CALL SPREADS**

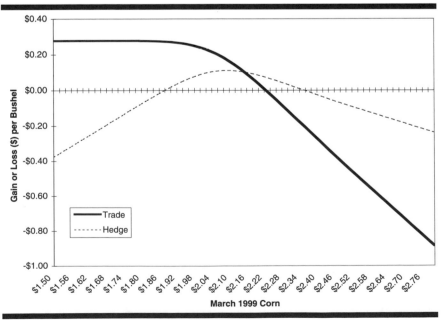

manageable trade size than does trade 18. However, this excess creates a profile resembling that of a short call option, and as a result, the hedge is efficient in only a small zone of static prices.

Intermonth Call Spreads

We can move now to the calendar call spreads. The same observations regarding the shape of the forward curve seen before obtain now as well. The first trade we examine is trade 24, a calendar bear call consisting of buying 5,731 May $2.20 calls at $0.16 and selling 5,731 March $2.10 calls at $0.15375, as shown in Figure 10.60. The trade's wholly unrealistic size results from the proximity of the two options' deltas. The large short position in the May $2.20 call gives this trade a disastrous hedge profile in higher prices and a negative gamma over most of the price spectrum.

Trade 26 is a calendar call backspread consisting of buying 200 May $2.20 calls at $0.16 and selling 532 March $2.10 calls at $0.15375, as shown in Figure 10.61. The excess short $2.10 call position makes this trade inefficient at both higher and lower prices. A deepening of

Figure 10.60 **PROFILE FOR 5,731 MARCH $2.10 TO MAY $2.20 CALL SPREADS**

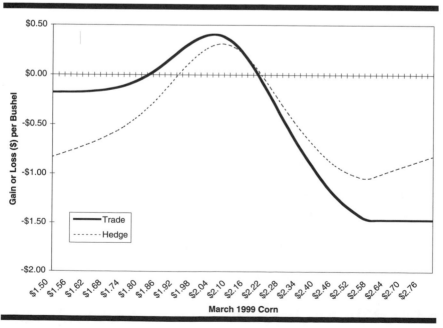

March 1999 Corn

Figure 10.61 **PROFILE FOR 200 MAY $2.20 TO 532 MARCH $2.10 CALL SPREADS**

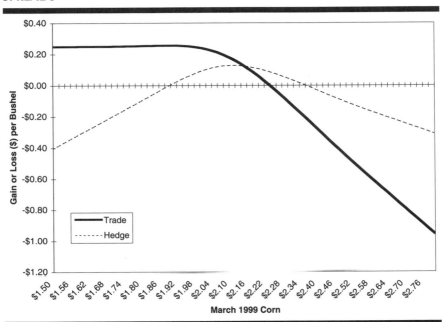

the March-to-May carry would expand the zone of modest efficiency at static prices.

The final trade in this class, trade 27, is a short calendar synthetic call consisting of selling both 295 May $2.10 puts at $0.0875 and 295 March futures at $2.1525, as shown in Figure 10.62. The small number of contracts involved moderates this trade's inefficiency at higher prices, but the small initial credit for the short $2.10 put also limits the trade's modest efficiency at higher prices.

We now move on to the backward calendar call spreads, starting with trade 7, which consists of buying 1,764 March $2.10 calls at $0.15375 and selling 1,764 December $2.00 calls at $0.1025, as shown in Figure 10.63. The unwieldy size of the trade derives from the small delta difference between the two options. The trade is efficient at higher price levels, but this is offset by a large inefficiency at lower prices.

Trade 9 is a backward calendar call backspread consisting of buying 200 December $2.00 calls at $0.1025 and selling 540 March $2.10 calls at $0.15375, as shown in Figure 10.64. The excess short $2.10 call position produces large hedge inefficiencies at higher prices, and these are barely offset at static prices, owing to the time decay on the

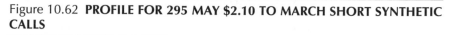

Figure 10.62 **PROFILE FOR 295 MAY $2.10 TO MARCH SHORT SYNTHETIC CALLS**

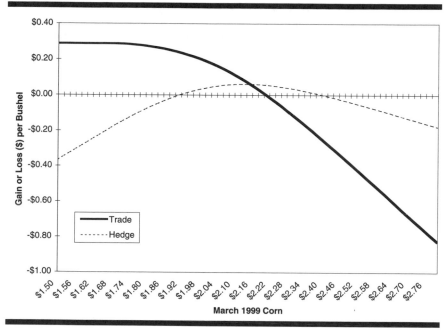

Figure 10.63 **PROFILE FOR 1,764 MARCH $2.10 TO DECEMBER $2.00 CALL SPREADS**

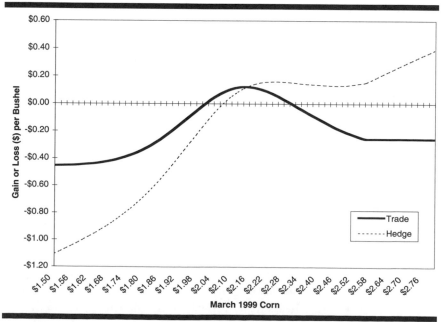

Figure 10.64 **PROFILE FOR 200 DECEMBER $2.00 TO 540 MARCH $2.10 CALL SPREADS**

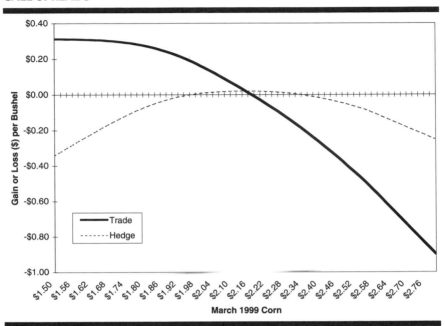

long $2.00 call. A narrowing of the December-to-March carry would benefit the trade.

Trade 10, a short backward calendar synthetic call consisting of selling both 271 December $1.90 puts at $0.04 and 271 March futures, as shown in Figure 10.65, completes the discussion of this trade class. The small number of contracts involved reduces this trade's inefficiency at higher price levels, but the small initial credit received makes its small zone of hedge efficiency unattractive as well. The trade would benefit from a narrowing of the December-to-March carry, but not significantly.

Synthetic Futures and Put–Call Combinations

We can turn our attention now to the class of trade that did not acquit itself very well in the long positions section of this chapter, the various combinations of buying and selling or selling and buying puts and calls together. Just as we did in the long positions section, we can skip over the most basic of these trades, the synthetic short future (SSF) defined in trade 2. We should note once again, however, that the short future will serve as the basis for comparison in deciding whether any

Figure 10.65 **PROFILE FOR 271 DECEMBER $1.90 TO MARCH SHORT SYNTHETIC CALLS**

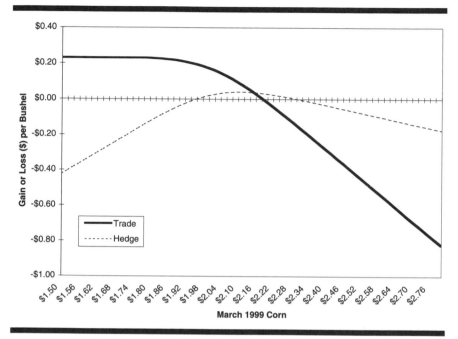

of these option-based short hedges is in fact adding any value to the hedge process.

Trade 1 consists of buying 232 March $2.10 puts at $0.10125 and selling 232 March $2.20 calls at $0.11, as shown in Figure 10.66. The small trade size and virtually nonexistent credit at initiation make this trade very close to the base case of simply selling 200 March futures.

Trade 39 consists of buying 302 March $2.20 puts at $0.1525 and selling 302 March $2.60 calls at $0.025, as shown in Figure 10.67. The spacing between the strikes and modest trade size allow this trade to produce an efficient hedge profile at both higher and lower prices in exchange for a modest zone of underperformance at static price levels. Only at much higher prices than illustrated will the hedge exhibit linear declines in efficiency.

Trade 40, which consists of buying 369 March $2.10 puts at $0.10125 and selling 369 March $2.60 calls at $0.025, widens the distance between strikes further, as shown in Figure 10.68. The smaller capital outlay at initiation produces greater hedge efficiency at lower prices than those seen for trade 39 while retaining the same curve shape at higher price levels.

Figure 10.66 **PROFILE FOR 232 MARCH $2.10 PUT TO $2.20 CALL SPREADS**

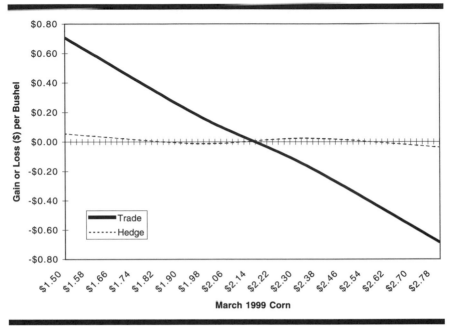

Figure 10.67 **PROFILE FOR 302 MARCH $2.20 PUT TO $2.60 CALL SPREADS**

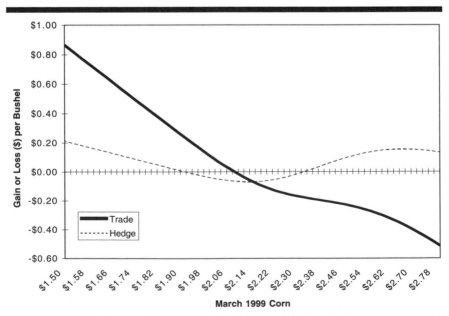

Figure 10.68   **PROFILE FOR 369 MARCH $2.20 PUT TO $2.60 CALL SPREADS**

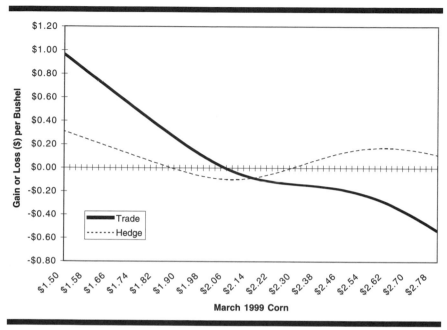

We now move on to the calendar variations on these trades. Trade 23 is a calendar SSF consisting of buying 200 March $2.20 puts at $0.1525 and selling 200 May $2.20 calls at $0.16, as shown in Figure 10.69. The trade exhibits modest efficiency at lower prices and near zero efficiency at higher prices. The trade would benefit from a deepening of the March-to-May carry.

Trade 22 is a calendar split-strike synthetic future consisting of buying 254 May $2.10 puts at $0.0875 and selling 254 March $2.20 calls at $0.11, as shown in Figure 10.70. This trade also has a very flat hedge efficiency profile, one that is generally positive at lower and static prices and starts to deteriorate at higher prices, owing to the short $2.20 call. The trade would benefit from a move toward backwardation in the March-to-May spread.

Trade 31 consists of buying 428 May $2.10 puts at $0.0875 and selling 428 March $2.60 calls at $0.025, as shown in Figure 10.71. The large number of $2.10 puts gives this trade good hedge efficiency at lower price levels, whereas the small initial capital outlay gives the trade good hedge efficiency at higher prices until the short $2.60 strike is approached.

Figure 10.69 **PROFILE FOR 200 MARCH $2.20 PUT TO MAY $2.20 CALL SPREADS**

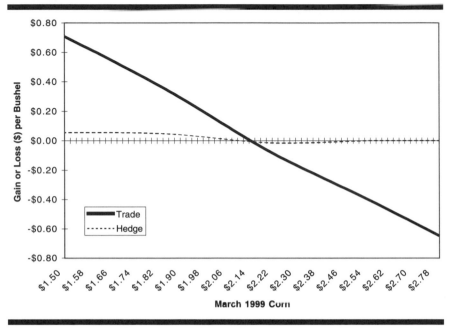

Figure 10.70 **PROFILE FOR 254 MAY $2.10 PUT TO MARCH $2.20 CALL SPREADS**

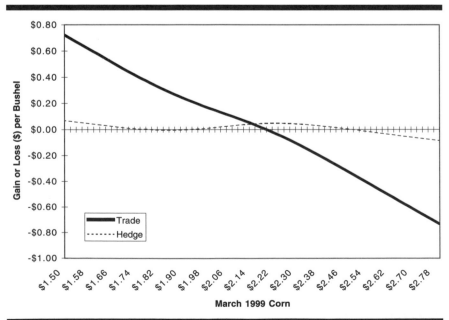

Figure 10.71 **PROFILE FOR 428 MAY $2.10 PUT TO MARCH $2.60 CALL SPREADS**

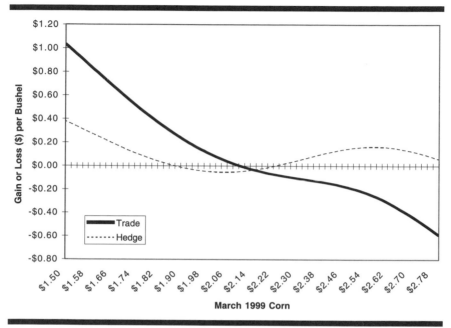

Trade 30 reverses the months of trade 31; it consists of buying 321 March $2.10 puts at $0.10125 and selling 321 May $2.60 calls at $0.05, as shown in Figure 10.72. The small number of contracts involved and the small initial capital outlay allow this trade to enjoy good efficiency at lower price levels and at higher price levels until the approach of the short $2.60 strike. The zone of underperformance at static prices is limited. The trade would benefit from a deepening of the carry between March and May.

We can now move to the backward calendar variations of these put–call combinations. Trade 6 is a backward calendar SSF consisting of buying 200 March $2.20 puts at $0.1525 and selling 200 December $2.20 calls at $0.03, as shown in Figure 10.73. The trade exhibits modest hedge gains at higher prices and modest hedge losses and lower prices. It would be hurt by a narrowing of the December-to-March carry.

Trade 5 consists of buying 275 December $1.90 puts at $0.04 and selling 275 March $2.20 calls at $0.11, as shown in Figure 10.74. The small trade size and the initial credit allow this trade to maintain hedge efficiency at static and slightly higher prices and to have good hedge efficiency at lower prices. The trade would benefit from a deepening of the carry between December and March.

Figure 10.72 **PROFILE FOR 321 MARCH $2.10 PUT TO MAY $2.60 CALL
SPREADS**

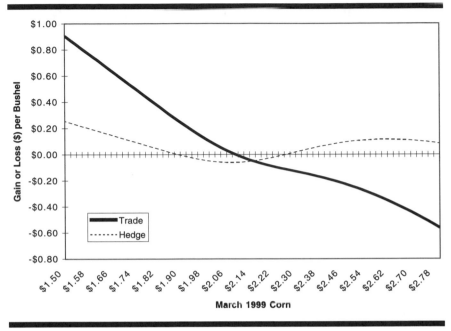

Figure 10.73 **PROFILE FOR 200 MARCH $2.20 PUT TO DECEMBER $2.20
CALL SPREADS**

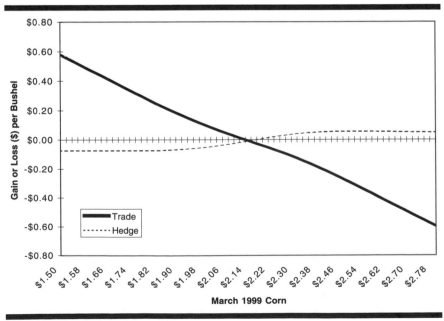

Figure 10.74 **PROFILE FOR 275 DECEMBER $1.90 PUT TO MARCH $2.20 CALL SPREADS**

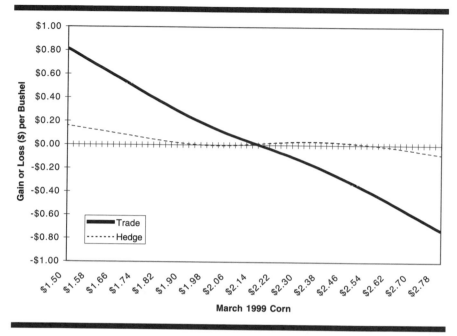

Trade 14 consists of buying 491 December $1.90 puts at $0.04 and selling 491 March $2.60 calls at $0.025, as shown in Figure 10.75. The small initial capital outlay and the large number of $1.90 puts make this a very efficient hedge at lower price levels. The trade's efficiency remains modestly positive until the approach of the short $2.60 strike, at which point it will become strongly negative. The trade will benefit from a deepening of the December-to-March carry.

Trade 13 completes the analysis of this class of trade. It consists of buying 415 March $2.10 puts at $0.10125 and selling 415 December $2.40 calls at $0.00875, as shown in Figure 10.76. As was the case for trade 14, the hedge gains for this trade are concentrated at the lower price levels, and once the short $2.40 strike is exceeded, the loss profile will be open ended.

Straddles

We now move to the final class of trades we will examine for hedging a long cash market position: the straddles. Trade 38 consists of buying 731 March $2.30 calls at $0.0725 and 731 March $2.30 puts at $0.2175, as shown in Figure 10.77. The large trade size and large initial capital

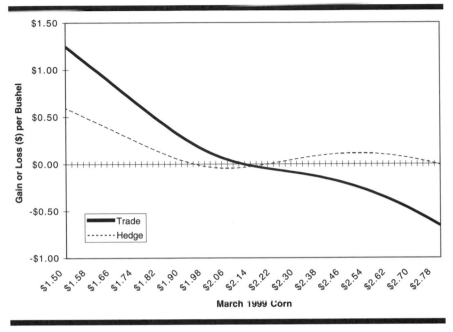

Figure 10.75 **PROFILE FOR 491 DECEMBER $1.90 PUT TO MARCH $2.60 CALL SPREADS**

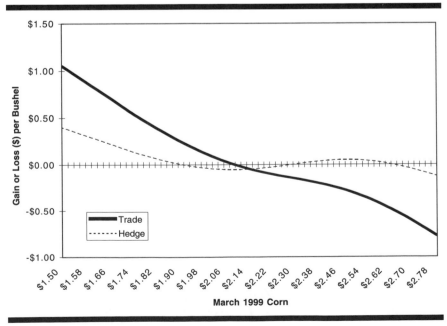

Figure 10.76 **PROFILE FOR 415 MARCH $2.10 PUT TO DECEMBER $2.40 CALL SPREADS**

Figure 10.77   **PROFILE FOR 731 MARCH $2.30 STRADDLES**

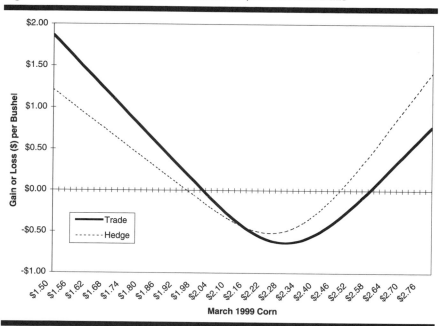

outlay make this trade highly susceptible to time decay and to any decrease in volatility. Large hedge gains are possible with early and strong price movement, but the risk in a static market is considerable, nearly $0.50 per bushel with 30 days left.

Trade 43, a short straddle consisting of selling 1,082 March $2.10 calls at $0.15375 and 1,082 March $2.10 puts at $0.10125, has the inverse profit profile, as shown in Figure 10.78. The large initial credit and large trade size place this trade in a position to capture a huge amount of time decay in a static market. Unfortunately, there is little assurance entering a trade that such a market will exist, and the risk profile of this gamma-negative trade at both higher and lower prices is terrible.

Trade 28 is a calendar long straddle consisting of buying 1,167 March $2.30 calls at $0.0725 and buying 1,167 May $2.30 puts at $0.19, as shown in Figure 10.79. Once again, the large initial capital outlay and massive exposure to both time decay and volatility reductions preclude this trade from active consideration as an active hedging instrument even though large hedge gains are possible at both higher and lower price levels. The trade would benefit from a move toward backwardation in the March-to-May spread.

Figure 10.78 **PROFILE FOR 1,082 SHORT MARCH $2.10 STRADDLES**

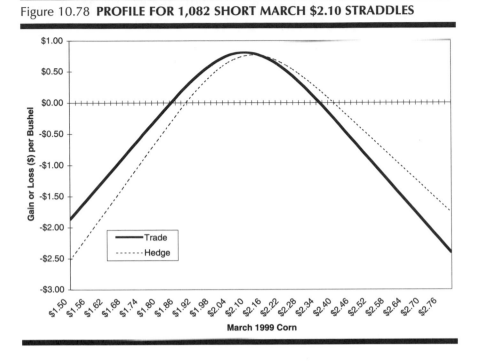

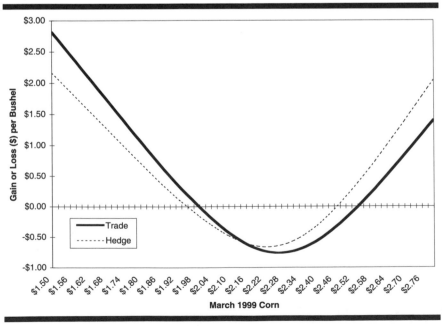

Trade 29, which consists of buying 1,126 May $2.30 calls at $0.12 and buying 1,126 March $2.30 puts at $0.2175, reverses the months from trade 28, as shown in Figure 10.80. The placement of the long call option in May increases the initial capital outlay of the trade and hence reduces its overall hedge efficiency.

Trade 32 is a calendar short straddle consisting of selling 771 May $2.10 puts at $0.15375 and selling 771 March $2.10 calls at $0.0875, as shown in Figure 10.81. The credit at initiation is not sufficient to cover the open-ended liabilities and negative gamma involved, even though the gains at static prices are attractive. The trade will benefit from a deepening of the March-to-May carry.

Trade 33 reverses the months involved in trade 32. It consists of selling 827 March $2.10 puts at $0.10125 and 827 May $2.10 calls at $0.215, as shown in Figure 10.82. Even though the initial credit for this trade is fairly robust, it is still not enough to overcome the risks associated with the open-ended liabilities at both higher and lower prices. A move toward backwardation in the March-to-May spread would benefit the trade.

Figure 10.80 **PROFILE FOR 1,126 MARCH $2.30 PUT TO MAY $2.30 CALL STRADDLES**

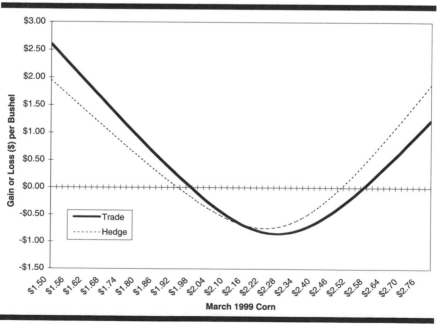

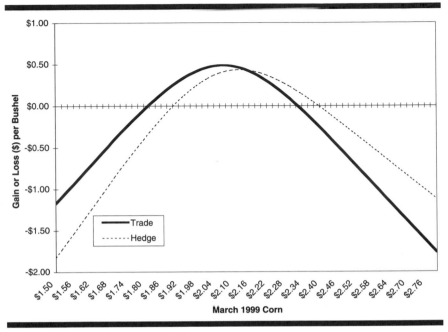

Figure 10.81 **PROFILE FOR 771 MARCH $2.10 CALL TO MAY $2.10 PUT STRADDLES**

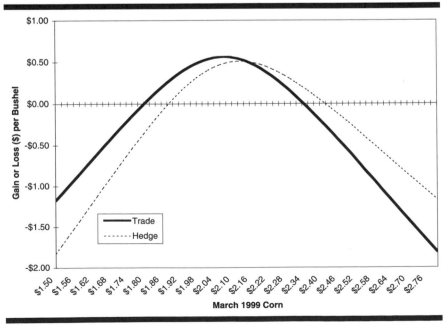

Figure 10.82 **PROFILE FOR 827 SHORT MARCH $2.10 PUT TO MAY $2.10 CALL STRADDLES**

The last set of trades we will examine are the backward calendar straddles, those involving a combination of December and March contracts. Trade 11 consists of buying 816 March $2.30 calls at $0.0725 and buying 816 December $2.10 puts at $0.12625, as shown in Figure 10.83. The distance between the strikes and the leverage of the initial capital outlay give this trade strong hedge efficiency at both higher and lower price levels at the cost of modest underperformance at static prices. The trade is structured to benefit from a deepening of the December-to-March carry.

Trade 12 reverses the months from trade 11 and thus puts the trade in position to benefit from a narrowing of the December-to-March carry. It consists of buying 851 December $2.10 calls at $0.05625 and buying 851 March $2.30 puts at $0.2175, as shown in Figure 10.84. Although the initial capital outlay and leverage of this trade are higher than those of trade 11, it retains the same strong hedge efficiencies at both higher and lower prices and only limited underperformance at static prices. Any narrowing of the carry level between December and March will work to the trade's benefit.

Figure 10.83 **PROFILE FOR 816 MARCH $2.30 CALL TO MAY $2.10 PUT STRADDLES**

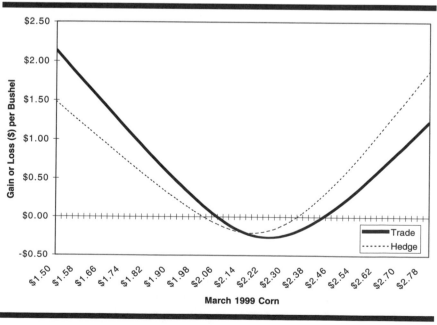

Figure 10.84 **PROFILE FOR 851 MARCH $2.30 PUT TO DECEMBER $2.10 CALL STRADDLES**

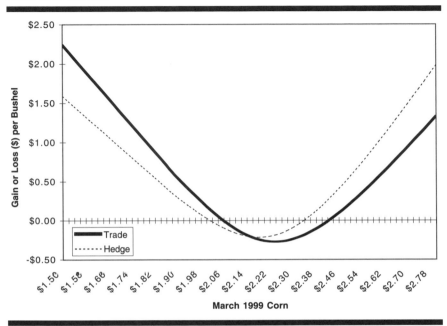

Trade 15 is a short backward calendar straddle consisting of selling 1,168 March $1.90 calls at $0.29 and 1,168 December $2.10 puts at $0.12625, as shown in Figure 10.85. Although the initial credit on this trade is substantial, it is clearly insufficient to compensate for the large open-ended liabilities at both higher and lower price levels. It will benefit slightly from a narrowing of the December-to-March carry.

Trade 16, the final trade we will examine in this set, reverses the months from trade 15. It consists of selling 601 December $1.90 calls at $0.1675 and 601 March $2.10 puts at $0.10125, as shown in Figure 10.86. Once again, the substantial initial credit cannot overcome the negative gamma of the short straddle, and the position is subject to substantial and open-ended losses at both higher and lower price levels.

POSITION SELECTION

The same considerations listed in on pages 155–156 in Chapter 9 for individual option strike selection can be used now to compare positions. One of these considerations, the need to maintain positive

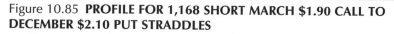

Figure 10.85 **PROFILE FOR 1,168 SHORT MARCH $1.90 CALL TO DECEMBER $2.10 PUT STRADDLES**

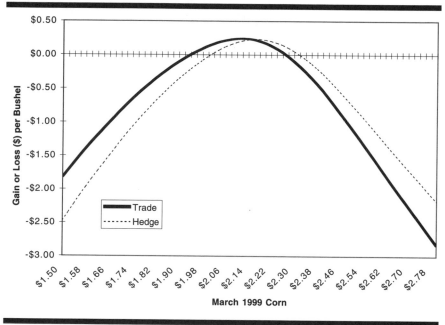

Figure 10.86 **PROFILE FOR 601 SHORT MARCH $2.10 PUT TO DECEMBER $1.90 CALL STRADDLES**

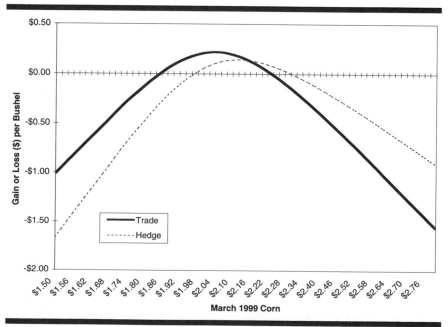

gamma, we make into a hard-and-fast criterion: Negative gamma at initiation removes the position from further consideration. A second, but more arbitrary, exclusionary rule is related to the problems created when the delta of an individual spread is small, resulting in some obviously unwieldy position sizes: The delta of each spread must be greater than .20 for long positions and less than −.20 for short positions. This will preclude contract leverage of greater than 5 : 1 to the underlying position.

Once these two exclusions are made, we can revert to the same analysis used in Chapter 9, including the second, sixth, and seventh points in the list of strategy components regarding the shape of the forward curve and the reduction of net borrowing costs by selling forward in a carry market and buying forward in a backwardated market. Our aim is simple: We wish to maximize the return on our position's delta while reducing the net borrowing cost. The tradeoff between maximizing return on delta, which occurs near the ATM strike, and minimizing time decay, which occurs near the deep-in-the-money (DITM) strikes, is the same problem we faced during our strike selection exercises, particularly for strikes 1 and 2.

We can characterize the general objective function as maximizing the potential return on the hedge's position for a given level of cost, where cost is a function of the expected borrowing cost of the position and not a function of the position's initial debit or credit level. The two subobjectives must be taken together; neither a simple maximization of potential return nor a simple minimization of borrowing cost will satisfy the total objective. Since both debit and credit spreads have a net borrowing cost at initiation if they have positive gamma, the position selection algorithm is indifferent as to whether the trade will be a debit or a credit, but experience has taught that traders themselves are never indifferent to this criterion!

The Long Hedge

The optimal position for our long hedge is trade 7, illustrated in Figure 10.20; the next four most attractive long hedge positions are Trades 19, 24, 20, and 14, in descending order. Trade 7 is a backward calendar bull put consisting of buying 489 December $2.00 puts at $0.0725 and selling 489 March $2.60 puts at $0.465. We can emplace this trade with the full knowledge that it will have to be rolled forward to another, completely different, position at a later date to hedge a March commitment because of the earlier expiration date of the December $2.00 put. We can depict the performance of this trade from four different perspectives. The first, shown in Figure 10.87, is the

Figure 10.87 **NET FINANCIAL GAIN ON TRADE 7**

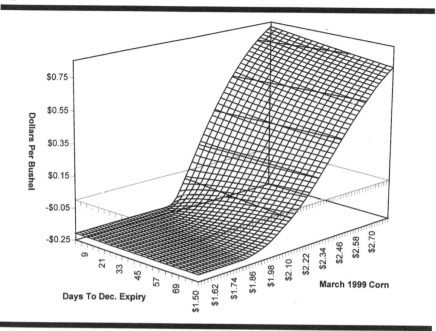

trade's profit and loss profile across the dimensions of March price and time remaining on the December option, with the December-to-March spread held constant.

The profit profile of the trade resembles that of a call option, but it has a much lower exposure to time decay than does the call option over a wide range of prices and time, as we shall see in Figure 10.90. Next, we can compare this profile to the base case of simply buying 200 March futures; this surface, shown in Figure 10.88, is also the net basis of the trade.

The zone of underperformance is centered around the static price level, which we expect, and it is also highly sensitive to time decay: At expiration, the worst-case loss on the basis is around $0.155 per bushel, but if the trade were exited with 30 days remaining, the worst-case loss would be only around $0.06 per bushel. The effects of time decay, as discussed in Chapter 8, are wholly predictable, and this would suggest that the negative effects of time decay could be avoided simply by exiting the trade when these effects start to damage the hedge's effectiveness.

The basis gains on the trade are open ended on the downside, owing to the effects of lower prices for the buyer, but the basis gains

Figure 10.88 **INCREMENTAL GAIN ON TRADE 7**

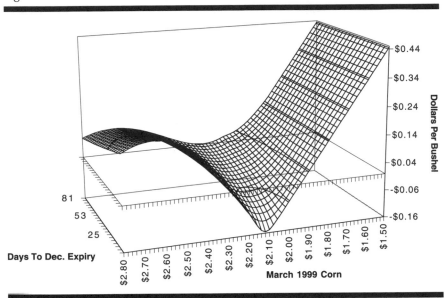

start to flatten out at higher prices, owing to the limited gains available on the short $2.60 put. This will require management of the position to maintain optimal hedge efficiency, as we discuss in Chapter 11.

Since the trade is sensitive to changes in the December-to-March spread, we should depict these effects to understand the risk that we are taking. We see in Figure 10.89 that the trade is hurt at lower prices by a move toward backwardation in corn; this is expected given the long December put and short March put. At higher prices, the net basis becomes insensitive to increases in backwardation, since the net gain on the put spread has already reached its maximum. The worst case lies within an interesting combination of circumstances: lower March prices and a shift in the December-to-March spread toward backwardation. The implications of this combination are that corn is scarce for December delivery but will be abundant for March delivery. Although nothing is impossible, this combination of circumstances defies both economic logic and fundamental realities, since there is no source of surplus corn available between December and March.

We can add yet one more comparison, the one between trade 7 and our plain-vanilla call option trade, trade 35, which consists of buying 288 March $2.00 calls at $0.21375. The difference between the two positions is depicted in Figure 10.90. Trade 7 outperforms trade 35 in all but two zones: significantly higher prices and static prices. Both

Figure 10.89 **NET BASIS GAIN ON TRADE 7**

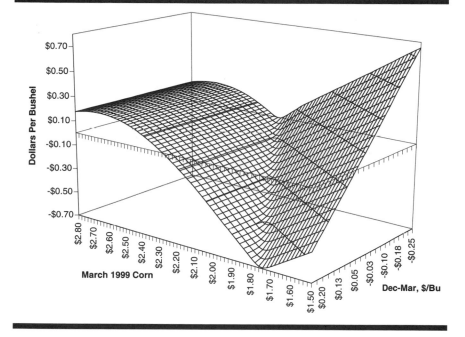

Figure 10.90 **INCREMENTAL ADVANTAGE OF TRADE 7 OVER TRADE 35**

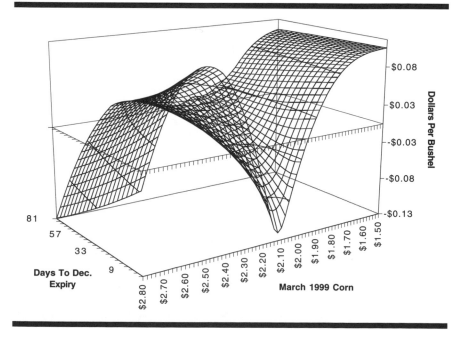

of these are to be expected. Trade 7 has a limited upside, and the presence of the December $2.00 put creates more rapid time decay at static prices.

At the static case, the expected borrowing cost of trade 35 over the period of comparison is its initial capital outlay per bushel, $0.2837, less its expected value at the time of the December expiration, $0.2518, or $0.0319. The expected borrowing cost, or net time decay, for trade 7 is a much larger $0.13817 per bushel, which may be a surprising answer given the fact that trade 7 is emplaced at a net credit of $0.9597 per bushel and trade 35, at a net debit of $0.3078 per bushel. The reason for the greater borrowing cost lies in the expected loss of the entire December $2.00 put premium of $0.1773 per bushel, which is offset only partially by the lending afforded by the short March $2.60 put. In exchange for this greater net borrowing, the owner of trade 7 gets much greater downside protection and much greater upside protection until the approach of the $2.60 strike.

The Short Hedge

The optimal position for our short hedge is trade 11, illustrated in Figure 10.91 across the dimensions of March price and time remaining on the December options, with the December-to-March spread held con-

Figure 10.91 **NET FINANCIAL GAIN ON TRADE 11**

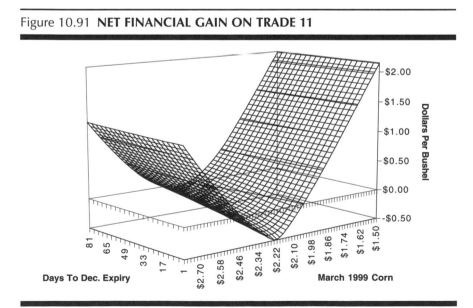

stant. This backward calendar long straddle consists of buying 816 March $2.30 calls at $0.0725 and buying 816 December $2.10 puts at $0.12625; the next four most attractive hedges are trades 41, 44, 20, and 42, in descending order. As was the case for our long hedge, we emplace this position with full knowledge that we will have to roll it forward into a completely different position as the long December $2.10 put expires.

Trade 11 has the typical profit profile of all long straddle positions, open-ended gains at both higher and lower prices offset by a zone of underperformance in the middle. This zone of underperformance is highly sensitive to time decay; at expiration, the worst-case loss is close to $0.50 per bushel, but if the trade were exited with 30 days remaining, the worst-case loss would be reduced to around $0.26 per bushel. The trade would benefit from any deepening of the December-to-March carry and from any increase in volatility.

The incremental financial gain of trade 11 to the base case of simply selling 200 March futures is depicted in Figure 10.92; this is also the net basis of the trade. The large leverage of the trade allows its incremental gain surface to retain the general straddle shape, with the larger incremental gains occurring in the higher price environment. The incremental gains remain open ended at both higher and lower price levels.

Figure 10.92 **INCREMENTAL FINANCIAL GAIN FOR TRADE 11**

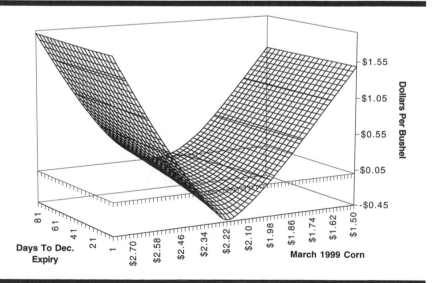

The economics of the trade are sensitive to the December-to-March spread, and we can depict in Figure 10.93 the net basis at the expiration of the December $2.10 put across a range of March prices and December-to-March spreads. We find that the worst-case outcome occurs once again at the unlikely combination of lower prices for March corn accompanied by a move toward backwardation in the December-to-March spread. The same comment applies as before: that while nothing is impossible, this combination of circumstances is highly unlikely.

Finally, we can make one more comparison, the one between trade 11 and the plain-vanilla put option position, trade 41, consisting of buying 280 March $2.40 puts at $0.29375, as shown in Figure 10.94. The same general straddle shape emerges, with trade 11 outperforming trade 41 in both higher and lower price zones, and with trade 11 showing greater sensitivity to time decay.

The net borrowing cost in trade 11 in a completely static environment is its initial capital outlay per bushel, $0.8109, less its value at the expiration of the December $2.10 put. Neither leg of trade 11 will expire worthless in the static case; the December $2.10 put will have an intrinsic value of $0.07 and the March $2.30 call will have time

Figure 10.93 **NET BASIS GAIN ON TRADE 11**

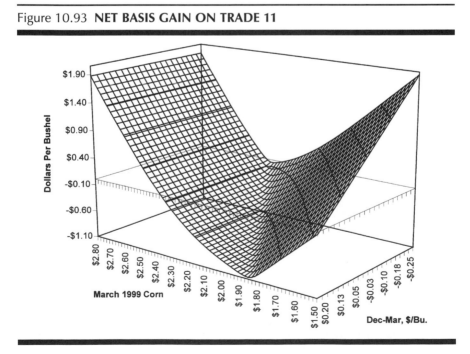

Figure 10.94 **INCREMENTAL ADVANTAGE OF TRADE 11 OVER TRADE 41**

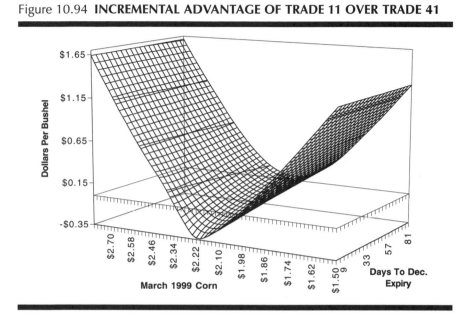

value of $0.049. At the trade's 4.08 : 1 leverage, the total value at December expiration should be $0.4858. The net borrowing cost is $0.3251 per bushel for trade 11. Trade 41, an ITM put, will have an expected time decay of only $0.0355 per bushel. What did we get for our greater borrowing cost? We got both greater downside protection and something that trade 41 cannot provide: upside participation.

CONCLUSION

The algorithms used for strike selection in Chapter 9 and the one used for position selection in this chapter use real-time market data, which in turn drives the calculation of option derivative statistics. The information contained in the forward curves of the underlying asset—be it a physical market, an expectation-driven financial market, such as short-term interest rates or currencies, or a market with little or no information in its forward curve, such as bonds and equities—is incorporated on a real-time basis as well.

Many option trading methodologies rely on trying to find mispriced assets or on making bets regarding the level and skew of volatility. The Dynamic Option Selection System does not. Even though finding a mispriced asset, like getting a free prize in the mail, is nice, one cannot rely on having free money handed to one. Prices reported by a quote service may indicate a discrepancy, but these are likely to disappear at execution time. The corollary to this is that the system must not be sensitive to anomalous prices, and within reason, it is not.

Making a bet on volatility, like making a bet on prices, transforms the external risk of the market into the internal risk of the trader making a correct decision. The notion of volatility being too high or too low begs the question: With respect to what norm? There are many predictable, scheduled events that may have a known volatility impact, such as the presence of a government report or a contract expiration, and we may have a reliable chance of, say, bond option volatility retreating after an employment report. In the case of unique times and events, however, volatility can extend well outside of a historical range and can stay there for some time, as we saw in our studies of crude oil and soybean volatility in Chapter 5. If the world has changed structurally, we cannot expect volatility to regress to some mean just because our GARCH (generalized autoregressive conditional heteroskedasticity) or ARIMA (autoregressive integrated moving average) model indicates that it is an outlier.

The three most important variables in position selection are the ordinal level of volatility, the shape of the forward curve, and time remaining to expiration. The ordinal level of volatility is critical in determining the rate of time decay and the net debit or credit at initiation for the position, and it affects both the strike selection algorithms and the position selection algorithm. The shape of the forward curve creates opportunities to shift position costs by buying in forward months in backwardated markets and selling in forward months in carry markets, but it affects only the position selection algorithm. Time remaining to expiration has the same effects as the ordinal level of volatility. Time moves in one direction and at a known rate, whereas the other two variables move in both directions and tend to jump in quantum fashion from broad and stable ranges to unstable zones.

These variables, in providing us with most of the information we need, allow us to let the market tell us how we should structure our trade. We thereby are relieved of the need to impose our will on the market. This is absolutely analogous to and consistent with letting the market tell us its internal tenor via the adaptive moving average and who, between buyers and sellers, is the more anxious via the Market Tension Index (MTI) and EuroTension Index (ETI) indicators.

The positions generated by the Dynamic Option Selection System, because they are initiated in conformance with the market and because they have limited risk, have, along with their position management methodology, a wide range of trading applications. This is where we shall turn our attention next.

11

Do the Right Thing

The irony of striving so hard to eliminate the need for making decisions about where the market is heading in any one of the dimensions we have examined—price, volatility, and expectations—is that we have wound up with a system requiring intensive position management. However, intensive management need not require subjective decision making on the trader's part; indeed, position management can and should be nothing more than a mechanical exercise.

POSITION MANAGEMENT AND HEDGE PRINCIPLES

The mechanical management of an option-based hedge will be illustrated with the long trade 19 from Chapter 10, a bull put consisting of buying 641 March $2.20 puts at $0.1525 and selling 641 March $2.60 puts at $0.465; this presupposes that a short cash position of 1 million bushels of corn for March delivery, 200 futures contracts, is behind this hedge. The two hedge principles offered in Chapter 9 and restated below, along with a third principle, will be our guide:

- The total delta of the hedge must be less than or equal to the delta of the cash market risk.
- The management of the position, especially the sale of this excess delta and the restructuring of the position as required, is the only way to reduce the overall cost of insurance and/or the initial net borrowing involved in the position.

- All buyers should convert their short linear profit profile into that of a put option, and all sellers should convert their long linear profit profile into that of a call option.

First, we should depict how the trade would perform in the absence of position management. Figure 11.1 illustrates the return on trade 19 across the dimensions of the March corn price and time remaining to the option expiration; this is a three-dimensional expansion of Figure 10.15.

Three features stand out in this profile. The first is the limited-loss feature inherent in bull put spreads; no matter what happens, the maximum loss per bushel will be $0.28. The second is the limited-profit feature once the short $2.60 strike is approached. The third is the leveraged gains that occur as upward price movement starts; this leverage is greater early on in the life of the trade. These three features can be highlighted by depicting the trade as a net hedge by adding in the underlying cash market gains and losses, as shown in Figure 11.2.

Figure 11.1 **NET FINANCIAL GAIN ON TRADE 19**

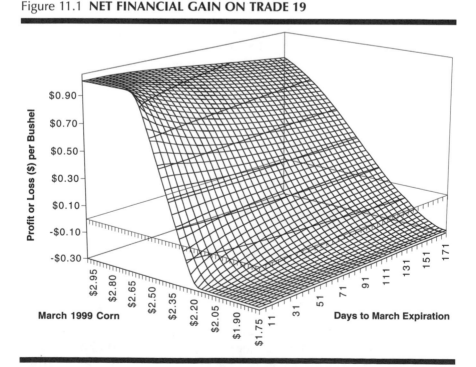

Figure 11.2 **NET HEDGE GAIN ON TRADE 19**

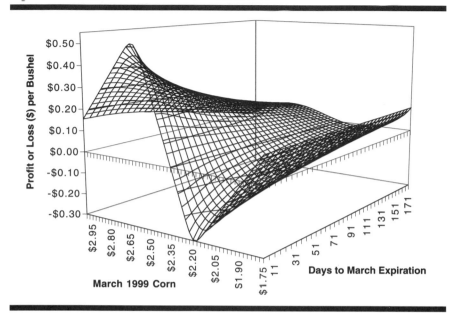

The nadir of hedge performance occurs at the long $2.20 strike, which is where the entire long option premium of $0.1525 is lost without any offsetting cash market gain from lower prices. The depth of this nadir increases with the passage of time and indeed is solely a function of net time decay on trade 19. At prices below $2.20, hedge gains occur as a function of lower prices and as a function of time remaining; by expiration, the net hedge gain at lower prices is a linear function of price. We should note in passing that avoidance of the deepening nadir is quite simple; since it is a function of time decay, and since time advances in one direction and at a known rate, all we need to do is roll the hedge forward at the point when time decay starts to accelerate noticeably. This point will vary, as illustrated throughout Chapter 8, according to both the relationship between the price and the strike and volatility, but a good rule of thumb for at-the-money (ATM) situations is 1 month prior to expiration.

The crest of hedge performance occurs at the short $2.60 strike, which is where the entire short option premium of $0.465 is absorbed without any offsetting cash market losses from higher prices. The height of the crest, just like the depth of the nadir, increases with the passage of time as the short $2.60 put decays. At prices above $2.60, hedge gains start to disappear as a function of higher prices and of time remaining; by expiration, the net hedge gain is reduced—and could change into a loss—as a linear function of price.

POSITION MANAGEMENT UNDER ADVERSE PHYSICAL MARKET MOVEMENT

Should we be concerned with this decline in hedge efficiency as the $2.60 strike is approached and with the negative efficiency thereafter? Only if we are locked into the existing structure of trade 19; otherwise, our mechanical discipline to our hedge principles should assure us that trade 19 will be nothing more than a memory by the time declining hedge efficiency is reached. This can be illustrated in several ways. First, we should look at a map of excess delta for trade 19, as shown in Figure 11.3, delta in excess of our requirement of the equivalent of 200 futures, across the dimensions of price and time remaining to expiration.

The total delta of trade 19 exceeds the equivalent of 200 futures fairly quickly, and this mandates that we sell the excess back to the

Figure 11.3 **EXCESS DELTA FOR TRADE 19**

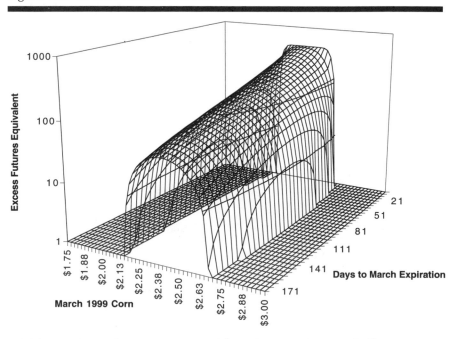

market. This is the same procedure we illustrated in Chapter 9 in the several tables regarding actions on September 4, 1998. These sales are critical to hedge performance for two reasons. First, our goal as buyers is to make our profit profile resemble that of a put option, and if the market becomes overhedged, our profit profile will start to look like that of the hedge instrument—in this case, a bull put spread. The opposite rationale would apply for a short hedge position: Our goal as sellers is to make our profit profile resemble that of a call option, and overhedging will cause our profit profile to deteriorate into that of the hedge instrument. Second, the sale of excess delta is functionally equivalent to a rebate of the insurance premium paid at the trade's initiation. This rebate serves several purposes, the most important of which is raising the break-even point of the trade. In addition, as the break-even is raised, the cross-section of prices where the net hedge performance is narrowed as well. Finally, the rebate frees up capital from hedging to other, more productive, uses.

We can illustrate these rebate effects by imposing an upward price movement of the daily $0.12-per-bushel limit on the first day of the trade, assuming that volatilities and other key variables will remain constant, which is an even less realistic assumption than it sounds. The position of our hedge is illustrated in Table 11.1. The increase in price leads to an increase in total delta from 200 to 236. At the new delta of the bull put spread, .368, we will have to close 98 spreads at a

Table 11.1 **SALE OF EXCESS DELTA**

Event/Aspect	September 1, 1998	September 2, 1998	Change
March corn	$2.1525	$2.2725	
$2.20 put	$0.15250	$0.09875	−$0.05375
$2.60 put	$0.46500	$0.36875	$0.09625
Net gain			$0.04250
Total delta	200	236	
Total gamma	387	217	
Delta/spread		0.368	
Excess spreads		98	
Total gain			$66,744
Gain per bushel			$0.067
After sale			
Total delta		200	
Total gamma		184	

gain of $0.425 per spread. Multiplied by the ratio of trade 19, this will result in a realized profit of $0.067 per bushel.

Once we close 98 of our original 641 spreads, we are still long a total of 200 futures. Our total gamma is drastically lower than its original value of 387. The price increase alone reduced total gamma to 217, and then the sale of 98 spreads reduced gamma even further to 184. This reduction in gamma is totally expected, but it means that each succeeding price movement higher will have a smaller effect on the total delta and on our ability to realize the rebate of insurance costs. We will need to pay attention to our gamma, for this determines when our second hedge principle involving position restructuring will be invoked.

The change in the break-even profile produced by the delta sale is illustrated in Figure 11.4. The capture of the rebate increases the relative advantage of the new position with its 543 spreads to the original position with its 641 in all lower and static price environments. This relative advantage is capped at $0.16 per bushel, whereas the zone of disadvantage at higher prices is floored at $0.04 per bushel.

This asymmetry of advantage following the sale of excess delta suggests that our new hedge position has acquired more of a put

Figure 11.4 **INCREMENTAL ADVANTAGE OF POST–DELTA-SALE POSITION**

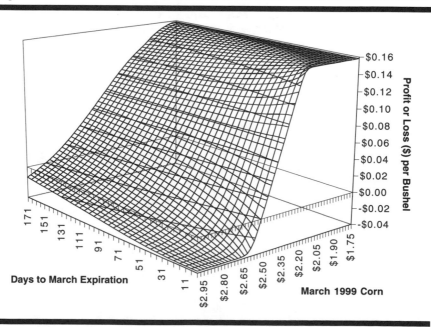

option character than did our original position, and this is true. We will now have fewer long positions, the number of contracts in our bull put spread, to block our cash market gains should the market reverse its initial burst higher. Figure 11.5 illustrates how even a single sale of excess delta can raise the worst-case point from nearly $0.30 per bushel in the initial scenario, displayed in Figure 11.2, to less than $0.15 per bushel. Moreover, the width of the price spectrum indicating a net hedge loss narrows considerably as well, from the $1.88-to-2.33 band in Figure 11.2 to the $2.05-to-2.28 band here.

If the market continues its burst higher, however, we will get to repeat the process shown in Table 11.1. We can impose a second consecutive $0.12 per bushel limit move higher for March corn. This process is illustrated in Table 11.2.

The smaller number of spreads at the start of the day, 543 instead of our initial 641, and the lower delta of our short $2.60 put lead to a much smaller excess delta number, only the equivalent of 12 futures contracts. We will sell 31 spreads back to the market, realizing another $0.04625 per bushel from the September 2 level and $0.08875 per bushel from the September 1 level. Our gamma, however, has shrunk from its original level of 387 to only 11. With the price of March corn already at $2.3925 and with knowledge that trade 19 will not protect us over the price of $2.60, we should move to restructure the position.

Figure 11.5 **NET HEDGE GAIN AFTER FIRST EXCESS DELTA SALE**

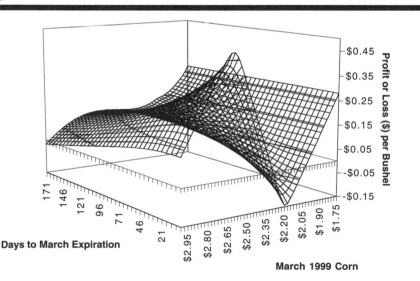

March 1999 Corn

Table 11.2. **SECOND SALE OF EXCESS DELTA**

Event/Aspect	September 2, 1998	September 3, 1998	Change
March corn	$2.2725	$2.3925	
$2.20 put	$0.09875	$0.06125	–$0.03750
$2.60 put	$0.36875	$0.28500	$0.08375
Net gain			$0.04625
Total delta	200	212	
Total gamma	184	11	
Delta/spread		0.391	
Excess spreads		31	
Total gain			$19,463
Gain per bushel			$0.019
After sale			
Total delta		200	
Total gamma		11	

Restructuring involves closing down the entirety of trade 19 and replacing it with an entirely new trade optimal for the new market conditions. In so doing, we capture a profit on the trade, money that can never disappear from the accounting for the hedge. We will also acquire a higher break-even point than the $2.29 at expiration seen in Figure 11.1. Since we are still physically short corn, our new call option–equivalent position will produce a synthetic put option at a higher strike. This latter point can be illustrated quite easily be supposing that trade 19 is replaced by a completely parallel trade structure, a bull put involving a long $2.40 put and a short $2.80 put applied in the same 641 spread quantity as the original trade 19. We can then redraw Figure 11.1, including the captured $0.08875 profit from September 1.

The most striking feature of Figure 11.6 is the elimination of the loss zone due to the effects of the retained profit from the original trade 19. This constitutes an upward shift in our expected net hedge profit profile. The hedge does not lose its efficiency until the short $2.80 strike is approached; this will constitute a shift in the location of the hedge's nadir. Our worst-case outcome, seen in Figure 11.7, is a $0.22 per bushel loss at $2.38, as opposed to the original worst-case outcome of $0.30 per bushel at $2.20.

This mechanical and systematic sale of excess delta provides us with an automatic procedure for capturing profits on a trade and elim-

Figure 11.6 **NET FINANCIAL GAIN ON SHIFTED TRADE 19**

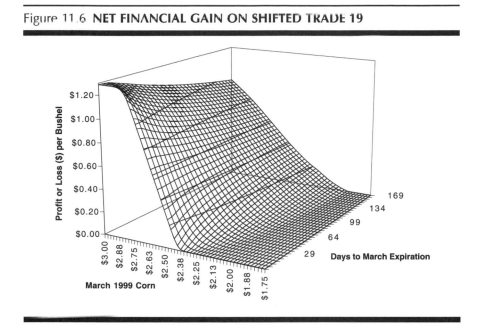

Figure 11.7 **NET HEDGE GAIN ON SHIFTED TRADE 19**

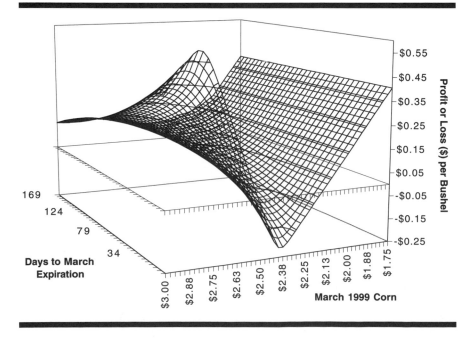

inates the problem of risk aversion in the domain of profits discussed in Chapter 1: We will take profits when our hedge exposure, as defined by the delta of the position, exceeds the exposure of the underlying asset—in this case, our physically short corn position. As stated above, failure to sell this excess delta changes our original and desired risk profile, that of a put option, into the opposite risk profile of our hedge instrument. We will sell only as much as we have to sell to bring our total exposure back to a maximum of zero; this assures that we are, at a minimum, fully hedged on our position going into the next day.

POSITION MANAGEMENT UNDER FAVORABLE PHYSICAL MARKET MOVEMENT

What if the price of corn had dropped, and dropped severely, instead of rising sharply as we have posited? Our goal as hedgers with a short position in the underlying market is to maintain a profit profile of a put option, not the profit profile of a short future. As the price of corn falls, the delta of the long $2.20 put decreases more rapidly than does the delta of the short $2.60 put, and this will eventually cause the delta of trade 19 to approach zero. It also leaves the buyer with a windfall gain on his short position in the physical corn market, one that he should be loath to abandon.

Table 11.3 illustrates how our original hedge position would look after three days of $0.12 losses. Our loss on trade 19 would be $0.272

Table 11.3 **SITUATION FOLLOWING 3-DAY PLUNGE**

Event/Aspect	September 1, 1998	September 4, 1998	Change
March corn	$2.1525	$1.7925	
$2.20 put	$0.15250	$0.41000	$0.25750
$2.60 put	$0.46500	$0.80750	−$0.34250
Net gain			−$0.08500
Total delta	200	39	
Total gamma	184	258	
Delta/spread		0.072	
Trade 19 gain			−$272,425
Gain per bushel			−$0.272
Cash market gain per bushel			$0.360
Net hedge gain per bushel			$0.088

per bushel, which is nearly the entire maximum loss of $0.28 per bushel. More important, however, is the decline in the position's delta to the equivalent of only 39 futures. This means that trade 19 will provide very inefficient protection against a subsequent rebound in prices and that our existing gain on the total hedge of $0.088 per bushel will be jeopardized. Since we have already achieved virtually our maximum loss of $0.28 per bushel and since our existing position is approaching that of a speculative short position, we should recognize our loss on trade 19 and restructure the trade. In practice, this restructure point can be whenever the net delta of the hedged instrument falls below −.80 or rises above .80, or whenever the loss on the hedge instrument exceeds 95% of the potential loss. If the sale of excess delta is equivalent to receiving a rebate on insurance expenditures, the resetting of a hedge is equivalent to rebuilding and reinsuring a house lost to fire.

Once a new hedge is in place—say, another parallel to the original trade 19 of long the $1.80 put and short the $2.20 put—we will need to manage the hedge according to the procedures above. Should the market rebound, we will need to sell the excess delta from the new bull put spread, and should it continue to plunge, we will eventually have to replace it once again.

This mechanical procedure for recognizing the loss on the hedge instrument eliminates the risk seeking in the domain of losses discussed in Chapter 1. In fact, the combination of the automatic delta sales and position restructuring at higher prices and position resets at lower prices follows the oldest known and most-violated maxim of the entire world of trading: Buy low and sell high.

SYNTHETIC INDEXING

We have now arrived at a critical juncture in our thinking. It should stand to reason that any instrument capable of being the best hedging tool should be the best position for trading a position as well. In our discussion above, trade 19 substituted for the time-honored base case of buying 200 March corn futures at a price determined by the trader. But what if there was no short physical corn position on the other side of trade 19, and yet we chose to emplace the trade and manage it just as if there were? Then we would have a long position in March corn that should, subject to the position management methodology outlined above, outperform the base case in both and higher and lower price environments, at the cost of underperformance in static price environments.

Over time in a volatile market, we should expect to have sufficient opportunities to manage the position according to the buy low–sell high, risk-neutral methodology outlined above to create a synthetic index capable of outperforming its base case. Given the difficulties that active stock portfolio managers have had in matching an index such as Standard & Poor's (S&P) 500, a synthetic index capable of out-performing this base case should be quite attractive. We should moderate the use of the term *index* somewhat in the interest of syntactical purity. A true index should have a stable correlation approaching 1.00 against its underlying cash market benchmark, and the tracking error of one against the other should be stable and predictable over time. The option-based index created by the Dynamic Option Selection System and managed in accordance with the methodology outlined above will not exhibit these attributes, except by coincidence, over any time segment.

Two separate but identical historical simulations suggest that an option-based equity index can outperform its underlying benchmark, in this case the S&P 500, over time. The first simulation was a walk-forward day-by-day study using data only available at the close of business each day over the June 1989–to–November 1997 period. The options on the S&P 500 futures traded at the Chicago Mercantile Exchange were used as the trading instrument. A hypothetical $100 million portfolio was traded, and the initial net asset value (NAV) of shares in the portfolio were set to $10.00. The benchmark was the S&P 500 index, with dividends reinvested. Commission costs were set at $9.00 per round-turn. Excess funds were credited at 90% of the 90-day treasury bill rate.

Over the period in question, the NAV of the option portfolio rose from the initial $10.00 to $62.31; the comparable figure for the unmanaged index itself was $39.47. Nearly all the outperformance occurred during the strong bull market for U.S. stocks during the 1995–1997 period as the pace of position management, both in the form of excess delta sales and position restructuring, became frenetic.

The second simulation began with the calendar year of 1998. The structure and procedures were identical to that listed above. By the end of October 1998, the NAV of the option portfolio stood at $12.48, as compared with $11.22 for the unmanaged index. Here, however, most of the outperformance began after the market instability seen in the July–September 1998 period, a period of intense price swings and surging implied volatility. The comparative performance during the market crash during the last week of August 1998 was particularly telling, as seen in Table 11.4. This was due to the fact that the existing position, a calendar call frontspread structured like the long trade 25

Table 11.4 **PERFORMANCE DURING AUGUST 1998 CRASH**

	Base Index ($)	Option Index ($)
August 24	11.11	11.43
August 25	11.16	11.42
August 26	11.07	11.34
August 27	10.65	11.11
August 28	10.49	11.02
August 31	9.78	11.06

from Chapter 10, reaching its maximum loss by August 31. The long position was reset on that day—a case, it turned out, of buying the low of the move.

Of necessity, there are periods of underperformance as well, and they occur in the expected conditions of choppy markets. The second half of 1994, a period characterized by narrow ranges and low volatility, did not provide good opportunities for position management. As a result, much of the relative outperformance the option portfolio accumulated over the 1989–1993 period was dissipated by the end of 1994.

CONCLUSION

As we have discussed, the mechanics of the Dynamic Option Selection System do not depend on finding mispriced assets; the assumption is and must be that all prices are efficient within the bounds of execution costs. This does not preclude the kind of outperformance seen in the above experiments, since the efficient market hypothesis is silent on the subject of whether a position is fairly priced for a stream of future events. It would be preposterous to suggest that this is so. Equally important, we cannot predict that an option portfolio will outperform its underlying index, for that is entirely dependent on the path of future events. We can state with confidence that it should underperform in a static market and outperform in a directional and volatile market, but we have no control over what the environment will be. We have put ourselves in the position, however, of always limiting our losses, always letting our profits run, always striving to raise the break-even point and shift it to a higher price, and always engaging in a methodology of buying low and selling high. We have put ourselves in the position where the accidents will work in our favor. This is all we as traders can ever do. Time and the market will take care of the rest.

Index